Between East
and West

# Between East and West

Trieste,
the United States,
and the
Cold War,
1941–1954

Roberto G. Rabel

Duke University Center for International Studies Publication
Duke University Press  Durham and London  1988

ROBERT MANNING
STROZIER LIBRARY

AUG 26 1988

Tallahassee, Florida

© Duke University Press
All rights reserved
Printed in the United States of America
on acid-free paper ∞
Library of Congress Cataloging-in-Publication
data appear on the last page of this book
Chapter 3 has been published previously in
substantially similar form as "Prologue to
Containment: The Truman Administration's
Response to the Trieste Crisis of May 1945,"
*Diplomatic History* 10 (Spring 1986): 141–60,
and is published here by permission of
Scholarly Resources, Inc.

# Contents

Preface vii
Acknowledgments xiv

1. A Zone of Strain: The Geohistorical Origins of the Trieste Dispute 1
2. Liberal Principles versus Military Necessity: Anglo-American Policy toward the Julian Region in World War II 17
3. Toward Containment? The Trieste Crisis of May 1945 52
4. The Cold War Sets In: Trieste in the Balance, June 1945 to September 1947 74
5. Cold War Pawn: Trieste and American Policy, September 1947 to December 1949 102
6. From Paralysis to Partition: Steps toward a Settlement, 1950 to 1954 131
7. Conclusion 163

Notes 169

Bibliography 199

Index 213

# Preface

> In the ideological conflict between East and West, between Communism and Western political concepts, individual political acts may have an importance far beyond their local consequences.—Frances B. Stevens to George Kennan, September 9, 1947, *Foreign Relations of the United States, 1947*

For a few weeks in May 1945 there was a serious possibility that Trieste (Trst) would be the setting for the first armed conflict between East and West in the postwar era. Claimed by both Italy and Yugoslavia, this port city in the northern Adriatic was liberated almost simultaneously by Yugoslav and Anglo-American troops in the closing days of the Second World War in Europe. The United States and Britain insisted that Yugoslav occupation of Trieste would prejudice a final settlement of the territorial dispute at the peace table. Tensions ran high, but an armed clash was avoided when the Yugoslavs agreed reluctantly in late May to accept temporary Anglo-American military administration of the city until a peace treaty was signed with Italy.

For almost a decade thereafter, Trieste was poised precariously between East and West in the Cold War. The city and its environs remained under joint British and American military government, while a larger zone south and west of the city was under Yugoslav military administration. The Allied peace treaty with Italy in 1947 included provisions to eliminate these supposedly temporary expedients by amalgamating the two zones into an internationalized Free Territory of Trieste. But Cold War discord among the great powers prevented implementation of the scheme. As a result, Trieste languished in a strange kind of international limbo until 1954, when the disputed territory was partitioned between Italy and Yugoslavia along lines approximating the existing zones. The city itself thereby reverted to Italian sovereignty.

The purpose of this book is to analyze the causes, consequences, and significance of American entanglement in the problems of this Italo-Yugoslav border region. Its fundamental thesis is that American involvement was intimately related to wartime intervention in Europe and to the subsequent unfolding of the Cold War. The particular details of the Trieste problem were of limited importance in themselves; the United States was drawn there by the pursuit of more general political and military objectives. Essentially, therefore, this work is a historical case study in American Cold War policy-making.

Historians have studied many aspects of the Trieste problem but there has been little scholarly analysis of its significance as an issue in postwar East-West relations. Most striking, with the possible exception of the crisis of May 1945, Cold War scholars in the English-speaking world have made almost no attempt to examine critically the extensive documentary record now available concerning American policy toward Trieste.[1]

The only book-length study in English concerning the dispute is Bogdan Novak's *Trieste, 1941–1954: The Ethnic, Political, and Ideological Struggle*. That work is valuable as a narrative account of the local Italo-Yugoslav struggle for control of the Trieste area, but perforce ignores many broader international dimensions of the problem because it was written before declassification of the relevant Anglo-American documents. Jean-Baptiste Duroselle's *Le conflit de Trieste* is also useful but is intended primarily as an abstract case study in crisis resolution between two conflicting nation-states rather than an analysis of the historical particulars of the Trieste problem.[2]

There is a richer Italian and Yugoslav historiography. Regrettably, much of it has been narrowly nationalistic, memorialistic, or ideologically polemical in tone, and has done little to illuminate Trieste's role in the Cold War. More recently, however, Italian scholars in particular have begun to produce more scholarly studies based on declassified British and American records concerning this issue. The most important of these as a contribution to Cold War history is Giampaolo Valdevit's *La questione di Trieste, 1941–1954*, a thorough study of the complex interactions between international diplomacy and local conflict in Trieste during the Cold War period.[3]

Most of the research for this book was completed before the publication of Valdevit's study. To some extent it unavoidably covers similar ground and presents a broadly similar analysis of the Trieste problem for an English-language readership. There are, however, differences of interpretation concerning the significance of that problem as a Cold War issue.[4] More important, the present study is focused not so much on the Trieste problem itself but on American policy toward that dispute and on its changing significance for American policymakers from 1941 to 1954.

For a time Trieste represented a microcosm of the unfolding Cold War for the United States. It was one place where the United States soon learned of the responsibilities, costs, and limits of its powers as a would-be "world policeman" at the end of World War II. In this small area American policymakers had to confront the same potentially explosive problems of nationalism, ideological confrontation, strategic security, mass dislocation of population, and economic disruption that they would have to face on a global scale after World War II. Trieste presented an early postwar opportunity for testing how American liberal democratic principles could be applied in response to such problems. As the American ambassador to Yugoslavia noted in 1947, Trieste was of "symbolic as well as intrinsic importance," and remained "a proving ground for both American and Soviet intentions."[5]

Of course neither the Trieste problem nor American reactions to it can be explained solely in Cold War terms. Accordingly, the first chapter of this study briefly analyzes the complicated geohistorical background of the Italo-Yugoslav frontier problem in order to explain why it was one of the classic territorial disputes in European history. The area's fate was subject to influence by the changing contours of power politics in southeastern Europe from early times well into the twentieth century.[6] Chapter 1 also evaluates the significance of the first American involvement in this dispute, which occurred long before the Cold War. President Woodrow Wilson's opposition to Italian claims to Fiume (now Rijeka), in accord with the principle of self-determination, brought the United States and Italy into direct confrontation at the Paris Peace Conference in 1919. His failure to limit Italian expansion into Yugoslav-inhabited areas in the northern Adriatic proved symptomatic of a larger failure of American liberal internationalism in the aftermath of World War I.

The United States was somewhat more successful in pursuing liberal democratic principles in Trieste after World War II. Chapter 2 discusses the reopening of the Italo-Yugoslav frontier question during that conflict, showing how the State Department's view of the issue was guided primarily by the abstract liberal principles embodied in the Atlantic Charter, while the War Department responded to the pressures of regional military exigencies. Despite British reservations, a policy was adopted of Anglo-American occupation of the whole disputed territory until its fate could be determined at the peace table. Chapter 3 examines the dramatic crisis which ensued at war's end when Josip Broz Tito challenged that policy head-on by occupying the area with his own forces. In contrast to an unwillingness to go beyond diplomatic rhetoric in 1919, the United States revealed in 1945 that it was prepared to use its considerable power to prevent Yugoslav occupation of Trieste because it was seen as a violation of the liberal principles on which Washington hoped peace would be based.

In the years from 1945 to 1948 Trieste came to exemplify for American officials the practice of categorizing diverse local disputes as skirmishes in a worldwide confrontation between liberal democracy and totalitarian communism—a practice which became a leitmotif of American Cold War policymaking. The rationale for United States interest in such disputes was that, as one State Department official put it, "in the ideological struggle between East and West, between Communism and Western political concepts, individual political acts may have an importance far beyond their local consequences."[7] Accordingly, chapters 4 and 5 illustrate how the American commitment to Trieste in those years evolved according to the anticommunist logic of the containment doctrine.

It was only after the Soviet-Yugoslav break of mid-1948 made it counterproductive that the United States began abandoning that line of approach to the Trieste problem. Although still influenced by broader Cold War concerns, after 1949 American officials could no longer define the Trieste problem even indirectly in terms of a Soviet-inspired threat and instead became primarily concerned with the local and Italo-Yugoslav implications of the dispute. Chapter 6 explains how the United States (and Great Britain) actively pursued a realistic resolution of the dispute on the basis of a direct Italo-Yugoslav accord. Although American policymakers were ultimately successful in facilitating such a settlement, the process was a difficult and frustrating one that was drawn out over five years—in part because of the legacy of their own earlier decisionmaking based on Cold War considerations.

Tracing the course of American involvement in the Trieste dispute in this fashion is not only of interest per se, but can contribute in some measure to the growing scholarly understanding of the Cold War as something more than a bipolar confrontation between the United States and the Soviet Union. In recent years Cold War historiography has moved beyond the acerbic debate over responsibility for originating the Cold War. There has been considerable blurring of the once inviolate trichotomy of orthodox, realist, and revisionist interpretations. The focus of Cold War historiography in this era of post-revisionism and depolarization has shifted from an exclusive preoccupation with Soviet-American relations at the summit level to a more diversified perspective on the Cold War that takes into account the roles played by other nations—most notably Great Britain—and examines policymaking processes at various levels.[8] These developments have led to revitalization of the field through monographic research on specific areas illustrating the complex interactions between multiple actors which defined the historical process subsumed under the label of "the Cold War."

In the Trieste case American policy was the product of a decade of shifting interactions between individuals and organizations at various policymaking levels in several countries as well as in the contested area itself—all responding to a dispute whose outcome would directly affect the lives of over half a million Italians and Yugoslavs, would have important political effects in both Italy and Yugoslavia, and would have economic repercussions throughout the port of Trieste's traditional hinterlands. More specifically, United States policy toward the Trieste problem was shaped by the interplay between several major factors: a liberal commitment to the principle of self-determination; the exigencies of maintaining local stability and effective administration as long as the hotly disputed area remained under Anglo-American military occupation; the need for close cooperation and consultation with Great Britain; and, finally, the larger realities of the Cold War, especially in terms of American perceptions of the respective roles of Italy and Yugoslavia in that East-West confrontation. As will be seen, these factors would receive differing priorities according to shifts in local, regional, and international circumstances. By examining the dynamic interplay between these factors in detailed fashion, this book seeks to explain the origins, evolution, and impact of American Cold War policy in one specific setting.

A few words on the scope of this book are also in order. Quite obviously its principal concern is to analyze the Trieste problem as a Cold War issue. Beyond its significance as such, however, the Trieste dispute was fascinating in itself as an entangled maze of conflicting but often overlapping national, ideological, social, and economic interests. Above all it was a human problem which profoundly affected the lives of hundreds of thousands of people in Trieste and nearby areas.[9] To tell their story would require a very different approach; in this study the local dimensions of the problem are examined only insofar as they illuminate the dynamics of Cold War diplomacy. There is only limited analysis of how the Anglo-American military government in Trieste responded to local imperatives and what impact its presence had on the rhythms of local life. For instance, an assessment of its efforts to promote economic reconstruction in the area falls beyond the purview of this book. Neither is there close examination of the complicated conflicts which divided local groups in Trieste during this period. This book also makes no attempt to address the once bitter debate on the respective merits of Italian or Yugoslav claims to the area, or to adjudge the "justice" of the final settlement.

The question of geographical focus is more problematical. Although

Trieste was the most important prize at stake in the Italo-Yugoslav dispute, for many years the dispute encompassed a larger area known as the Julian Region.[10] This study concerns other parts of the Julian Region only until 1947 when the Italian peace treaty was concluded. Discussion thereafter is limited to the abortive Free Territory of Trieste, which became the area of contention and of direct United States involvement.

Finally, the question of toponymy should be mentioned. As a result of ethnic diversity and shifts in national frontiers, most localities in the Julian Region have had two or even three names: Italian, Yugoslav (Croatian and/or Slovenian) and, in a few cases, even German (although those are almost forgotten now). For example, the Italian "Trieste" is rendered as "Trst" in Slovenian and "Triest" in German. To avoid inconsistency this study will generally refer to each locality according to its official name since 1954. The relevant Italian or Yugoslav equivalent will be given in parentheses when a place name is first mentioned.

# Acknowledgments

⦿ I have accumulated numerous debts of gratitude—intellectual, emotional, and financial—during the course of researching and writing this book.

I owe thanks for financial assistance to the History Department and Graduate School of Duke University, the Fulbright-Hays Program of the New Zealand and United States governments, the Harry S Truman Library Institute, and the History Department of the University of Otago. I am also grateful to the many archivists and librarians at the following institutions who eased the course of my research: the National Archives, the Federal Records Center at Suitland, Maryland, the Library of Congress, the Dwight D. Eisenhower Library, the Harry S Truman Library, the United States Military History Institute, the Princeton University Library, Perkins Library at Duke University, the Public Record Office (London, England) and the New Zealand National Archives.

For their counsel, encouragement, and criticism of early drafts of the manuscript, I offer sincere thanks to William Scott, Bruce Kuniholm, Richard Watson, James Miller, and especially Calvin Davis, who ably supervised the dissertation on which much of this book is based. I owe a special debt of gratitude to Giampaolo Valdevit, who has been grappling for many years with the same problems and wading through the same documents as I did for this study. We have enjoyed a fruitful scholarly collaboration, sharing primary resources and exchanging ideas on the Trieste question.

I also wish to thank Alfred Bowman, John Campbell, Joseph Greene, and Leonard Unger for their generosity in sharing their reminiscences with me and for answering my many questions about their views on American involvement in the Trieste dispute.

My parents-in-law, Al and Acee Hughes, deserve thanks for their continuous encouragement of all my endeavors. Bobbi Rubinoff provided hospitality and a sympathetic ear during several extended visits to the archives in Washington.

I owe my greatest debts of gratitude to three exceptional women. My mother and grandmother were torn from their birthplace in Istria by the very problem this study examines and had to struggle to build new lives in a distant land. They have given me more opportunities than I can thank them for. My wife, Kathleen, has shared in almost every aspect of my work. She has been my typist, critic, and inspiration.

Consequently, this book is dedicated to my mother and grandmother, who lived it, and to my wife who made it possible for me to write about it.

Map 1 The Julian Region, 1866–1947

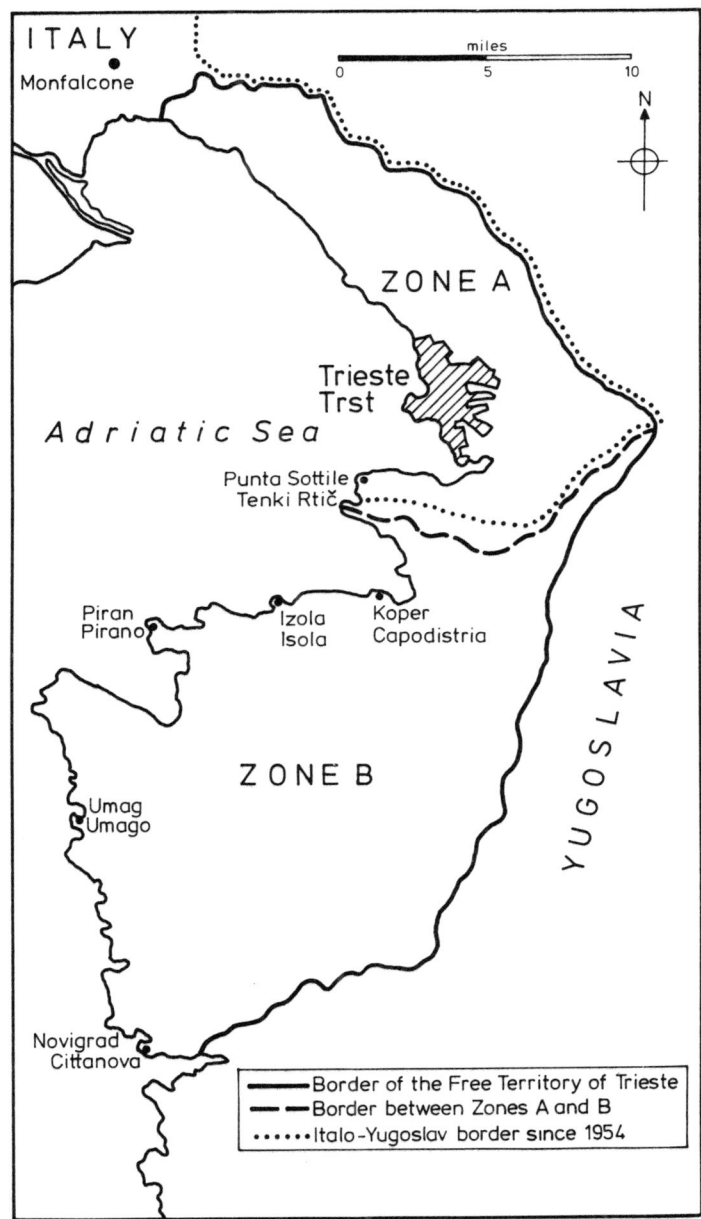

Map 2 The Free Territory of Trieste, 1947–1954

# 1

## A Zone of Strain: The Geohistorical Origins of the Trieste Dispute

⊙ ANYONE who becomes immersed in international affairs soon realizes that no important issue exists in isolation; rarely is it only bilateral. A problem which may seem of interest to only two countries almost invariably affects a third and, as often as not, a fourth or more.—Dwight D. Eisenhower, *Mandate for Change, 1953–1956*

The United States emerged from World War II as the most powerful nation in the world. Cognizant of this power, American leaders hoped to foster the creation of a liberal world order. They feared that the Soviet Union in particular posed a major threat to their objectives. To counter that threat American policymakers felt compelled to take on a broad range of external political and military commitments. From Western Europe to the Far East, the United States became an influential arbiter of events in many areas outside its previous realm of interests. The port city of Trieste (Trst) at the head of the Adriatic was one locality that fell within the bounds of the new *Pax Americana*.

On one level, American intervention in the Trieste question can be explained as one of the many unforeseen consequences of World War II and the emerging Cold War. That involvement, however, did not simply materialize in a vacuum but was, in significant ways, an outgrowth of European power struggles in the region dating back two millennia. Therefore, to understand fully the reasons for American involvement in the Trieste dispute, it is necessary to begin by analyzing the history of the area itself to determine how its specific problems were swept up in the broader currents of international power politics in the twentieth century.

## A "Zone of Strain"

Throughout its history Trieste has shared the fortunes of a larger area known as the Julian Region, which has been of long-standing significance in European political geography. For two thousand years this area at the head of the Adriatic was a strategic thoroughfare or frontier zone where the clash of rival expansionist forces caused frequent changes in sovereignty. Since the nineteenth century it has also been the setting for a conflict between opposing national and political ideologies which would culminate in the struggle for Trieste and nearby territories after World War II.

One consequence of these rivalries and shifting sovereignties has been that the area in question—now divided between Italy and Yugoslavia—is difficult to define. For the purpose of this study it may be described as the territory between the Austro-Italian frontier of 1866–1918 and the Italo-Yugoslav frontier of 1924. Italians came to call this region Venezia Giulia (Julian Venetia), while Croats and Slovenes adopted the term Julijska Krajina (the Julian March) to describe an almost equivalent territory. In English, the area became known as the Julian Region.[1]

Physically, the Julian Region constitutes a natural portal between the Italian plain of the Po Valley and the Danubian Basin, in large part because of the excellent mountain passes found at the meeting point of the Julian Alps and the Dinaric Range. Its shores mark the point where the Adriatic reaches toward the landlocked states of Central Europe, and the Gulfs of Trieste and Fiume (Rijeka) on the two sides of the Istrian peninsula represent the most convenient northern outlets to that sea. In effect, the area is a natural crossroads between the Italian peninsula, the Balkans, and Central Europe.[2]

The strategic and economic implications of this geographical setting prompted frequent conflict among nearby states for its control. The character of the Julian Region as a "zone of strain" was further reinforced by the fact that it was one of the few points of direct contact between all three of Europe's major ethnic groupings: Latins, Slavs, and Germans. It is hardly surprising that throughout history this area has been directly affected by the broader power struggles in the lands around it.[3]

The strategic and economic significance of the Julian Region was evident as early as Roman times. After conquering the Illyro-Celtic peoples who originally inhabited this area, the Romans used the Julian Region as a major military and commercial thoroughfare. When the Roman Empire disintegrated the area became a chronic battlefield and an open corridor into Italy for successive waves of invaders: Byzantines in 394; Goths in 400; Huns in 454; Ostrogoths in 488; and Lombards and Avars in 568. By 811 the whole Julian Region had been incorporated into the Carolingian Empire but was soon broken up into various feudal holdings whose rulers constantly intrigued against each other. After the tenth century the region became the focal point of a broader rivalry between the ambitious Venetian Republic and the rising Habsburg Empire. The two powers clashed repeatedly in the area until the eighteenth century, when the Habsburgs finally dislodged the Venetians from their last footholds on the western Istrian coast. Excepting a brief interlude under French rule during the Napoleonic era, the Julian Region remained under Habsburg control until the First World War.[4]

## The Nationalistic Factor

The rise of nationalism in Europe in the nineteenth century introduced a new element into the historic struggle for these borderlands. Rival expansionist powers had hitherto contested the area because of its importance as a strategic frontier zone, a land of passage, and an outlet to the sea. Although the region had been inhabited primarily by Italian and Slavic peoples (usually under German overlordship) since the seventh century, the mixed ethnic composition of the local population had little influence on these struggles. During the nineteenth century, however, the focus of international rivalry in the Julian Region shifted to this "ethnic" and nationalistic level.

The Italian ethnic presence originated in Roman times and the influence of Latin culture persisted in the Julian cities long after the collapse of the Roman Empire. Italianization was reinforced after the tenth century by Venetian influence on the western coast of Istria (Istra) and by general acceptance of Italian as the lingua franca of the Adriatic. Italian domination of urban culture in the Julian Region continued into the nineteenth century despite Habsburg political control.

The Slavic presence also has a long history, dating from the sixth century when Slavic peoples accompanied the Avars into the Julian Region. Slavic migration into the Julian Region continued thereafter, and parts of Istria were even incorporated into an independent Croatian kingdom from the ninth to eleventh centuries. By the fifteenth century most of the Julian countryside was populated by Slavic peoples—Croats in Istria, and Slovenes from Trieste northward.[5]

There was considerable intermingling of the Italian and Slavic populations of the Julian Region over the centuries, and by the nineteenth century it was difficult to discern clear-cut "ethnic" distinctions between the so-called Italian and Slavic communities. Cultural practices, principally linguistic preferences, provided the only practical criteria by which to distinguish national groupings in the Julian Region: Italian was the favored tongue of the coastal urban centers; Croatian or Slovenian was spoken in the rural interior. Even then, distinctions were often imprecise, for bilingualism was common and there were significant Italian-speaking minorities in the interior (and vice versa).[6]

This long-standing ethnic diversity of the Julian Region was of no real significance in political terms until nationalism became a major force in Europe during the nineteenth century. The rise of nationalism brought the realization that the Julian Region was not only a focal point of strategic and economic rivalries but also a frontier zone between the Italian and South Slav "nations." The notion that the boundaries of political states should correspond to those of national groupings raised particularly intractable problems in areas of mixed ethnic population—especially those incorporated within a multinational empire.

Animated by the *Risorgimento* quest for Italian unification, Italians were first to claim the Julian Region on ethnic grounds in the early nineteenth century. The question was academic as long as an Italian nation-state remained a dream but took on serious proportions after Italy was unified in 1861 and gained Venice from the Habsburgs in 1866. Many Italian nationalists began to agitate for the remaining areas of Italian population still in Austrian hands: namely, the Julian Region and the Trentino. At first the aspirations for these *terre irredente* ("unredeemed lands") symbolized the quest for fulfillment of the *Risorgimento* and, as such, drew support primarily from Italy's republican Left, inspired by Giuseppe Mazzini's ideals of democratic nationalism. Gradually, however, the campaign for redemption of all Italians from foreign control became the driving wedge of Italian imperialism in Europe as irredentism became absorbed in a more strident, dogmatic nationalism exalting Italianism above all other principles. By the early twentieth century its ardent supporters claimed all the Julian Region and much of Dalmatia, with scant regard for the large number of Slavs living in those areas.[7]

In the Julian Region itself, Italian irredentism manifested itself largely through aggressive cultural organizations sponsored by Triestine intellectuals and the Italian bourgeoisie of Istria. Eschewing the fraternal sympathy for other oppressed nationalities characteristic of the early *Risorgimento*, these organizations sought to defend the *italianità* ("Italianness") of the area not only against its Austrian overlords but, more directly, against the perceived threat of a newly awakened Slavic national consciousness. Though punctuated by occasional acts of terrorism against Austrian political figures, the Italian nationalist movement in the Julian Region increasingly drew its impetus from the struggle against growing Slavic influence as the twentieth century approached.[8]

Ultimately, irredentist success depended on military or political action by the Italian government. But until the First World War Italian political leaders were unwilling to sacrifice the practical diplomatic advantages of smooth relations with the Habsburgs on the altar of irredentism. Renewal of the Triple Alliance between Italy, Austria-Hungary, and Germany for the fifth time in 1912 made redemption of the Julian Region seem a dim prospect and Italian leaders tended to discourage irredentist agitation.[9]

Nevertheless, irredentist sentiment in Italy increased after 1890. Italian nationalist agitation in the Julian Region itself also intensified, reaching new heights in the early twentieth century and creating serious strains in Italo-Austrian relations. Animosity over the Julian problem raised the question of how long the Italian government could afford to resist the domestic pressure of growing irredentism before jettisoning its Austrian alliance. The First World War broke out with that question unresolved.[10]

By that time Slavic national consciousness was another major factor in the power struggle for the Julian Region. That consciousness had not manifested itself as early among local Croats and Slovenes as among Italians, but in the mid-nineteenth century a "Slav awakening" occurred in the region. It was a result of the general European impact of nationalism and of the liberation of the Slavic peasantry in 1848 from the remnants of feudalism. Slavs who moved to the cities thereafter were no longer automatically assimilated into the dominant Italian urban culture. Some Slovenes and Croats now envisaged the Julian Region as part of a future South Slav national homeland. This sentiment exerted further influence after 1860 when Slovenian and Croatian cultural, economic, and political organizations appeared in the region. Initially pursuing anti-Habsburg goals, these organizations soon clashed with Italian nationalism in the area and threatened Italian cultural domination. Like local Italian irredentists, Slavic nationalists were supported by fellow nationals outside the Julian Region, in this instance from neighboring parts of the Habsburg Empire. By 1914 many exponents of Slavic nationalism were as adamant as Italian irredentists in claiming almost the entire Julian Region.[11]

The advent of nationalism inserted a dynamic new element into the traditional rivalry for the Julian Region. When World War I erupted the clash between Italian and Slavic nationalism was already a serious local problem. The persistence of Habsburg power held in abeyance direct Italo-Yugoslav confrontation on the international level but World War I would realign international rivalries in the Julian Region along primarily nationalistic lines. As in earlier centuries, this realignment occurred because of major changes in the balance of power in surrounding regions—in this case, the disintegration of the Austro-Hungarian Empire.

## The Economic Factor

The impact of nationalism was not the only local development in the nineteenth century with international implications for the Julian Region. Although the area remained of some strategic significance, its primary importance for the Habsburg Empire was economic. These economic considerations made the Habsburgs willing to absorb the political costs of suppressing Italian irredentism and playing off Slavic nationalism against its Italian counterpart.

Historically the Julian Region had held little intrinsic economic significance. It had been used since Roman times as a commercial thoroughfare, but the trade of Trieste and other Julian ports did not generally extend beyond the Adriatic. It was only in the second half of the nineteenth century that Trieste was transformed into a major international port.

At that time the Habsburgs dramatically expanded Trieste's harbor facilities and linked the port to a large central European hinterland by extending the Südbahn Railroad from Vienna to Trieste in 1857. After the Habsburgs lost Venice and the Suez Canal opened in the 1860s, Trieste became the principal seaport of Austria proper and much of Central Europe. By 1914 it was a thriving city of over 200,000 people and the world's eighth busiest port. Less traffic flowed through Rijeka, but it also expanded and functioned as the central port for the Hungarian portion of the Empire after the *Ausgleich* of 1867. These ports were developed at considerable expense and linked to hinterlands in Central and southeastern Europe by the application of great engineering expertise. In an important sense their economic success was an artificial creation because it rested on the political unity of their hinterlands under Habsburg control and on the active intervention of the Habsburg state to encourage their expansion by such means as favorable rail charges.[12]

The privileged economic relationship between the Julian ports and their Danubian hinterlands created a particular predicament for

Italian nationalists in the Julian Region. Quite simply, the extension of Italian sovereignty to the area would sever that relationship. Thus the "antithesis between the economic factor and the national one" was already identified by a local Italian historian in 1912 as a "consistent theme in Trieste's history."[13] It would remain so throughout the twentieth century.

By the early twentieth century the Julian Region was once again a focal point of international rivalry. It retained some of its historic importance as a strategic transit route and frontier zone between the Italian peninsula and the Danube as well as serving as a base for naval operations in the Adriatic. As a consequence of developments in the nineteenth century, a complex of nationalistic, ideological and economic interests were now also at stake there. The stage had been set for one of the most intractable European territorial disputes of the twentieth century.

### The Fiume Crisis: *Sacro Egoismo* versus the New Diplomacy

The first act of that drama would be played out in Fiume[14] in the aftermath of World War I, and the United States would play a leading role. The story of Woodrow Wilson's unyielding stand against Italian claims to that area at the Paris Peace Conference is well known and has been told from several perspectives. Indeed, the incident stands as an important example of the interaction between European regional struggles for power at the end of World War I and the emergence of the United States as a global power seeking a liberal world order. Yet the Fiume episode has received scant attention as an antecedent of the post-1945 Trieste problem.[15]

There are, in fact, ample grounds for comparing the Fiume and Trieste disputes. Both emerged from a matrix of traditional power politics and became serious problems because of fundamental shifts in the regional balance of power caused by war. Both disputes were related to political and social problems within the nations most immediately concerned: Italy and Yugoslavia. Moreover, albeit in different senses, the Fiume and Trieste issues each represented part of a broader challenge to European political structures—protofascistic nationalism after World War I and communism after World War II. Most significant for the purposes of this study, the United States became enmeshed in both clashes over the Julian Region as a result of an evolving commitment to pursue European political stability under liberal auspices. The degree of American involvement however, differed markedly in each case.

The origins of U.S. involvement in the Fiume dispute can be traced back to the differing war aims of the United States and Italy. Italian leaders entered World War I intent on the pursuit of *sacro egoismo* ("sacred self-interest"), a policy which sought to exploit the First World War as an opportunity to advance specific nationalistic and expansionist objectives: strategic security for Italy on its northern and northeastern frontiers; redemption of those Italians still under Habsburg rule; mastery of the Adriatic; and the extension of Italian economic influence into the Balkans. Consequently, Italy entered the war against the Central powers in 1915 only after the secret Pact of London was signed, by which Britain, France and Russia agreed to support Italian postwar claims to the Julian Region, parts of Dalmatia, and the Trentino and Alto Adige (South Tyrol) to the Brenner Pass. Italy's frustrating wartime experience only strengthened its leaders' commitment to these postwar claims, even though they included territories inhabited by ethnically "Yugoslav" peoples and thereby violated the principle of self-determination.[16]

American entry into the war in 1917 and Woodrow Wilson's subsequent enunciation of a New Diplomacy represented a direct challenge to the Italian program for a victors' peace—at least in principle. As a consequence, wartime relations between Italy and the United States were strained. When Wilson sought to define Allied war aims in terms of his Fourteen Points, the Italian government refused to accept point nine, which stated that "a readjustment of the frontiers of Italy should be effected along clearly recognizable lines of nationality." Nevertheless, disagreement never gave way to open confrontation during the war, largely because the perceived need for wartime cooperation with the Allies led Wilson to hesitate in insisting on their compliance with his liberal principles. The president did not move beyond an abstract commitment to the concept of self-determination and did little to encourage tangible expressions of self-determination in the territories of the Central powers. Wishing to avoid partisan involvement in specific conflicts between competing national groups, Wilson hoped that at war's end the United States could be the arbiter of an integrated peace settlement, under whose aegis individual political and territorial problems could be solved by applying the appropriate liberal principles.[17]

In reality, when the time came to translate Wilson's general policies into practical terms at the Paris Peace Conference, the United States became embroiled in European disputes not as an impartial judge but as a litigant with its own interests at stake—albeit interests of a different order than the European disputants. Facing a complex postwar situation in which the clash of rival European national interests interfaced with a broader struggle between reaction and revolution, the Wilson administration had to weigh the democratic, anti-imperialist thrust of the New Diplomacy against its antirevolutionary commitment to order and stability. The Fiume question illustrated this difficulty perfectly.

After the war the Italians persisted in their territorial demands. These now included the city of Fiume, which had a small Italian majority but was surrounded by Slav-inhabited lands claimed by the new Kingdom of the Serbs, Croats, and Slovenes. Italian leaders felt obliged to insist on total fulfillment of their claims to justify the war's great costs to the Italian public, to appease the ultranationalist forces which had consistently supported intervention and, allegedly, to preempt a revolutionary crisis. As the historian Arno Mayer has noted, domestic politics and foreign policy became fatally intertwined in Italy in the months after November 1918. Prime Minister Vittorio Orlando staked his domestic political legitimacy on the consummation of the foreign policy of *sacro egoismo*.[18]

Wilson and the United States represented the most serious obstacle to that goal. In the months preceding the Paris Peace Conference, the president carefully studied the Italian claims. For reasons that are unclear he quickly agreed to the Italian demand for a frontier on the Brenner, thereby consigning some 150,000 Austrians to Italian rule in clear violation of his own principle of self-determination. He also accepted some other Italian demands. But Wilson agreed with his territorial experts that Italy should not have Fiume or Dalmatia.[19]

Circumstances would dictate that Wilson stand firm on this issue. By the time Italy's claims were discussed at the Paris peace conference, the president had seriously compromised his liberal program by various concessions to the other Allied powers. He seized upon the Fiume issue as an occasion for a symbolic stand on the integrity of the New Diplomacy. There were several reasons for doing so. Quite plainly, if his liberal democratic program were to prevail, he had to oppose demands such as those of Italy in the Adriatic, smacking so blatantly as they did of the Old Diplomacy. Italy was a weaker power than Britain and France and one whose wishes could more easily be denied. He also feared that the new Yugoslav state might be drawn toward the Bolshevik example if treated unfairly by the great powers.[20] On the other hand, in opposing Italy Wilson was unwilling to use force or direct economic pressure for fear of precipitating domestic disorder there and forfeiting Italian participation in the overall peace settlement and the League of Nations.

The Fiume problem illustrated a fundamental dilemma bedeviling Wilson's policy at the end of World War I. Should he stand firm on the New Diplomacy at all times, despite the peril of alienating the Allied governments and possibly plunging their nations into disorder; or should he ensure European stability by compromising with the Allies, even at the cost of forsaking liberal-democratic principles? Given the duality of American interests, Wilson had little chance of success when he chose to turn Fiume into a test case for the fate of liberal internationalism.

This development occurred at the Paris peace conference in April 1919 when Italy's claims were considered by the Council of Four (Wilson, Orlando, David Lloyd George of Great Britain and Georges Clemenceau of France). During these discussions Italian representatives tried to use the specter of imminent revolution in Italy to gain support for their claim to Fiume and protested that their country was being denied the just reward of its war effort. Some members of the American delegation had shown sympathy toward this argument in the preceding weeks and urged Wilson to seek a realistic compromise with the Italians on Fiume. But Wilson chose to listen to a group of his territorial experts who argued that giving Fiume to Italy would not only violate the principle of self-determination and leave Yugoslavia without a viable port, but would show the world that "a big power has profited by the old methods: secret treaties, shameless demands, selfish oppression." In a key meeting of the Council of Four on 19 April, Wilson echoed this view, arguing that the Fiume issue should be considered in a broader context:

> We are trying to make peace on an entirely new basis and to establish a new order of international relations. . . . to put Fiume inside Italy would be totally inconsistent with the new order of international relations. . . . the Italian population at Fiume was not connected with Italy by intervening Italian population. Hence to unite it with Italy would be an arbitrary act, so inconsistent with the principles on which we were acting that he [Wilson] for one could not concur in it.

Despite this plea the Italians remained intransigent.[21]

Angered and frustrated, Wilson contemplated economic pressure but in the end decided to appeal directly to the Italian people. On the evening of 23 April he issued a press statement reiterating the arguments he had made privately to Italy's leaders. The Fiume question thereby presented the occasion for public reaffirmation of the New Diplomacy—a move Wilson had been considering for weeks. This statement had some impact in the United States and Europe in reassuring liberals that the president had not abandoned the tenets of the New Diplomacy, but was a complete failure in Italy, where it only intensified the national passion for Fiume and strengthened the hand of an aggressively nationalistic new Right.[22]

Thereafter the issue remained stalemated. Despite successive compromise proposals by the other Allied powers and a new Italian government, Wilson remained obdurate. The issue was left unsettled until Wilson faded from the scene in 1920. The Yugoslavs knew they could no longer rely on American support after Congress rejected the League of Nations and the Democrats lost the presidential election in November. Warren Harding was elected on a promise of "normalcy not nostrums" and his administration would quickly abandon the active pursuit of liberal internationalism insofar as it entailed political entanglements in Europe. Realizing their consequent weakness, the Yugoslavs came to an agreement with the Italians. On 12 November 1920 they signed the Treaty of Rapallo, granting most of the Julian Region to Italy but creating a free city of Fiume.[23]

At that time the city had been under the control of Gabriele D'Annunzio for over a year. This blustering Italian nationalist poet had led a motley band of Italian adventurers, disgruntled soldiers, and Fascists to Fiume in September 1919 and seized it in a bold coup. His presence there was an embarrassment for successive Italian governments, none of which tried to remove him for fear that the armed forces would not comply and that the Right would object. Only after the Treaty of Rapallo was signed did the Italian army oust D'Annunzio from Fiume, on 1 January 1921, and establish a free city.

Fiume's status as such was troubled and brief. Local Italo-Slavic friction led to frequent Italian intervention. In 1924 a group of Italian Fascists seized the city. Soon after, Benito Mussolini, Italy's new premier, concluded the Treaty of Rome with the Yugoslavs by which Italy annexed Fiume in return for minor concessions. It was fitting that Mussolini should be in power when Italy finally obtained Fiume, for the unfolding of the Adriatic problem had been coterminous with the rise of Italian fascism. And who would be better fitted to consummate the tradition of *sacro egoismo* than *il Duce*?

For Italy the acquisition of Fiume in 1924 thus marked a victory of sorts for *sacro egoismo*. But the costs were considerable. By then the myth of a "mutilated victory" was entrenched, according to which Italy had been denied the just rewards of its war effort by opportunistic allies and ineffective political leaders. The postwar agitation over Fiume and the northern Adriatic contributed fatally to the debilitation of liberal Italy and abetted the rise of fascism. The pursuit of extreme claims on Italy's eastern frontier by successive governments did nothing to diminish domestic instability and merely placed the nation in thrall to expansionist nationalism as the panacea for the threat of socialism. Having attained power by creating that illusion, Italy's new Fascist rulers themselves became entranced by its allure.

Moreover, the outcome of the Fiume dispute did not satisfy Yugoslav aspirations in the Julian Region. Yugoslavs did not consider the settlement just and believed they had been denied part of their national patrimony by superior Italian might. They continued to covet the ports of Fiume and Trieste, and still hoped for redemption of over 500,000 Croats and Slovenes.

For American policy in Europe the Fiume imbroglio represented part of a larger failure. The United States had drifted into involvement in the issue as a consequence of a more general wartime and peacemaking policy of international stability based on self-determination, liberal political and economic institutions, and a community of power. At Paris Wilson had made the Fiume question a test case of liberal internationalist principles but was unprepared to use military or economic pressure to oppose Italy's claims. As a consequence, the Fiume affair represented in microcosm the foundering of American liberal internationalism after World War I because of the incapacity of Wilsonian diplomacy to maintain a consistent course between the European shoals of reactionary nationalism and revolutionary socialism.

## The Interwar Period

From a local perspective the post–World War I settlement of the Italo-Yugoslav frontier dispute was far from satisfactory. The assertion of Italian control after 1918 failed egregiously to eliminate the Italo-Yugoslav animosity which had begun during the period of Habsburg rule. Instead a new level of confrontation was superimposed over that of nationalistic rivalry so that by 1941 there would emerge a three-cornered ideological struggle among the local agents of fascism, socialism and liberalism, replicating in microcosm the clash of those ideological forces throughout wartime Europe.[24]

This complex pattern of local conflict was the unanticipated outcome of fascist efforts to consolidate Italy's grip on its post–World War I territorial gains. After 1918 the Julian Region was a fecund seedbed for the early growth of the Italian Fascist party. As fervent nationalists and antisocialists, the Fascists were able to exploit the twin anxieties of the local Italian bourgeoisie: Slavic nationalism and revolutionary socialism.

After Mussolini gained power in Italy local Fascists pressed the central authorities to eliminate the "Slavic problem" by initiating a harsh program of Italianization and antisocialism in the Julian Region. The central government complied by introducing such measures as compulsory use of Italian in schools, enforced Italianization of Slavic surnames, imprisonment or deportation of Croatian and Slovenian leaders, disbanding Slavic cultural and economic organizations, and even physical persecution in cases of suspected resistance to Italianization. The policy dealt a severe blow to the public institutions of Slavic nationalism in the Julian Region; but it also radicalized Slavic ethnic consciousness on a visceral level, stimulated terrorist activities, and helped forge an enduring connection between local Yugoslav nationalism and communism. Nevertheless, as ardent defenders of the area's *italianità*, the Fascists would continue to draw extensive support from the local Italian population well into World War II—much to the frustration of the Italian antifascist resistance. The net effect of Fascist policy during the interwar years was to create a climate of tension and polarization that eventually exploded into a fragmented local struggle among diverse political and national forces after war broke out.[25]

This repressive policy also harmed Italian relations with Yugoslavia. Fascist diplomacy toward its Adriatic neighbor had initially followed the course set by former foreign minister Carlo Sforza, who sought peaceful Italian penetration of southeastern Europe through economic expansion and political cooperation with Balkan states—in effect, an Italian version of the American "Open Door." As a result, Italo-Yugoslav relations were relatively amicable for a few years. By 1926, however, Mussolini began to yield to the Slavophobia of the many Fascists from the Julian Region who obtained high office in his regime. The harsh Italianization policies subsequently pursued in the Julian Region became a major source of tension in relations with Yugoslavia and stimulated the growth of a powerful irredentist movement in that country. Mussolini sought to play down this problem when he reverted to a more accommodating approach toward Belgrade in the late 1930s because of Italian concern at the prospect of German expansion into southeastern Europe. The Italians signed a nonaggression pact with Yugoslavia in 1937 and Italo-Yugoslav relations improved briefly. The Yugoslav government even saw fit to suppress the noisy irredentist movement within Yugoslavia. For a short time the Julian problem lay dormant.[26]

With the onset of World War II, however, the two Adriatic nations soon became direct adversaries. Mussolini now discarded his policies of regional cooperation to join Adolf Hitler in seeking to redefine the map of post-Versailles Europe by force. Italy formally entered the war in 1940. After an abortive assault on Greece in October of that year, Mussolini joined Hitler in a successful invasion of both Greece and Yugoslavia in April 1941. Thanks to the Nazi war machine Italy was able to secure total domination of the Adriatic, but that control would be short-lived.

## Conclusion

One of the direct repercussions of Italian and Yugoslav involvement in World War II was the abrupt reopening of the Italo-Yugoslav frontier question. The particular nationalistic, ideological, and economic issues which had fueled the local struggle for the Julian Region since the nineteenth century would now be swept up in the general wartime struggle for international dominance in Europe. As had been the case at so many times in its history, the fate of the Julian Region would be once again dependent on the outcome of a much broader politicomilitary conflict.

The United States had been drawn into the Italo-Yugoslav frontier dispute in 1919 as a result of its participation in World War I. On that occasion its views had failed to prevail. It remained to be seen if American policies would have any greater success when involvement in a second global conflict obliged the United States to give renewed attention to the problems of the Julian Region.

# 2

## Liberal Principles versus Military Necessity: Anglo-American Policy toward the Julian Region in World War II

> IN this global war, there is literally no question, political or military, in which the United States is not interested.—Franklin D. Roosevelt to Joseph Stalin, 4 October 1944, *FRUS: The Conferences at Malta and Yalta, 1945*

As in World War I, American involvement in the struggle for the Julian Region came about indirectly during World War II as an outgrowth of more general political and military objectives. Of seemingly peripheral importance, the question of who should occupy Trieste would nonetheless bring the United States and Great Britain close to armed conflict with Yugoslavia in May 1945 and was an additional source of tension in their relations with the Soviet Union. The firm Anglo-American stance during that crisis was not due to direct interest in this locality per se, but was related to larger American and British aims in Europe, to their pursuit of postwar stability, and to the intensification of East-West tensions within Allied ranks during the war's final phases.

The showdown with the Yugoslavs in Trieste has been described frequently as the first confrontation of the Cold War.[1] To explain how an initially marginal involvement could lead to such a strong American stand on the Trieste question at the end of the European war, one must trace in detail the evolution of the Julian problem during World War II. American policymaking on this seemingly narrow and unimportant territorial dispute was invariably conditioned by more general considerations. These include wartime developments in Italy and Yugoslavia as well as in the Julian Region itself; the interdependence of Allied military strength and political-diplomatic objectives in those countries; divergent American and British policies; deteriorating Anglo-American relations with the Soviet Union and related suspicions of leftist movements throughout Europe. The parameters of the Julian problem during World War II were thus defined by a complicated interplay between military and political considerations at both the local and international levels.[2]

### The Anglo-Yugoslav "Secret Agreements"

A secret British initiative in early 1941 prompted the first broader international consideration of postwar revision of the Italo-Yugoslav boundary. At a time when Britain's wartime situation was at its lowest ebb, Prime Minister Winston Churchill became convinced that Hitler was preparing an advance into the Balkans. The British began considering various expedients to harden local resistance to German penetration, hoping especially to persuade the Yugoslavs and Turks to enter the war.

In the case of Yugoslavia, one expedient was to promise postwar territorial compensations in the Julian Region. In January 1941 the Yugoslav minister in Moscow, Milan Gavrilović, suggested that "it might help the Yugoslav government to strengthen their own position, and through them that of their neighbors against the Germans," if Britain were to support Yugoslav claims in the Julian Region. Officials in the British Foreign Office noted that the proposal smacked of "bribery" and was reminiscent of the 1915 Pact of London but, in order "to be armed at all points," they requested Arnold Toynbee's Foreign Research and Press Service to study the Yugoslav case for frontier rectifications. A report was duly produced in early February concluding that Yugoslavia had sound claims on ethnic grounds to most of Istria and the Italian islands off Dalmatia, but not to the cities of Trieste, Gorizia (Gorica), Rijeka, and Zadar (Zara). The Foreign Office only needed cabinet approval "to hold out this bait to the Yugoslavs." But the British war cabinet showed little interest when the subject was raised, and there the matter might have rested.[3]

Only days later the Yugoslav stance became more critical when the war cabinet decided on 24 February to send British forces to Greece. The Foreign Office now recommended that, despite the British policy of not discussing territorial changes during the war, "the decision of the Yugoslav Government at the present juncture is of such importance that it would be worthwhile to disregard this rule on this occasion if by doing so we could induce Yugoslavia to intervene forcibly on behalf of Greece." The cabinet concurred. At the time Foreign Secretary Anthony Eden was meeting with the Yugoslav government. The cabinet notified him that if he thought it "necessary or useful" he could indicate that "his Majesty's Government are studying with sympathy the case for revisions of the Italo-Yugoslav frontier which they are disposed to think could be established and advocated by them at the Peace Conference." Notwithstanding the importance placed on Yugoslav support, the cabinet specified that British policy on the matter should not move beyond this vague formula, which did not commit Britain to a precise frontier line. British representatives apparently mentioned the territorial issue to the Yugoslavs, but the whole question became irrelevant in April when Italy and Germany invaded Yugoslavia.[4]

Though inconclusive, the British initiative introduced the pattern according to which Allied policy on the Italo-Yugoslav boundary issue would unfold during the war. The British had deliberately limited themselves to a vague proposal for favorable consideration of Yugoslav claims in the Julian Region and were careful not to suggest a specific location for an ethnic boundary. While willing to tack somewhat, they did not believe the issue justified a significant deviation from the policy of not committing themselves on postwar boundaries. In 1941 British interest in Italo-Yugoslav frontier rectifications was based on short-term military expediency. It was of a piece with historian Elisabeth Barker's general description of British wartime policies in southeastern Europe as "a story of last-minute improvisation and the undertaking of commitments without the resources to fulfill them. Policies, if that is the right word for them, were largely dictated by negative outside factors."[5] Insofar as Allied policies impinged on the Italo-Yugoslav struggle for the Julian Region during World War II, their influence would generally remain indirect—a reverberation of broader military and political objectives of the different Allied nations.

This early British foray into the boundary dispute also foreshadowed later Anglo-American disagreements on military and political goals in southeastern Europe. Rumors of "secret agreements" on the Julian Region prompted concern among American policymakers, who were advocating an even more rigorous policy of no political or territorial settlements during the war—in part because of experiences during World War I with secret accords such as the Pact of London. In July 1941 President Franklin D. Roosevelt queried Churchill about "the stupid story that you promised Trieste to Yugoslavia." Recalling that in 1919 there were serious problems "over actual and alleged promises to the Italians and others," Roosevelt asked Churchill to consider stating publicly "that no post-war peace commitments as to territories, populations or economies have been given." At the Atlantic Charter discussions in August, Sir Alexander Cadogan, the British permanent under secretary of state for foreign affairs, assured Sumner Welles, the American under secretary of state, that Britain had made no such commitments, with the possible exception of an oral statement to the Yugoslav government that at war's end "the subject of jurisdiction over Istria was a matter which might well come up for reconsideration." Cadogan added that this statement manifestly did not constitute "a firm commitment" and that Trieste or Gorizia had not been mentioned. "Heartened" by this assurance, Welles emphasized that the United States wished to avoid repeating the problems caused in World War I when secret accords involving Great Britain were disclosed. The British did not formally disavow secret treaties but Washington's concern about their territorial agreements, which had been sparked by the "secret agreements" with Yugoslavia, was somewhat allayed by the signature on 14 August 1941 of the Atlantic Charter. The first two points of that document declared that neither Great Britain nor the United States sought "aggrandizement, territorial or other" and that both countries wished "to see no territorial changes that do not accord with the freely expressed wishes of the peoples concerned."[6]

Despite this affirmation of Anglo-American unity, the chance appearance of the Julian issue had already evinced differences in the two nations' fidelity to a formula of no wartime agreements on politicoterritorial questions. British interests in southeastern Europe would lead to further wartime disagreements with the United States on such matters.

## Early Anglo-American Policies toward the Julian Region

From the outset of American participation in the war, Roosevelt resolved that his country's primary objective would be military victory as soon as possible.[7] The president thus stressed the need for unity within the Allied coalition. He appeared to obtain common affirmation of this principle with the "Declaration of the United Nations," which most of the Allies signed on 1 January 1942.[8] An important corollary of this policy was that political and territorial questions arising during the war would be settled at the peace table in line with the principles of the Atlantic Charter, thereby not detracting from the combined war effort against the Axis powers. Accordingly, Roosevelt cautioned the American people in 1943 that "we must not relax our pressure on the enemy by taking time out to define every boundary and settle every political controversy in every part of the world." He disdained those who wanted to know "what are you going to do about such and such five-square-kilometer area in the world?"[9]

Despite Roosevelt's desiderata, American policymakers would eventually have to confront precisely such questions. Political objectives were invariably enmeshed in Allied warmaking, especially after 1943 when it became evident that the Allies would prevail. Problems such as those of the Julian Region became sources of inter-Allied discord and were approached in terms of more general military and political strategies.

In the early stages of American involvement the Julian problem did not loom large in Washington. It was, nonetheless, studied as part of the State Department's general postwar planning. In late 1942 members of Harley Notter's Advisory Committee on Postwar Foreign Policy produced several reports bearing on the Julian Region.

The most illuminating study was one by John C. Campbell, on 22 December 1942, on the "Italo-Yugoslav Frontier: Alternative Boundaries." Campbell evaluated various possible frontier lines in the area and urged that the United States be guided by the principles of the Atlantic Charter in determining a suitable boundary. He noted that the precise application of these principles would depend on American interest in imposing either a punitive or rehabilitative peace settlement on Italy. He added that "were moderate Italian opinion to be alienated by a harsh peace creating a new Italia Irredenta, the problems of establishing a stable regime in Italy and of bringing Italy back into the concert of nations might prove very difficult." This observation implied that the Julian problem should be considered as part of the more general question of what to do with Italy. But Campbell also realized that "American policy will necessarily be affected by the state of affairs which may emerge among the Yugoslavs." He referred in particular to an idea current in American and British policymaking circles that Yugoslavia and other Habsburg successor states might form a decentralized Danubian federation after the war. Trieste would be a logical major port for such a political entity.[10]

Campbell's report was significant in that it effectively delineated the parameters within which American policy concerning the Italo-Yugoslav frontier would unfold during World War II. The United States government would not adopt "a fixed position as to where the postwar frontier should be drawn," but would make plans for postwar consideration of that issue within a framework of Atlantic Charter principles such as ethnic self-determination and economic rationality.[11] At the same time Campbell's report correctly assumed that Washington's final decision on a particular boundary line would depend not only upon these broad principles but also upon American objectives in both Italy and Yugoslavia and on the political configuration of southeastern Europe at the war's end. In view of subsequent developments it is interesting that Campbell assumed the United States would have a decisive voice in determining the future location of the frontier, but did not consider the possibility that the Julian Region might become a frontier zone between two antagonistic systems of international political economy as well as between two nations. The vagueness and abstraction evident in this early analysis would perforce continue to typify American wartime policymaking on the Julian problem.

British policy developed along substantially similar lines in 1942 and 1943. The Foreign Office, however, took a more active interest in the Julian problem than the State Department because of traditional British interests in the Mediterranean area and, more specifically, because of the controversy over the "secret Anglo-Yugoslav agreements." The British were at pains to play down earlier assurances to the Yugoslavs and were careful not to encourage further Yugoslav claims to the Julian Region. The Foreign Office studied the question intermittently during these years but British plans for the Julian Region also remained vague because they were thought to depend on the direction of future political developments in Europe. The overriding concern of the British was to retain a free hand to influence the precise postwar location of the Italo-Yugoslav boundary in accord with more general objectives.[12]

While preliminary Anglo-American policy planning proceeded falteringly, military decisionmaking during 1943 helped shape the geopolitical context in which the future of the Julian Region would be determined. At the Casablanca Conference in January 1943 Churchill and Roosevelt agreed to exploit Allied strength in North Africa to embark on Mediterranean operations culminating in the invasion of Sicily (Operation Husky). Although Anglo-American planners agreed at the Trident Conference in May that Operation Husky must remain secondary to a cross-channel invasion, they recognized that it might lead to Italy's early elimination from the war. There was, however, Anglo-American disagreement concerning the extent to which an Italian campaign should be waged. In fact, as a British historian has noted, "the curious situation obtained ... that when Allied armies landed in Sicily on 10 July, nobody had yet decided where they were to go next."[13]

As it happened, Italy was nearing collapse. An internal coup overthrew Mussolini two weeks later, encouraging the Allies to invade the Italian mainland. The new Italian military government of General Pietro Badoglio immediately opened negotiations which led to Italy's withdrawal from the war in early September.

Shortly before Italy's surrender Roosevelt unexpectedly expressed interest in the Julian question while meeting with Churchill at the first Quebec Conference. The Foreign Office learned from the British embassy in Washington on 20 August that the president was "strongly of the opinion that Trieste, Fiume and Pola should constitute three outlets for countries in the interior and be free ports for all countries." Roosevelt advocated that these ports should become free cities under international administration (which might include the United States). The president's motives are unclear, but this rather specific and unanticipated pronouncement concerning the three cities seems exemplary of his well-known practice of conducting American wartime diplomacy on a personal, improvisational basis without working through the State Department. In the absence of specific coordination with the president, State Department officials were usually left to rely on the abstract principles enunciated in the Atlantic Charter—as evidenced in the case of their planning for the Julian Region. In this instance, despite comments similar to Roosevelt's by Secretary of State Cordell Hull at Quebec, the president's specific suggestions for the area do not even appear to have been noted within the State Department, let alone acted upon.[14]

The Foreign Office, however, reacted at once by preparing a study of his proposals. In suggesting the terms of reference for this study, Arnold Toynbee underlined the potential significance of Roosevelt's views in the context of general American policy: "It is noteworthy that the President's plan appears to assume that the United States will accept some permanent responsibility for maintaining the postwar settlement in at least one area of Eastern Europe." Indeed, this specific proposal for the future organization of the Julian Region's key cities marked a departure from Roosevelt's own policy of not discussing territorial settlements during the war. In early September the Foreign Office produced a paper entitled "The Future of Trieste, Fiume and Pola," outlining alternative arrangements depending on various circumstances. As one British official observed, the problem remained that, "like all similar papers, and, like Roosevelt's putative proposal this one suffers from ignorance of the future international background."[15]

By September wartime developments were altering the likely configuration of the "future international background" in the Julian

Region itself. On 8 September 1943 Italy became the first Axis power to surrender. The repercussions were immediate and dramatic in the Julian Region, where the Italian army failed to defend the northeastern gateway into Italy.

Italy's collapse caused the local struggle in this troubled area to crystallize along the lines it would assume for the rest of the war. The Germans seized the major cities, while Yugoslav Partisans took control of much of the Istrian countryside. Within a month the Germans drove out the Partisans and secured effective control of the Julian Region. Following the Habsburgs' example, the Germans exploited Italo-Slav animosities to good effect and governed with the objective of incorporating this zone directly into the Third Reich as its outlet to the Adriatic—the culmination of a quiet but longstanding *Drang nach süd-osten*.

A number of local Italian and Yugoslav political groups collaborated with the Germans: Mussolini's newly organized Republican Fascist party; anti-Slavic Italian nationalists forming an autonomist, local Fascist bloc; some Slovenian anticommunists; local supporters of the pro-Fascist Ustashi government of Croatia; and a few Chetniks (supporters of the Serbian anticommunist leader Draža Mihailović) who had fled from other areas. Ranged against the Germans and these groups—but not necessarily cooperating with each other—were Italian "democratic" parties, the Italian Communists, the Yugoslav Communists (Tito's Partisans), and several noncommunist parties. The lines of conflict and cooperation between these diverse political forces would fluctuate and overlap along the axes of national competition (German, Italian, Yugoslav, autonomist, internationalist) and ideological opposition (communist, fascist, liberal).[16]

The Allies would eventually have to confront this bewilderingly complex situation, but during the war it was virtually ignored. Instead, policies were determined by more general American, British, and Soviet objectives in southeastern Europe, particularly with respect to Italy and Yugoslavia. After the Italian armistice policymaking on the Julian Region was therefore influenced by Allied occupation policies in Italy, military progress against Germany, Allied relations with the Yugoslav Partisans, and growing inter-Allied tensions.

## Defining the Anglo-American Occupation Policy

The Italian armistice inaugurated a new phase in the Second World War during which the transition to the postwar era began. As the first Axis power to surrender and undergo Allied occupation, Italy became a critical testing ground for the unity of the anti-Nazi coalition and for Allied postwar planning. At the same time parts of the country (including the Julian Region) remained active war zones until a few days before the final Allied victory in Europe.

The Italian campaign was a veritable "political-military labyrinth" after September 1943.[17] Roosevelt himself remarked to Churchill in early October that Allied occupation policy in Italy would "set the precedent for all such future activities in the war." In view of his comment, it is noteworthy that the British and Americans excluded the Soviet Union from any meaningful role in the political mechanisms of control established in Italy—most important, the Allied Control Commission. Justified primarily by considerations of military efficiency, this action was nevertheless an initial step in ensuring Italy's place in a postwar Western system and gave the Soviet Union a precedent for avoiding Anglo-American influence in the occupation of Eastern Europe.[18]

The Julian Region received specific attention in late 1943 at the Teheran Conference as part of a larger inter-Allied debate on military strategy. The major strategic decision made at the conference related to the planned Anglo-American invasion of France (Operation Overlord), which would open the second front long demanded by the Soviet Union. The Americans were committed to a cross-channel assault but believed such a landing could not be undertaken before the spring of 1944. One of their aims at Teheran was to ascertain if the Soviet Union favored interim Mediterranean operations as a means of immediately alleviating pressure on the Eastern front—even at the cost of delaying Operation Overlord. Roosevelt suggested to Churchill and Joseph Stalin that one possibility would be a landing in Istria that would lead to combined operations with Yugoslav partisans and to a subsequent advance northeastward to meet the Soviet armies in Romania. Ironically, some of the president's own advisers were taken aback, fearing his suggestion signalled acceptance of Churchill's "strategic opportunism" in the Mediterranean and would delay Overlord. Harry Hopkins, Roosevelt's close confidant, could not understand who was "promoting that Adriatic business that the President continually returns to?" In reality, as historian Mark Stoler has noted, the idea had been suggested to Roosevelt by General Dwight D. Eisenhower (with the approval of the Joint Chiefs of Staff) as a way of satisfying Soviet demands for prompt action without destroying Overlord. Churchill was enthusiastic, foreseeing definite military advantages accruing to the British from more extensive operations in the Mediterranean theater. Roosevelt, however, had no strong personal attachment to the scheme and soon discarded it when Stalin indicated he would prefer Overlord to proceed on schedule rather than risk delay by action elsewhere. American planners also favored an unequivocal commitment to the cross-channel invasion; only the British were disappointed that the Mediterranean would remain a distinctly secondary theater of Allied operations. As far as the Julian Region was concerned, the outcome of the Teheran debates on military strategy removed any prospect of an early liberation by Allied forces.[19]

The possibility of Allied military actions in the Julian Region did not arise again until after the Normandy landings in June 1944. Having established important beachheads, the British and Americans had to decide whether to proceed with a supporting operation in southern France (Operation Anvil). The American Joint Chiefs of Staff favored this plan because it would open up vital ports for reinforcements. The British Chiefs of Staff, however, backed Churchill's proposal that more resources be applied to an Anglo-American advance up the Italian peninsula, which might be supported by an Istrian landing and a subsequent thrust through the Ljubljana Gap. The debate about Anglo-American strategy in the Mediterranean theater had been renewed.[20]

This time political factors impinged directly on the debate. Roosevelt pointedly reminded Churchill that military operations must not be subordinated to political objectives and that the Allies' first priority must be to strike at the heart of Germany—a goal that would be most quickly achieved by supporting Overlord with an assault on southern France. The British eventually deferred to this viewpoint, but Churchill was especially disappointed at American objections to the proposed landing in the Julian Region. He complained in his memoirs that

> it was his [Roosevelt's] objections to a descent on the Istrian peninsula and a thrust against Vienna through the Ljubljana Gap that revealed both the rigidity of the American military plans and his own suspicion of what he called a campaign "in the Balkans. . . . I cannot agree," he wrote, "to the employment of United States troops against Istria *and into the Balkans. . . . For purely political considerations over here, I should never even survive a slight setback in 'Overlord' if it were known that fairly large forces had been diverted to the Balkans."*
>
> No one involved in these discussions had ever thought of moving armies into the Balkans; but Istria and Trieste were strategic and political positions, which, as he saw very clearly, might exercise profound and widespread reactions, especially after Russian advances.

It is well known that by this time Churchill was alarmed at the Red Army's advance into Eastern Europe and the Balkans. While he did not stress political motivations when advocating an Adriatic thrust, he clearly had them in mind. Roosevelt, however, was facing an election and had no desire to endanger his domestic political standing by a "Balkan entanglement." Such a development, he knew, could be construed as a departure from the general American policy of placing military victory against Germany above all other considerations. For practical purposes the debate over the Mediterranean strategy was over. Italy thereafter remained quite definitely a secondary theater of Anglo-American operations.[21]

The possibility of imminent liberation of the Julian Region had again been forestalled by larger strategic imperatives. American officials in Italy nonetheless assumed that the area would eventually be captured in the course of the Italian campaign. They now began to ponder what problems its postliberation administration might entail, for they realized that the area was the object of rival Italian and Yugoslav claims.

In late July 1944 Captain Ellery Stone, the American deputy chief of the Allied Control Commission, asked for guidance "on what provinces should be included within ACC/AMG [Allied Control Commission/Allied Military Government] administration on the boundaries of Italy." He noted that there was a specific problem in the Julian Region where Yugoslav forces seemed to be preparing to take over the area "at the earliest possible moment." Stone was particularly adamant about the need for a clear policy on the Julian Region to avert "unfortunate incidents and complications between Allied authorities and the Yugoslav forces" and he outlined several possible courses by which that aim might be achieved.[22]

Washington's response ignored the idea of a compromise with the Yugoslavs embodied in some of Stone's suggestions. The State Department opted instead for his most inflexible alternative by directing that "Allied Military Government should be extended to all metropolitan Italian territory, as it is liberated, within the 1939 frontiers. No military forces other than the Anglo-American forces operating through AMG, should be permitted to administer Italian metropolitan territory as defined above." Acknowledging the special problems involved in Italy's disputed frontier zones, the department argued that it was a matter of maintaining a "general principle" and that "any other procedure would prejudice final disposition of territories and settlement of frontiers." Officials in Washington appeared to ignore the likelihood of Yugoslav objections and expected implicitly to impose their occupation policy on both litigants in accord with Atlantic Charter principles.[23]

Nominally in agreement, British policy was actually based on different premises. The Foreign Office also advocated the imposition of AMG as the most appropriate temporary solution, but stressed that the success of this policy required Yugoslav cooperation—meaning the cooperation of Josip Broz Tito's Partisans. By 1944 this predominantly communist group had emerged as the dominant resistance force in Yugoslavia, and the Allies had recognized it as such. Both British and Americans were giving military assistance to the Partisans, but the British were particularly interested in retaining influence over Yugoslav developments and did not wish to alienate Tito unnecessarily. Eden therefore recommended in early August that Churchill and British military officials should sound out Tito on the proposed Anglo-American policy during a planned meeting in Italy.[24]

That meeting took place in Naples on 12 and 13 August. During these discussions Churchill and British military commanders outlined to Tito the plan to establish AMG throughout northern Italy (including the Julian Region) when captured from the Germans. Churchill stated that the purposes of the policy were to avoid prejudicing the final status of any disputed area, to accord with the general American policy of opposing wartime territorial changes and to prevent discouraging the Italians who were contributing usefully to the war effort. The British also argued that AMG would be required in the Julian Region for military reasons, "to safeguard the bases and lines of communication of the Allied troops of occupation in Central Europe." Tito was prepared to accept these anticipated military needs and agreed that Anglo-American authorities could exercise operational control in the area for this purpose. He insisted, however, that local civil and military administration should be conducted by Yugoslav authorities, who had "already established a considerable measure of control there." Two contending conceptions of postliberation administration in the Julian Region had clashed for the first time. The British attempt to secure preliminary Yugoslav acquiescence to the AMG plan failed and the issue was left unsettled.[25]

Despite Yugoslav objections there was no change in Anglo-American policy toward the Julian Region. But the nonmilitary ramifications of the question were becoming more prominent. The Anglo-American plan was not based solely on grounds of military necessity but reflected a conviction that an equitable postwar settlement depended upon temporary exclusion from the area of both interested parties. It was confirmed in mid-September that this nonmilitary consideration was the key assumption underpinning policy on the Julian Region. While Roosevelt was at the second Quebec Conference the State Department submitted for his approval a memorandum explaining that

> certain areas of Italy's northeastern frontier will probably be in dispute after hostilities. In order that the final disposition of these disputed areas would not be prejudiced by occupation of

the armed forces of claimant states, it is suggested that Allied Military Government be extended to all Italian metropolitan territory within its 1939 frontiers.... Allied Military Government would thus be maintained until the disputed areas are finally disposed of by treaty or other settlement. Any other course such as letting the Tito forces occupy the Istrian peninsula ... would undoubtedly prejudice the final disposition of these territories, cause deep resentment on the part of the Italian people and result in the loss of considerable prestige by the Allies in Italy.

The president duly approved the recommendation after conferring with Churchill. This high-level decision raised the possibility of an American political commitment to maintain forces in at least one part of Europe after hostilities ended—presumably to avert the sort of development that Woodrow Wilson had been unable to prevent in the Julian Region twenty-five years earlier. This implicit commitment was particularly noteworthy given the strong aversion of the United States to "Balkan" entanglements expressed in opposition to the British-sponsored Adriatic strategy. On a military level American policymakers may have remained wary of using the Julian Region as a gateway to the Balkans, but on a political level they obviously viewed it as the terminus of Italy—a "legitimate" zone for American military operations and one in which the Americans were gradually questioning the dominance of their British partner. The department's memorandum also revealed that, though not interested in the precise ultimate location of the Italo-Yugoslav frontier, some Washington policymakers were already conscious of the Julian problem's potential impact on domestic political stability in Italy. Having established a firm policy, the Americans did not really take into account the probability of continued Yugoslav opposition to the AMG plan nor did they consider how to overcome that obstacle to its implementation.[26]

Churchill meanwhile adopted a more pragmatic approach clearly conceived to further his general political objectives in southeastern Europe. In late August, with a new Allied offensive under way in Italy, the prime minister had reminded Roosevelt of his remarks at

Teheran about Istria, commenting that he was certain that "the arrival of a powerful army in Trieste and Istria in four or five weeks would have an effect far outside military values." Roosevelt's reply stressed the need to continue pursuing the main Italian campaign in order to tie down German divisions that could be used elsewhere, but he did indicate that "we can review our Teheran talk about Trieste and Istria" at the Quebec Conference. At that conference Churchill again proposed a "righthanded movement to give Germany a stab in the Adriatic armpit." He justified the scheme on military grounds but confirmed in his memoirs that "another reason . . . was the rapid encroachment of the Russians into the Balkan Peninsula and the dangerous spread of Soviet influence there." He was beginning to regard Tito as part of that "Soviet influence" and realized that one effect of an Allied landing at the head of the Adriatic would be control of the Julian Region by Anglo-American forces. Roosevelt did not object directly to this proposal, but it would have required the diversion of precious resources to a new front, which might compromise Roosevelt's overriding aim of winning the war against Germany as soon as possible. It was agreed at Quebec to keep open the "Istrian option" but only to act on it if the current Allied offensive in Italy resulted in a significant German retreat. That offensive became bogged down in the following weeks. Although the proposal for an Adriatic operation received serious consideration by British and American generals in October, they eventually rejected it for reasons of logistic impracticability.[27]

Realizing that Britain would have to accommodate itself to a significantly altered postwar balance of power in southeastern Europe, Churchill did not rely on military strategy alone to secure British interests in this region. In mid-October 1944 he visited Moscow, where he and Stalin concluded their famous "percentages" agreement, seemingly dividing southeastern Europe into spheres of interest. As part of this accord the Soviet leader conceded to the British an equal share of influence in Yugoslavia.[28]

There has been much controversy concerning the precise significance of the Moscow accords, but it is clear that they did indicate Churchill's willingness to sanction a spheres-of-influence approach to European affairs. Though such an approach might be viewed as a "realistic" reconciliation of British and Soviet interests in this region, it obviously ran directly counter to the principles of the Atlantic Charter espoused publicly by the United States. This divergence in British and American approaches toward Soviet action in Eastern Europe held important implications for the subsequent development of the Cold War. As Vojtech Mastny has noted, "there was much to be said for both the British and American approaches, provided that the one chosen had been applied jointly and consistently by the two governments. But this did not happen ... a deficiency that only tended to confuse the Russians and encourage them to act unilaterally." This general disparity in British and American policies was also reflected in their respective approaches to the Julian problem.[29]

The Americans still intended to establish AMG in the disputed area but had given no further thought to its practical implementation and failed to define their specific interests in the area. In contrast, the British now considered a local compromise with Tito that squared with the accommodationist philosophy of the Moscow accords and recognized the military realities of the situation. Given that Yugoslav Partisans were already operating in Istria, the Combined Chiefs of Staff (CCS) feared that Tito's men "may suceed in establishing [a] considerable measure of control" in the Julian Region at the time of a German withdrawal. This joint Anglo-American body thus agreed with the British and advised Allied Force Headquarters (AFHQ) in Italy on 30 October 1944 that it would eventually "be necessary to reach some agreement with Marshal Tito about establishment of Allied Military Government." Their view was reinforced by reports from British and American field missions with Tito's Partisans in Slovenia and the Julian Region that the Yugoslavs intended to seize the area and were increasingly hostile toward Britain and the United States.[30]

Policymakers in Washington took little note of these reports. In London, however, there was alarm at the prospect of a potentially explosive encounter between Anglo-American and Yugoslav forces in the Julian Region unless prior agreement were reached with Tito. At the Foreign Office, the War Office, and AFHQ in Italy, British officials anxiously debated the problem as part of a more general reassessment of British objectives in southeastern Europe. These discussions were conditioned by London's interest in maintaining influence on Yugoslav developments and by recent experiences in Greece, where British troops had to be deployed directly against the forces of the Left in an internal civil war. Mindful of this precedent, the British wished to avoid a similar confrontation with the Yugoslavs. The Foreign Office recommended in mid-December that existing policy on the Julian Region be amended to allow for a provisional line of demarcation between Anglo-American and Yugoslav zones of military administration.[31]

In early 1945 Eden formally proposed such a scheme at the Yalta Conference.[32] The demarcation line suggested by the British satisfied Allied military requirements by leaving Trieste and lines of communication to Austria under AMG control, but assigning most of the Julian Region to Yugoslav military administration on the basis of Slavic ethnic predominance. Such a line, of course, would also serve British political objectives with respect to Yugoslavia. In the event, the question was not taken up by the principals at Yalta because more pressing issues crowded the agenda. The opportunity was thereby lost for agreement on a clearly defined occupation scheme for the Julian Region that would have had inter-Allied support at the highest levels.

### A Race for Trieste?

By late 1944 the Anglo-American coalition with the Soviet Union was visibly strained by the pressure of divergent national interests. As Soviet forces advanced rapidly throughout Eastern Europe, British and American observers witnessed with dismay the realization of Stalin's now famous maxim: "This war is not as in the past. Whoever occupies a territory also imposes on it his own social system. Everyone imposes his own system as far as his army has power to do so. It cannot be otherwise."[33] While the Soviet Union appeared to be erecting a sphere of influence around its European borders, the United States remained wedded in principle to the Atlantic Charter program of an open world and the postponement of territorial settlements until the peacemaking. Churchill's politically minded military strategy and his visit to Moscow suggested that Britain would adopt a primarily realpolitik approach, excluding the Soviets where possible but accommodating them where necessary. The general trend toward growing inter-Allied distrust and discord was reinforced as the war against Hitler neared its end. Despite a veneer of camaraderie and some measure of agreement, the Yalta conference in February 1945 failed to resolve underlying tensions. In the following months British and American leaders grew increasingly wary of the Soviet Union and of powerful European movements of the Left, such as Tito's Partisans and the Italian Communists.

The question of temporary military administration of the Julian Region became associated indirectly with this emerging pattern of general antagonisms in southeastern Europe. In the final months of the European war both British and American policymakers gave increasing attention to the political connotations of the Julian problem. Their divergent interpretations of that problem were influenced strongly by their equally divergent objectives in Italy and Yugoslavia.

In Italy, friction between Britain and the United States had long been evident and reflected differing assumptions about the desired character of the postwar world. Hoping to ensure renewed influence in the Mediterranean after the war, the British sought to treat Italy as a vanquished nation as long as possible, using the monarchy to realign domestic political life along conservative lines. The United States, in contrast, was interested primarily in the rapid democratic rehabilitation of Italy as a viable partner in a new liberal world order. Britain was the "senior partner" in Italy for most of the war but, by virtue of its preponderant economic and military power, the United States gradually eclipsed the British during the final months. Roosevelt told Churchill at Yalta that the Allies should seek to foster the regrowth of democracy in Italy as quickly as possible and urged that "some constructive steps should be taken to move away from the present anomalous situation of onerous and obsolete surrender terms which are no longer pertinent to the situation today." Despite their differences, both nations wished to maintain firm control over the leftist-dominated Italian resistance movement in the north. Both Britain and the United States regarded political stability as a crucial postwar objective in Italy.[34]

In early 1945 the British also still hoped to retain meaningful influence in Yugoslavia. Pragmatism demanded maintaining a dialogue with Tito, whose communist Partisans constituted the country's most powerful political force. Although providing Tito with military supplies, the United States had few specific interests at stake in Yugoslavia and generally sought to avoid entanglement in Yugoslav political affairs. Nevertheless, the Americans hoped for the establishment of a nominally democratic regime there in accord with the high-sounding principles of the Yalta Conference's "declaration on liberated Europe." As the year wore on, however, they would increasingly come to view Tito as a Soviet pawn seeking to impose a totalitarian system on Yugoslavia. His stand on Trieste would reinforce that image in Washington.[35]

As 1945 opened the war against Germany was far from over in the Mediterranean theater. The Julian problem thus continued to receive attention primarily on the military level. Military planners discovered, however, that it was not possible to eschew the political implications associated with temporary administration of this disputed area.

While Allied forces slowly fought their way up the Italian peninsula, Field Marshal Sir Harold Alexander, Supreme Allied Commander in the Mediterranean theater (SACMED), began contemplating how to organize the Julian Region for military purposes in the likely event that Tito's Partisans arrived there before Anglo-American forces. Shortly after the Yalta Conference Alexander suggested at a meeting of the Political Committee of the Supreme Allied Command in the Mediterranean that an agreement be sought with Tito in regard to the Julian Region on "purely military grounds." The American representatives present disagreed. Admiral Stone of the Allied Commission objected that the Italian government had been told that "all Venezia Giulia would pass under AMG when liberated" and any alternative course would contravene the surrender instrument concluded with the Italians. Alexander Kirk, the United States political adviser to SACMED, who had just been named ambassador to Italy, was even more forceful in affirming existing American policy but he did not explain how the Allies would deal with Yugoslav opposition. Harold Macmillan, the British resident minister in Italy, noted in his diary at the time that the American position was "all very well in theory; in practice it is difficult to see how we are going to eject Tito." He concluded regretfully that this debate on Julian policy, which had begun in the field, would now have to be resolved by consultation between London and Washington.[36]

In the interim Alexander could only sound out Tito's opinion when he went to Belgrade a few days later to discuss the coordination of possible military operations in northeastern Italy. Having failed to secure an inter-Allied agreement on the diplomatic level to its Yalta proposal for the Julian Region, the British government had hoped that Alexander might reach a compromise on the operational level. But, given the American refusal to modify their policy, Alexander was unable to suggest to Tito a provisional line of demarcation in the Julian Region for operational purposes. Instead, he told Tito on 21 February that it would be necessary to establish AMG control throughout the Julian Region to protect the lines of communication between Trieste and Austria. The Yugoslav leader was still willing to accept AMG where necessary for operational purposes, but only if any Yugoslav civil administration already established by his Partisans was recognized. Tito objected, quite correctly, that establishment of AMG over the entire region (especially the Istrian Peninsula) was not essential for military communications—a view Alexander tacitly shared. Although Alexander may have been heartened by Tito's willingness to concede his military requirements, Yugoslav opposition to official Anglo-American policy had clearly not faltered since the talks with Churchill six months earlier. Like that earlier meeting, these discussions in February 1945 were thus no more than "an exchange of views," and no formal agreements were concluded.[37]

The Americans did not become any more conciliatory after learning of the Tito-Alexander talks. A few days after that meeting State Department officials instructed Kirk that the United States could not permit Yugoslav administration of predominantly Italian districts. They rejected the British suggestion of a provisional demarcation line, reaffirming that AMG was to be the final authority in all the Julian Region. The department considered this stand a direct application of the American "nonpolitical" policy of not prejudicing the resolution of postwar territorial disputes, and criticized "the persistent desire of the British to go as far as possible, for political reasons, in meeting whatever position the JCNL [Jugoslav Committee for National Liberation] has chosen to take in recent months." There was some truth to this charge, but the American policy was equally "political" insofar as it represented an application of Atlantic Charter principles rather than those of military necessity. Indeed, British officials were quick to question the viability of American policy on the military level. Alexander pointed out to Kirk that "the possibility of Allied forces reaching Venezia Giulia before Tito's forces will never arise as Yugoslav forces are already distributed throughout the area." Although they insisted that the problem was no longer theoretical and had to be treated on a practical level, the British did not force the issue. By March the official Anglo-American policy remained that of imposing AMG over the whole Julian Region.[38]

Tito had by now concluded that the Anglo-Americans would not sanction Yugoslav occupation of the disputed territories, especially the predominantly Italian localities of which the most important was Trieste. Yet the Yugoslavs were convinced that they could best assure postwar possession of the Julian Region by a preemptive armed occupation. As Vladimir Velebit, then chief of the Yugoslav military mission in London, explained later, "we thought . . . that whoever is in the possession of a certain territory has a ninety-nine percent chance of keeping it. . . . For this reason we made our preparations to concentrate our troops for the final quick advance against the Germans in a northwestern direction, in order to be in Austria and Trieste before the British and American troops." Those "preparations" included an effort in late 1944 to bring the Italian resistance movement in northeastern Italy under Yugoslav operational control. This objective was partially attained when the Italian Communist party's Garibaldi-Natisone Division agreed to come under the command of Tito's Slovene Ninth Corps in Friuli and parts of the Julian Region, thus splitting the local Italian resistance forces along ideological lines because the Christian Democratic party's Osoppo units refused to accept Yugoslav military control. The other element in Tito's strategy was to postpone the liberation of other parts of Yugoslavia in order to capture the disputed territories and present the British and Americans with a fait accompli. On 20 March 1945 the Yugoslav

Fourth Army began an offensive drive from Dalmatia. Its ultimate objective was Trieste.[39]

Alexander was aware of Tito's intentions but his own armies were not due to launch their final offensive in Italy until April. In a memorandum of 2 March, he cautioned the Combined Chiefs of Staff that Yugoslav troops were likely to control much of the Julian Region before his forces reached the area. He still argued that his forces needed to control Trieste and the lines of communication to Austria for military purposes but recognized that any "solution" of the problem must take into account two additional factors: the political objective of not prejudicing "the final disposition at the peace conference of disputed territory," and the need to avoid armed conflict with Tito's forces. Noting that political considerations had precluded approval of a provisional demarcation line, Alexander suggested as an alternative that Yugoslavia be invited to participate as an ally in AMG of the Julian Region after securing agreement to the plan by the three great powers. Aware that this proposal departed from standard Allied occupation policy in Italy, Alexander had once again suggested a pragmatic compromise solution that would secure his military objectives without risking an inter-Allied military clash. Its capacity to fulfill the political purpose of not prejudicing a final territorial settlement was less certain.[40]

American policymakers remained adamantly opposed to such an adjustment of the existing AMG policy. On the same day that Alexander made his suggestion Kirk complained to Washington that "it has been difficult to bring SAC [Supreme Allied Command] around to our point of view on this question. . . . We have persistently urged them that instead of asking Tito what he would like, we should tell Tito what we intend to do in the area and state that we expect cooperation." Messages from Washington later that month confirmed that Kirk's views were in line with American policy. The State Department explicitly rejected Eden's provisional line of demarcation in the Julian Region and also opposed Alexander's latest compromise suggestion on the grounds that the Yugoslavs were a party to the dispute.[41]

Washington's insistence on the AMG policy obliged the British to rethink their plans, and a rift now emerged within British ranks concerning the most appropriate policy to adopt. By and large the Foreign Office from Eden downward concurred in Alexander's view that a provisional line of demarcation or Yugoslav inclusion in AMG was required to fulfill immediate military purposes without risking armed confrontation with Tito's forces. In mid-March the Armistice and Post-War Committee of the British cabinet also favored the idea of a demarcation line but was more concerned about getting the Americans to promise to provide part of the forces required to occupy and administer the area. Having examined four alternative proposals for the postliberation administration of the Julian Region, the committee stressed the need to consult the Americans before making an approach to the Yugoslavs and concluded that the British government should support any of these plans the Americans would back with force. This decision was symptomatic of London's general endeavors to secure an American commitment to postwar security in Europe.[42]

Though sharing that general objective with his subordinates, Churchill had given up hope of retaining British influence over Tito and saw no reason to accommodate the Yugoslavs on the Julian issue. He expressed his views forthrightly to Eden on 11 March:

> My feeling is that henceforth our inclination should be to back Italy against Tito. Tito can be left to himself in his mountains to stew in Balkan juice which is bitter. But the fact that we are generally favourable to Italian claims at the head of the Adriatic will give us an influence over Italian internal policies as against Communists and wild men which may assist the reintegration of the Italian State. I have lost my relish for Yugoslavia.... On the other hand, I hope we may still save Italy from the Bolshevik pestilence.

A few days later the prime minister proposed informing Roosevelt "that we were favourably disposed towards Italy in the Northern Adriatic as against Tito's claims." Eden sought to persuade Churchill that Britain might still be able to influence the Yugoslav situation and should not write off Tito because there was no one else the British could usefully support in Yugoslavia. Indeed, it was more important than ever to counter anti-British feeling in Yugoslavia and try "to keep Marshal Tito on the right lines" rather than to leave Yugoslavia "to him and the Russians." A realistic compromise should therefore be reached concerning the disputed territory, if only because Tito's forces were likely to occupy it first. Despite Eden's admonitions of caution, Churchill became the most forceful and highly placed advocate of a strong Anglo-American line on the Julian question. This division in British ranks was left unresolved in the short term and would create some confusion for American policymakers in approaching the issue.[43]

While British and American policymakers groped for a viable policy, Tito's forces were advancing rapidly toward the Julian Region. In early April the Anglo-American armies were still stalled around Bologna. There had been some hope that successful completion of the Operation Sunrise negotiations (the projected secret surrender of German forces in Italy) would facilitate a speedy Allied takeover of northern Italy, including the Julian Region. Those negotiations, however, had halted—in part because of Soviet objections.[44]

The need for a coherent and realistic Anglo-American policy on the Julian Region was becoming urgent for both military and political reasons. The British thus presented the Armistice and Post-War Committee's four alternative plans to the Americans for consideration on 4 April, noting pointedly that they would back whichever plan Washington preferred, "providing the U.S. and U.K. Governments jointly contribute forces . . . required to back the plan until the final settlement is made by the peace treaty." After obtaining State Department clearance, the Anglo-American Combined Civil Affairs Committee approved one of the plans on 12 April. The plan provided for establishment of a jointly supported Anglo-American military government throughout the Julian Region but accepted the continuation of civil authorities of the predominant nationality in each locality. Soviet cooperation was to be sought in requesting the Yugoslavs to withdraw any of their forces in the area. The plan allayed British apprehensions concerning the inclusion of American forces in the occupation and administration of the Julian Region. It was, moreover, a compromise which attempted not only to meet Alexander's operational requirements but also the State Department's and Churchill's more long-term political concerns. The plan nevertheless was deeply flawed in that it failed to offer a realistic mechanism for defusing Yugoslav opposition peacefully and provided no practical guidelines for those who would be charged with setting AMG in place.[45]

Franklin D. Roosevelt died that same day and Harry S Truman became president of the United States. The State Department promptly presented the new American leader with a report on the major foreign policy problems confronting the United States. The section of the report concerning Italy suggested the importance the Department now placed on the Julian Region: "Our gravest problem at present, aside from the country's economic distress, is to forestall Yugoslav occupation of an important part of northeastern Italy, prejudicing by unilateral action a final equitable settlement of this territorial dispute and precipitating serious trouble with Italy. Difficulties may be encountered in maintaining Allied (Anglo-American) military government in this area."[46] Truman treated the issue cautiously while the war continued in Europe but would eventually be convinced by the State Department and Churchill that the United States should at least prevent Yugoslav control of Trieste and its environs. Whether or not Roosevelt would have dealt otherwise with the Yugoslavs is a moot point.

The final Allied offensive in Italy began at last in mid-April. By then the Yugoslavs had already thrust deeply into the Julian Region and were moving rapidly toward Trieste. Kirk anxiously cabled the State Department on 24 April, questioning the wisdom of maintaining Allied air support and supplies to the Yugoslavs at current levels in view of their rapid military progress in the Julian Region. Washington's reply echoed the "British position" that such support must be continued "during the operational phase." The main justification given was that the Allies could thereby rebut possible later charges that they had not cooperated with Tito against the Germans or that the entire Julian Region had been liberated without Anglo-American assistance. Ironically, although State Department officials may have thought they were emulating the "British position," both Churchill and Sir Orme Sargent of the Foreign Office seriously questioned the wisdom of continuing to provide Tito with military assistance. Sargent even went so far as to suggest that the CCS give Alexander a full explanation of current British policy toward Yugoslavia because there was reason to believe that "in recent months Field Marshal Alexander has been pursuing a policy of generosity and consideration towards Tito which differs considerably from the Prime Minister's and our own present ideas." This debate about continuing military cooperation was, in fact, of little significance for immediate practical purposes, since it now seemed that the Anglo-American contribution to the liberation of any part of the region might consist only of air support and military supplies. By 27 April Tito's forces were within 41 kilometers of Trieste while the closest British or American troops remained 222 kilometers away.[47]

During the next week military developments in Italy moved at lightning speed, generating their own political momentum. Occupation plans for the Julian Region could no longer be discussed at leisure in Washington and London. As the Yugoslavs neared Trieste Anglo-American policymakers had to confront directly the unresolved question of how to handle Yugoslav resistance to AMG in the Julian Region. The emerging prospect of armed confrontation with a wartime ally obliged these policymakers to make a hasty reappraisal of their political and military objectives in the area and the means they were prepared to use in attaining them.

Field Marshal Alexander was fully cognizant of the pace of military developments in northeastern Italy and of their consequences for Trieste and surrounding areas. The Sunrise negotiations for a separate German surrender had been revived and were now almost concluded. This surrender did not include German forces in the Julian Region, but Kirk, in particular, hoped that its successful conclusion would release Anglo-American forces for a speedy invasion of the Julian Region. He urged the State Department to apply pressure in Washington to persuade the military to exploit this opportunity promptly. Alexander, however, had decided that even with the "secret surrender" it was too late to implement the official Anglo-American plan because the Yugoslavs had already captured parts of the Julian Region and were expanding their control rapidly. The field marshal was seriously concerned about "drifting into a state of war with Tito." On 26 April, he advised the CCS that unless instructed otherwise, he would order his forces to establish AMG only in "those parts of Venezia Giulia which are of importance to my military operations." The areas in question comprised Trieste, Pula (Pola), and the lines of communication to Austria. The rest of the Julian Region was to be left to the Yugoslavs, and Tito was to be advised of Alexander's precise intentions in advance.[48]

Churchill advocated a different policy. He cabled Truman on 27 April, seeking to persuade him that Alexander should be ordered to make a dash for Trieste.

> It seems vital to get Trieste if we can do so in the easy manner proposed, and to run the risks inherent in these political military operations.
>
> The late president always attached great importance to Trieste, which he thought should be an international port forming an outlet into the Adriatic from the regions of the Danube Basin. . . . The great thing is to be there before Tito's guerillas are in occupation. . . . The actual status of Trieste can be determined at leisure.

A day earlier Kirk had dispatched an urgent request for similar instructions to the State Department. While Alexander was advocating a policy based on military realities, Churchill and Kirk were each emphasizing political considerations.[49]

The next day the Combined Chiefs of Staff, with Truman's approval, reaffirmed existing Anglo-American policy. They ordered Alexander to establish AMG throughout the Julian Region "if military necessity so requires before Soviet and Yugoslav agreements have been obtained." He was to consult the CCS for further instructions only if "Yugoslav forces refuse to cooperate in the plan for interim administration." Given the respective Anglo-American and Yugoslav field positions, this vague directive was virtually meaningless from an operational point of view.[50]

Not surprisingly, Alexander remained convinced that the plan was dangerously impractical. Nevertheless, he did want complete control of Trieste so that it could serve as an effective base for further military operations. Consequently, on 30 April he ordered his field commanders to secure only purely military objectives in the Julian Region: Trieste and the lines of communication linking it to Italy and Austria; Pula and the lines of communication leading to Trieste; and the anchorages between Trieste and Pula. Alexander advised Tito of his intentions and cautioned his forces to exercise "maximum care" in linking up with Yugoslav troops. A frustrated Kirk reported to the State Department that "this decision, of course, was made on purely military grounds" and effectively represented "no great change" in Alexander's plan as set forth on 26 April. Alexander clearly did not believe there was military justification for control of the whole Julian Region. Unlike Kirk, who continued to insist on the need to implement the full-blown AMG policy, Alexander was unwilling to risk an armed clash with the Yugoslavs for nonmilitary reasons. The field marshal hoped to reach a working compromise with the Yugoslavs, forged in the field on the basis of operational requirements rather than political considerations.[51]

Given the rapid Yugoslav advance, Churchill agreed that it was unlikely that the British and Americans could impose AMG on all the Julian Region. He cabled Truman on 30 April that it would be "a delusion to suppose the Yugoslav Government, with Soviet Government behind them, would agree" to such a policy. Churchill believed, however, that Trieste could still be salvaged if Alexander were to advance toward the city "as quickly as possible before informing the Russians or Yugoslavs." His rationale was that "we are as much entitled to move freely into Trieste, if we can get there as were the Russians to win their way into Vienna. We ought if possible to get there first and in turn talk about the rest of the Province." The prime minister was continuing to trade in the realities of power politics, wherein armed occupation was a more valuable commodity than diplomatic requests. Moreover, Churchill now sought to persuade Truman that Yugoslav aspirations were part of a broader wave of Soviet-inspired expansion:

> While the Allied forces will arrive in Trieste as liberators . . . the Yugoslavs will arrive as conquerors laying their hands on territory which they vehemently covet. . . . in view of the United States' friendly sentiments toward Italy, some defence of Italian rights at the head of the Adriatic might be the means of harmonious combination between the United States, the British and

the Italian Governments and would split or render ineffective the Communist movement in Italy. . . . There will be a great shock to public opinion in many countries when the American armies of the north withdraw, as they have to under the occupational zone scheme, . . . and when the Soviet advance overflows all those vast areas of Central Germany which the Americans had conquered. If at the same time the whole of the northern Adriatic is occupied by Yugoslavs who are the Russian tools and beneficiaries, this shock will be emphasised in a most intense degree.

He expressed similar views to Alexander the next day. Churchill's recommendations were part of a concerted effort to ensure that Anglo-American forces occupied key points in Europe at the end of the war to facilitate an "early and speedy showdown and settlement with Russia." In this particular case his additional hope of weakening the appeal of the Italian Communist party (PCI) was not without foundation, for the Trieste issue involved an awkward choice between upholding the city's Italian character or maintaining international solidarity with the Yugoslav Communists. During the war the PCI consistently argued that the national problem in the Julian Region had to be "subordinated to the local and international class interests of the proletariat." That policy offered Churchill a convenient political rationalization for his suggestions regarding Trieste, but his proposal for a "secret" assault on the city was itself a "delusion," for Alexander had already advised Tito of his intentions to advance into the area.[52]

The Yugoslav leader had promptly replied that he was not even willing to accept Alexander's limited objectives. Noting that Yugoslav troops were now attacking Trieste, Tito declared that the Yugoslav operational zone extended to the Isonzo (Soča) River (to the west of Trieste). He was willing to let Alexander use the ports of Trieste and Pula and rail connections for supplying Anglo-American troops in Austria, but he emphasized that in the Yugoslav zone of operations east of the Isonzo "our military and civil authorities will naturally continue to function." If there had been doubt earlier, Tito's messages made clear that the Yugoslavs did not intend yielding administrative control of any parts of the Julian Region captured from the Germans.⁵³

As Alexander had long expected, most of the Julian Region was in Yugoslav hands by 30 April and he saw little advantage in challenging that control. Trieste, however, had not fallen. That city was now the real issue in the field.

As Anglo-American and Yugoslav forces closed in on Trieste from opposite directions caution prevailed in Washington. Secretary of War Henry Stimson sensed that the situation contained the potential for disaster. He believed that Churchill hoped to exploit it to pursue traditional British interests in southeastern Europe. Fearing American military involvement in the area, the pragmatic Stimson suggested to General George Marshall, the Army chief of staff, that Truman be briefed "as to the background of the past differences between Britain and America on these matters." On 30 April he warned Acting Secretary of State Joseph Grew of the dangers of armed confrontation with the Yugoslavs, recalling that "Woodrow Wilson's hand was forced last time in the same locality." Despite continuing exhortations from Kirk in Italy urging the necessity for an unyielding AMG policy, Grew seemed to share Stimson's apprehensions. The acting secretary advised Truman the same day that Yugoslav Partisans appeared to have occupied Trieste and Pula, but that the State Department deemed it "unwise to employ American forces" to oust them if they refused to withdraw. The president replied that "he did not intend to have American forces used to fight Yugoslav forces nor did he wish to become involved in Balkan politics." It seemed the ambivalence in American policy would be resolved in favor of avoiding conflict with an ally rather than by securing Atlantic Charter principles or heeding Kirk's warnings of instability in Italy. The Americans replied cautiously to Churchill's earlier message, explaining that Alexander had sufficient guidance and that the United States was unwilling to commit forces to a conflict "in the Balkan political arena."⁵⁴

The United States appeared to be relenting in its commitment to impose AMG on Trieste and the rest of the Julian Region, yet the talk in Washington was about avoiding involvement in the Balkans, not about changing Alexander's orders or renouncing the AMG policy.

American policymakers were awaiting developments in the field before modifying their official policy. These were politics of inertia and uncertainty.

Military developments in the Julian Region during the first days of May had a decisive impact on the future complexion of the problem. On 1 May elements of the Second New Zealand Division of the British Eighth Army crossed the Isonzo. Overcoming scattered German resistance, they encountered Yugoslav forces in Monfalcone (Tržić), a few miles west of Trieste. By then Yugoslav Partisans had already entered Trieste following an Italian uprising in the city on 30 April. The German garrison had resisted vigorously and the fighting did not end until 2 May when New Zealand troops entered the city. As a result, some of the Germans surrendered to Yugoslavs while others gave themselves up to New Zealanders. The "race" for Trieste had ended somewhat ambiguously.[55]

### Conclusion

Upon liberation Trieste immediately became the setting for a potential inter-Allied crisis. American wartime policies had certainly contributed to that tense situation, and in the following weeks the United States would prove willing to risk armed conflict with Yugoslavia—possibly backed by the Soviet Union—to obtain military control of the Trieste area. But American actions in May and thereafter should not necessarily be seen as the ineluctable culmination of wartime developments, for the Julian question had played only a peripheral role in American wartime diplomacy. The involvement of the United States had developed indirectly and incrementally.

American policymakers had not seriously confronted the problem posed by the Italo-Yugoslav frontier dispute until 1944, when they formulated the policy of imposing Anglo-American AMG. This policy had the advantage of excluding both of the direct contenders from the disputed area and appeared justified on grounds of military necessity. It coincided with the general American objective of postponing political-territorial questions for settlement at the peace table where, as one former State Department planner recalled, "they could be considered rationally without pressure from the military situation, and in the context of a new world order." Implicitly, American policy on the Julian Region also rested on the assumption that the dispute should eventually be resolved according to the criteria of self-determination and economic rationality so that the location of the postwar frontier would "be such as to maximize the chances for peace, stability and mutual acceptance." This assumption was evident in American thinking, from early planning studies on the area completed at low levels in the State Department to President Roosevelt's own comments on the future of Trieste, Pula, and Rijeka at the first Quebec Conference.[56]

Nevertheless, the United States took no effective steps until war's end to implement its objectives in the Julian Region. On the operational level American military planners consistently rejected Churchill's "Mediterranean strategy." Such action would probably have ensured Anglo-American military control of significant portions of southeastern Europe (the Julian Region included), but American strategists considered their first priority to be victory against Germany in northwestern Europe and relegated the Mediterranean theater to a distinctly secondary status. Indeed, Americans were somewhat disturbed by British wartime policy, which was grounded in traditional European balance-of-power concepts and was designed consciously to preserve British interests in the region. In contrast, policymakers in Washington recoiled at the prospect of "Balkan entanglements" and had no intention of deploying extensive American military resources to secure political objectives there.

By 1945 American policy in the Julian Region was unrealistic. East-West relations were deteriorating, American officials in Italy were becoming increasingly concerned about containing a perceived leftist threat, and there was Yugoslav opposition to the official Anglo-American policy of imposing AMG over the whole Julian Region. Despite British exhortations for a compromise on the operational level, the State Department steadfastly refused to modify the policy of establishing AMG throughout the Julian Region.

A few American officials, such as Alexander Kirk, began to conceptualize the problem in terms prototypical of the Cold War. They believed that Anglo-American control of the Julian Region would help stabilize the Italian government as well as halt communist aggression. Like Churchill, Kirk sought to insert a definite political impetus into the final stages of the Anglo-American campaign in Italy to attain this objective.

In Washington, however, continued adherence to the original AMG policy largely represented a pro forma reaffirmation of Atlantic Charter principles. No attempt was made to negotiate seriously with the Yugoslavs to permit peaceful implementation of the policy, but neither were preparations made for using military force against them. Only when the issue was nearing a dangerous denouement in the final week of April 1945 did high-level American policymakers, led by Henry Stimson, reassess the AMG policy and reject the idea of risking American lives in an armed confrontation with an ally for temporary control of an area of no great importance to the United States. Even at that crucial moment they did not reject outright the AMG policy but merely urged caution, preferring to await developments in the field before making any clear-cut decisions. The confusion in American policy persisted until the German surrender in Trieste to Yugoslav and New Zealand forces. For that reason, in the case of Trieste, it would be incorrect to say that the Cold War had begun before the Second World War ended. Quite simply, the rigid dichotomies of the Cold War had not yet crystallized.

Only after Trieste's liberation on 2 May would the Julian problem be set in a new transitional framework between the politics of World War II and those of the Cold War. The United States had hitherto given little attention to the implementation of postwar objectives in the Julian Region because the problem of Yugoslav opposition to the AMG policy remained theoretical as long as the area was in Nazi hands. By the first week of May those wartime considerations no longer applied. Germany was defeated, there was an Anglo-American presence in Trieste, and Tito's forces appeared to be attempting an armed takeover. Trieste had become a *post*-war problem. The United States now had little choice but to decide between accommodation or confrontation in responding to a direct Yugoslav challenge to its objectives in the area. That American response would have to be framed in the new context of international relations in the postwar world—a world in which the United States could not afford the vacillation and inconsistency characteristic of its wartime policies toward the Julian problem. The backdrop was in place for one of the first inter-Allied crises of the postwar period to be played out.

## 3

# Toward Containment? The Trieste Crisis of May 1945

⊙ Our policy publicly proclaimed is that territorial changes should be made only after thorough study and after full consultation and deliberation between the various Governments involved.

It is, however, Marshal Tito's apparent intention to establish his claims by forces of arms and military occupation. Action of this kind would be all too reminiscent of Hitler, Mussolini and Japan. It is to prevent such actions that we have been fighting this war.—Field Marshal Sir Harold Alexander, "Message Issued to Allied Armed Forces in the Mediterranean Theater," 19 May 1945

When dawn broke on 3 May 1945, Trieste found itself under an uneasy dual occupation. The fortunes of war had brought two very different liberating armies to the area at the same time. New Zealand soldiers held most of the strong points but Tito's Fourth Army controlled the rest of the city. Each force had been charged by its superiors with the responsibility of establishing a military government. Not suprisingly, relations between the two armies were tense and confused.

This unanticipated situation represented a conspicuous failure of inter-Allied wartime diplomacy. Its consequences would have to be dealt with in a rapidly changing context of international relations, for the Second World War ended in Europe only a few days later. The occupation of Trieste was no longer a hypothetical problem that could be postponed and finessed in various ways in accord with the principles of military necessity. Partly as a consequence of ambiguous and poorly integrated Anglo-American wartime policies on the Julian question, it now became a matter of direct political-military confrontation within Allied ranks which would test rival postwar objectives.

The timing of the Trieste crisis coincided with the first moments of transition between the politics of World War II and those of the Cold War. It resembled other problems confronting the Truman administration insofar as it represented a failure of earlier Allied wartime diplomacy, but it was the only problem that assumed crisis proportions during the very week in which the European war ended, raising the immediate possibility of a military clash between East and West. American policymakers were obviously alarmed and recognized the need for urgent action, but they had no coherent strategy for dealing with the sort of threat posed by the Yugoslavs in Trieste.

Fumbling for a suitable response, policymakers in Washington eventually stood firm against Yugoslav occupation of the city on the basis of a tacit spheres-of-influence approach. In doing so they anticipated in certain ways the later development of the Truman administration's basic Cold War strategy: containment. American policy on Trieste in mid-1945 was neither preconceived nor rationalized in the same terms as the full-blown containment policy of 1947. It was, moreover, a policy adopted tentatively under crisis conditions against a complex background of wartime confusion, presidential uncertainty, and bureaucratic disagreement. Nevertheless, there is a case for interpreting the Truman administration's response to the Trieste crisis as an early step on the road to containment.[1] To determine the strength of that case it is necessary to examine in detail the actions of relevant American policymakers and their interaction with British officials during this first direct postwar confrontation with a communist regime.

## Crisis in the Field

A climate of inter-Allied tension prevailed in the Julian Region from the moment New Zealand and Yugoslav forces made contact near the Isonzo in those final days of war. Geoffrey Cox, an intelligence officer with the New Zealand division, recalled an abrupt change in the reception accorded the New Zealanders when they entered the Yugoslav zone of operations in Northern Italy: "Suddenly ... the atmosphere was completely changed.... We felt like strangers in a strange land, as if at the Isonzo we had passed some unmarked but distinct frontier. As indeed we had. We had driven from Italy into what was to become a No Man's Land between Eastern and Western Europe, and like any other No Man's Land it was extremely unpleasant." Surprised by the rapidity of the final Anglo-American advance, Yugoslav field officers sought to delay the New Zealand force in Monfalcone on 1 May. Realizing, however, that the battle for Trieste was not over, the New Zealand commander, General Bernard Freyberg, ordered his division to resume its advance toward that city as stipulated in Alexander's instructions. Despite Yugoslav protests his troops arrived in Trieste the next day in time to share in the surrender of the city. According to his earlier orders, Freyberg was to have established AMG in Trieste. But the Yugoslavs had already installed their own civil administration and the New Zealanders soon encountered overt Yugoslav hostility. General Freyberg found himself confronted with a menacing demand from the chief of staff of the Fourth Yugoslav Army, General Pavle Jaksić: "We request Allied troops immediately to withdraw to west bank river ISONZO and that Allied Military authorities do not mix in our internal affairs. After this warning 4 Army will not be responsible for anything that might happen if our request is not met. This is categorical." Prudently, Freyberg made no attempt to establish AMG and sought further instructions from his superiors at AFHQ.[2]

These unexpected developments in the field quickly gave rise to confrontation at a higher level. On 3 May Alexander received a message from Tito protesting that "Allied Forces, which are under your command, without any previous notice have entered Trieste, Gorizia and Monfalcone, the cities which have been liberated by the Yugoslav Army." Tito demanded an immediate explanation. Alexander himself had just dispatched a note to the Yugoslav leader suggesting that the overlapping of the two armies' operational zones need not cause "serious difficulties" and restating his intention to establish "the necessary organization in Trieste, and elsewhere in the Communications Zone, to ensure that my line of communication is brought into operation rapidly and can function efficiently." It is significant that the two cables—based on such radically different assumptions—crossed each other in transit. The two documents clearly exposed the gulf separating Anglo-American and Yugoslav intentions.[3]

Tito and Alexander exchanged further cables protesting each other's actions. After failing to reach immediate agreement, Alexander sent his chief of staff, Lieutenant General William Morgan, to Belgrade in an attempt to break the impasse. Alexander informed the CCS on 5 May that he had instructed Morgan to seek Tito's agreement to a provisional demarcation line which would satisfy his essential military requirements. In effect Alexander was proposing the plan which he and the Foreign Office had long favored. This time the CCS approved his proposal, providing Tito was informed such an agreement was "purely military" and would "not affect the ultimate disposal of any pre-war Italian territory which will be a matter to be decided at the peace settlement." Morgan presented the proposal to Tito on 9 May.[4]

Tito's response made it clear that a "purely military" settlement was no longer possible now that the war had ended. The Yugoslav leader still offered Alexander full use of the port of Trieste and the lines of communication required for military purposes but insisted on continued Yugoslav civil administration of the area. He also observed that the matter had taken on a predominantly political significance. Noting that Tito had raised a political issue, Alexander replied that he "must now refer the whole question to the British and American governments." Despite Alexander's efforts to reach a compromise settlement on the operational level, the attempt to secure a military solution had failed.[5]

## Reactions in Washington

These negotiations had been followed closely in Washington from the moment Trieste was liberated. Indeed, the week or so during which Alexander sought a compromise with Tito was a critical period in the evolution of American policy toward the problem. During this time some American policymakers came to view the Trieste situation as an example of totalitarian aggression and demanded firm opposition to it.

The course of American policy after 10 May is especially noteworthy in view of the mood in Washington during the final days of the military "race" for Trieste. Despite Kirk's emphasis on the political necessity of establishing AMG in as much of the Julian Region as possible, Stimson's caution had initially prevailed. Officials in Washington had seemed to accept that perhaps only Alexander's operational requirements could be met. Grew had even notified Kirk on 1 May that, if the Yugoslavs opposed the extension of AMG, "we cannot contemplate the use of American troops to enforce this policy." This apparent repudiation of the State Department's own policy stemmed largely from the fear of dangerous clashes with the Yugoslavs if they controlled most of the Julian Region.[6]

Trieste's liberation on 2 May had complicated the situation insofar as an armed clash was now possible even in fulfilling Alexander's minimum operational requirements. Officials in Washington continued to react cautiously, recognizing that direct contact between the two armies at Trieste could be more explosive than the contingencies hitherto foreseen. The War Department advised strongly against risking an armed clash, and Stimson repeated to Grew his usual line that "the American people would not sustain our getting embroiled in the Balkans." Stimson believed that the problem was "another case of these younger men, the subordinates in the State Department, doing dangerous things." Grew was noncommittal, but the State Department risked no major initiatives while Alexander negotiated with Tito.[7]

This caution was also due to Truman's attitude. The president had been quick to tell Grew on 30 April that he did not want American forces fighting the Yugoslavs. The reasons for this wariness are set out quite clearly in Truman's own description of his early reactions to the Trieste crisis:

> I did not want to become involved in the Balkans in a way that could lead us into another world conflict. In any case, I was

anxious to get the Russians into the war against Japan as soon as possible, thus saving the lives of countless Americans. Churchill, on the other hand, was always anxious to do what he could to save British control of the eastern Mediterranean in order to maintain Great Britain's influence in Greece, Egypt, and the Middle East.

Truman's comments indicate that he viewed the Trieste situation in a much broader context and that when the crisis first broke he shared Stimson's apprehensions concerning its possible ramifications.[8]

Even with a crisis looming and Anglo-American control of Trieste itself uncertain, the State Department did not readily abandon its unrealistic AMG policy. While Alexander tried to secure a working compromise, Kirk repeatedly warned his superiors in Washington of drastic consequences in Italy if the original AMG strategy were set aside. The Italian government also protested to the Americans, urging total AMG control of the Julian Region as promised. State Department officials were not unreceptive to these arguments. H. Freeman Matthews, Director of the Office of European Affairs, told Grew on 2 May that "when it becomes publicly known that Tito's forces are assuming control in that area we may expect serious outbursts both in Italy and on the part of our large and influential Italian-American population here." Grew himself expressed similar views to the president, suggesting that American troops might have to be used to maintain order in northern Italy if Yugoslav occupation of the Julian Region persisted. Some State Department officials would have preferred to maintain the original AMG policy but their hands were tied by Stimson's and Truman's opposition as well as by Alexander's insistence on securing only essential military requirements. The president's reluctance to use armed force finally brought them face to face with the basic inconsistency of having a forcefully articulated policy but no realistic means of implementing it.[9]

There is evidence, moreover, that the State Department was not content merely to await the outcome of the Tito-Alexander negotiations. The department wished to consult the Soviet Union in the hope that Moscow might persuade the Yugoslavs to withdraw from the Julian Region. Such a hope was predicated on the assumption—

already evident among American policymakers—that Stalin could control Tito. It was of a piece with Washington's faith in the efficacy of summit-level negotiations among the great powers as a means of defusing local conflicts, assuring inter-Allied harmony and, presumably, securing the triumph of Atlantic Charter principles. Both Matthews and Ambassador Patterson in Belgrade recommended sounding out the Soviets even though Moscow had not yet replied to the earlier notification of American intentions in the Julian Region.[10]

The British Foreign Office, however, strongly favored Alexander's plan for an operational compromise with the Yugoslavs—as long as the arrangements did indeed fulfill military needs and included Anglo-American control of Trieste. British diplomats believed that contacting Moscow would only hamper Alexander's and Morgan's efforts. There was considerable apprehension in London concerning the State Department's proposal to involve the Soviet Union. The Foreign Office, on 7 May, instructed the British ambassador in Washington, Lord Halifax: "please do your utmost to induce U.S. Government to suspend their communication to Moscow which will clearly put General Morgan in an embarrassing position and might imperil the success of his negotiations. As soon as negotiations are completed we will be prepared to discuss with U.S. Government what to say to the Russians." As it happened, the CCS had just approved Alexander's plan, and Halifax was able to reassure London that the "State Department now agrees not to make any démarche in Moscow until [they] can do so without prejudicing Morgan's discussions in Belgrade." Once again the State Department had been restrained—this time by the British.[11]

A greater degree of practicality now became evident within State Department ranks. The plan for extending AMG to the whole Julian Region was set aside as patently unrealistic. Instead, State Department officials now sought to ensure that their objectives could at least be achieved in the Trieste area, where Anglo-American forces were already present.

Having limited their interest to Trieste, they still had to shape American policy to coincide with their objectives. Kirk believed that the most pressing issue was to alleviate the risk allegedly posed to Italian political stability by Yugoslav occupation of Trieste. His view was not widely shared in Washington, even though the Italian government put forward similar arguments. But officials in Washington did concur in Kirk's analysis when he pointed out in a dispatch of 8 May that there was a more general goal that the United States should pursue. Likening Tito's justification for Yugoslav occupation of Trieste to those once advanced for expansion by Hitler and the Japanese, the ambassador to Italy concluded that "I do not see how we as a nation can meet our responsibilities before the world unless we challenge ... Tito's championship of illegal methods." This sentiment coincided closely with the interpretation of the Trieste affair evolving in Washington.[12]

Cavendish Cannon, a member of the State Department's Southern European division, had raised the same point two days earlier as part of a tactical plan to ensure that the department's views prevailed in Washington. In a revealing memorandum (whose influence would surpass that of Kirk's cable), Cannon argued that "top people" in the War Department opposed the State Department's recommendations on the Julian Region because they saw them as "part of a policy with which our military have never been overly sympathetic, namely the program for building up the Italians." He suggested that, in interdepartmental talks to be held the next day, the State Department should shift the emphasis from the Italian aspect of the question to that of the "fundamental principle of territorial settlement by orderly processes." They should point out that Tito "would never dare taking this strong line unless counting on full Soviet support" and that success in the Julian Region would encourage Tito to press similar claims to parts of Austria, Hungary, and Greece. Cannon's conclusion resembled Kirk's but specifically invoked a Soviet threat: "It is not a question of taking sides in a dispute between Italy and Yugoslavia, or of becoming involved in internal Balkan politics. The problem is essentially one of deciding whether we are going to permit the Soviet Government which operates directly on territorial settlements in the case of Poland which lies in the Soviet theater, to set up whatever states and boundaries look best for the future power of the U.S.S.R." Interestingly, both Cannon and Kirk saw fit to apply the general "lessons" of prewar appeasement to the specific situation in Trieste. Even more noteworthy, perhaps, was Cannon's hasty assumption that the Soviet Union was ultimately responsible for Tito's actions. Yet Cannon's arguments (complemented by Kirk's) shaped the State Department's tactics in its attempts to dominate American policy on Trieste.[13]

When Alexander's negotiations with Belgrade broke down on 9 May, the basic elements of the State Department's postwar policy on Trieste were in place. They were in large measure a logical extension of wartime goals but they also carried intimations of an emerging Cold War atmosphere. Trieste policy would be guided by three major concerns, to be given differing emphases at appropriate times.

The most prominent objective was to secure complete control of Trieste. The State Department accepted the realistic British approach of a demarcation line and discarded its own wartime policy of establishing AMG over the entire Julian Region. Publicly, American policy was still couched in terms of upholding Atlantic Charter principles of self-determination and orderly territorial settlement, but this new limited goal marked an implicit acceptance of spheres of influence in this area. Indeed, the second element affecting Trieste policy was a more general anxiety about Soviet-backed pressure on a strategic locality that fell within the Western sphere of influence. At war's end it was still uncertain whether the United States would seek to resolve such problems through cooperation or confrontation with the Soviet Union and the newly emerging communist states of Eastern Europe. That ambivalence was evident in American responses to the Trieste crisis, but the fact that the State Department was now willing to risk an armed clash to end Yugoslav occupation of Trieste was an indirect measure of the extent to which attitudes were hardening toward the Soviet Union and its putative "satellites." Finally, but of lesser importance in shaping immediate Trieste policy, was the need felt by Foreign Service officers such as Kirk for postwar stability in Italy to ensure a "democratic" form of government there. All three considerations figured in Cannon's memorandum, and the State Department established them as cornerstones of American policy on Trieste.

After Tito rejected Alexander's proposal, State Department officials lost no time in presenting their analysis to the president. They asserted that the Trieste dispute not only threatened Italian stability but was a microcosm of a larger problem in East-West relations with vital implications for "the future peace of Europe." Grew sent a memorandum to Truman on 10 May outlining this interpretation in language prototypical of Cold War diplomacy. The document was a synopsis of all that had transpired within the State Department since 2 May. It was very much the work of those "younger men" in the department whom Stimson distrusted and much of it was based on Cannon's proposal of 6 May. Grew repeated verbatim the passage alleging Soviet influence on Tito, and added that "Yugoslav (Russian) occupation of Trieste . . . would have most far-reaching consequences beyond the immediate territory involved." He even borrowed Kirk's comparison of Tito's methods with those of Hitler, and dramatically concluded that:

> at a time when we have at last achieved military victory in Europe and have a force of millions of men in arms on that continent, we must decide if we will acquiesce in unilateral action by force as a method of drawing the future boundaries of Western Europe. There is no doubt that Prime Minister Churchill sees the implications in these developments and feels, . . . that we should not give way to Tito. . . . Tito's acquiescence to even an unsatisfactory minimum now seems questionable. In these circumstances we may be faced with the necessity of withdrawing completely from this area, with all its consequences, or of implementing our present policy by threat of force to secure complete and exclusive control of Trieste and Pola, the keys to the region.

There was little doubt which alternative Grew favored.[14]

It is noteworthy that his arguments concerning Trieste were based on certain more general assumptions about the contemporary international political situation. The most important of these was that the Soviet Union was intent on pursuing expansionist policies and was directing communist organizations throughout Europe to serve its own purposes. Closely related to this assumption was the view that such expansion represented a direct threat to American international interests. Plainly Grew and those below him saw Trieste as another Munich in the making—unless the United States stood firm.[15]

Nevertheless, future policy depended on the president. In order to gain Truman's support for the State Department's policy Grew followed up his memorandum with a personal briefing on 10 May. During this briefing Grew reiterated the key points in his memorandum, stressing his conviction that "Russia was undoubtedly behind Tito's move with a view to utilize Trieste as a Russian port in the future." The president required no further persuasion. He told Grew that developments at Trieste left the United States with no alternative but to "throw them out." Only days after declaring categorically that "American forces should not be used to fight Yugoslav forces or for political purposes in the Balkans," Truman was prepared to sanction that risk. This reversal typified the fluidity and uncertainty which some historians have identified as a general characteristic of Truman's foreign policy during his early months in the White House. As Robert Messer has noted, "in truth, during the first weeks of his presidency he often fluctuated in his views and actions, depending on the circumstances and advice of the moment." In this case Grew and the State Department were providing the advice; and they had put forward a very persuasive argument for firm action in Trieste.[16]

The State Department promptly drafted a cable to advise Churchill of the hardening of policy toward Tito. This dispatch of 11 May repeated most of the points in Grew's memorandum and concluded that Tito should be told that the minimum acceptable settlement was "complete and exclusive control of Trieste and Pola, the lines of communication through Gorizia and Monfalcone, and an area sufficiently to the east of the line to permit proper administrative control." The State Department also released a press statement declaring that the United States believed a disinterested military government essential in the Julian Region and that disposition of the area must await a peace settlement. The message to Churchill and the press statement together affirmed Washington's intent to resist Tito's occupation of Trieste.[17]

Churchill was delighted. The Americans finally appeared to be coming into line with his argument that they should accept a tangible postwar commitment in Europe and use their current military strength to withstand communist aggression there. Foreign Secretary Eden, who was in Washington that week, further confirmed this impression by writing to Churchill that the American government was ready to use force in Trieste, "if it came to the worst." He added that a senior State Department official had told him that "in this particular issue the Americans and ourselves were more favourably placed than in any other to take up a challenge on behalf of the principles for which we stood." For his part the prime minister hoped this stiffening of resolve in Washington could be extended beyond "this particular issue." In his zeal to exploit the president's stand on Trieste, Churchill requested that a general order be given halting the removal of American forces from Europe.[18]

This message caused uneasiness in Washington. Replying on 14 May, Truman declined to give a general stand fast order unless justified by further developments. The president was concerned about the need to transfer troops to the Pacific to ensure victory against Japan and was sensitive to pressure to "bring the boys home." He explained, with reference to Trieste, that "unless Tito's forces should attack, it is impossible for me to involve this country in another war." He did, however, inform Churchill that he had instructed the American ambassador in Belgrade to join his British colleague in informing Tito of the firm Anglo-American stance on Trieste. Truman told Eden in person that he wanted to await Tito's response before finally committing the United States, but added that "we have had enough of being pushed around." The American position was becoming clear. The Truman administration, though unready to go as far as Churchill wished, was prepared to oppose apparent aggression in the Julian area, where it had forces in place and where the outcome affected a country whose stability it desired.[19]

Despite occasional bursts of tough-sounding rhetoric, flexibility was still evident in American responses to the actions of the Soviet Union and its "satellites" in mid-1945. Although Truman had been persuaded to take a relatively strong stand in the case of Trieste, he also sent Harry Hopkins on a conciliatory mission to Moscow at about the same time. Truman recorded the objectives of that mission in his diary on 22 May:

> [To] make it clear to Uncle Joe Stalin that I know what I wanted —and that I intended to get it—peace for the world for at least

90 years. That Poland, Rumania, Bulgaria, Czeckosovakia [sic], Austria, Yugo-Slavia, Latvia, Lithuania, Estonia et al make no difference to U.S. interests only so far as World Peace is concerned. That Poland ought to have 'free elections,' at least as free as [Frank] Hague, Tom Pendergast, Joe Martin or [Robert] Taft would allow in their respective bailiwicks. That Tito should be restrained at Trieste and Pela [sic] and Uncle Joe should make some sort of gesture—whether he means it or not—to keep before our public that he intends to keep his word. Any smart political boss will do that.

This entry is couched in the language of realpolitik, not that of ideological commitment. It suggests that Truman appreciated the limits of his capacity to influence developments in Eastern Europe and was willing to accept, with minor concessions for the benefit of American public opinion, the existence of Eastern and Western spheres of influence. Truman also seemed to assume that, unlike Eastern Europe, Trieste fell outside an emerging Soviet sphere of influence and was an area where American power could reach. This assumption was in perfect accord with the general quid pro quo approach to Soviet-American relations that historian John Lewis Gaddis has noted was readily embraced by the new president in his first few months in office.[20]

Washington and London remained slightly out of step in their positions on Trieste in the following week but their ambassadors did submit joint notes in Belgrade along the lines proposed by Truman on 14 May. The Soviet Union was also informed of the Anglo-American démarche. As Tito's response was negative, the Americans and British had to ponder their next move. It remained unclear whether Washington would revert to a more tentative policy.[21]

Churchill, for one, was worried about that possibility. He sought to ensure that the Americans remained firm and to allay their concerns about his apparent belligerence. The prime minister cabled Truman on 19 May that he certainly did not envisage "a war with the Yugoslavs" but that Tito's negative reply demanded immediate action. Citing messages from Alexander deploring Yugoslav behavior in Trieste, Churchill asserted that the positions of Anglo-American troops there were being endangered by Yugoslav infiltration. He called for pressure to be put on Tito to withdraw from Trieste and Pula.[22]

To Churchill's satisfaction Truman agreed that immediate action was necessary. The president's first step was to write to Stalin, carefully explaining that his government intended to stand firm against Tito's occupation of Trieste but also stressing that the United States would not take any actions to prejudice "legitimate Yugoslav claims" to the territory in question. This message was probably intended to dissuade Moscow from intervening on Tito's behalf so that the British and Americans could confront Tito alone. Truman's next step was to propose to Churchill that they urge Tito to reconsider. At the same time he recommended that they instruct Generals Dwight D. Eisenhower and Alexander to organize "a show of force, both air and ground, and that the presentation in Belgrade of our rejection of Tito's stand be timed . . . so that our commanders' troop movements will already be evident to Tito." The Americans had moved from a policy of extreme caution to one of direct pressure. According to Truman's memoirs, the rationale for this shift was that "I believed that all that it was necessary for us to do to impress Tito was to show such overpowering strength that he would back down before undertaking anything foolhardy." Truman was aware of the potentially disastrous consequences of this policy and expressed doubt about Churchill's belief that if armed conflict broke out it could be limited to "frontier incidents." Yet reinforcement of Anglo-American forces in the Julian Region began and, on 21 May, the CCS ordered Alexander to proceed with a show of force.[23]

American policy had reached a critical point. Only three outcomes were possible: diplomatic victory, military conflict with Yugoslavia, or a humiliating withdrawal from a publicly stated position.

## The Local Situation

Trieste itself remained in limbo while negotiations were proceeding. It was not surprising that the immediate aftermath of war would be accompanied by dislocation and tension in a city which had been the focus of intensely competing ethnic, ideological and strategic interests. In this particular case those problems were exacerbated by the fact that the Yugoslav and Anglo-American contingents, both of which were reinforced after 2 May, were thoroughly intermingled and lacked clear definition of their respective lines of authority and responsibility.

In view of the Yugoslav presence, Anglo-American commanders on the spot had chosen not to establish AMG before consulting their superiors—despite pleas from local Italian resistance leaders. The Yugoslavs, however, promptly assumed administrative authority, beginning a period of Yugoslav control later dubbed the "forty days" by Triestines. On 5 May, Yugoslav and Anglo-American field commanders reached a working agreement which approved the existing situation. Yugoslav administration was to continue throughout the Julian Region on a temporary basis pending the outcome of negotiations between Tito and Alexander. At the same time Anglo-American forces would remain in Trieste and would control the lines of communication to Austria. This agreement helped prevent serious incidents, but relations between the two occupying forces in Trieste remained strained.[24]

The character of Yugoslav administration was a major source of tension. Trieste was under direct Yugoslav military administration until 13 May and the Yugoslavs moved quickly to assert authority over all aspects of Triestine life. A curfew was imposed, Italian police and resistance groups were disarmed, large numbers of so-called Fascists were arrested summarily, and some were even deported to Yugoslavia proper. After 13 May a civil administration (based on "popular institutions") was introduced with certain nominal powers, but it bore a strongly pro-Yugoslav stamp and Yugoslav administrative policy changed little. Throughout the forty days, the two principal objectives of that policy were to eliminate any anticommunist forces (Italian or Slovene) and to consolidate the Yugoslav grip on this formerly Italian territory so that it might become an integral part of Yugoslavia.

Many members of the Anglo-American forces in Trieste perceived these policies as unnecessarily harsh and they grew increasingly hostile toward the Yugoslavs. General John Harding of the British Thirteenth Corps complained of "systematic and unconcealed victimisation by the Yugoslav authorities of the local population," and Alexander himself informed the CCS that "our men are obliged to look on without power to intervene whilst actions which offend their traditional sense of justice are committed. Further, our men feel that by taking no action they are condoning such behavior. As a result feeling against Jugoslavs is now strong and is getting stronger daily." The reaction of his soldiers was probably due as much to other factors as to their sense of fair play. These troops had spent a long time in Italy and had acquired a certain sympathy for its people, whereas Yugoslav culture was alien to them. Another important factor was the understandable disgruntlement felt against the Yugoslavs by the ordinary soldiers, who could not relax and were obliged to remain in a state of readiness even though the war was over. Whatever the sources of this hostility, Alexander clearly spelled out its implication to the CCS on 17 May: "It is now certain that any solution by which we shared an area with Jugoslav troops or Partisans or permitted Jugoslav administration to function would not work." Advice from the field thus added a further justification for adopting a firm line in London and Washington.[25]

## The Resolution of the Crisis

As it happened, Tito yielded—almost unexpectedly. Ambassador Richard Patterson reported from Belgrade on 21 May that the Yugoslavs had agreed to accept AMG under Alexander's control on the basis of the proposed demarcation line. The Yugoslavs demanded certain qualifying conditions, but they had backed down.[26]

The reasons for the sudden change in Yugoslav policy are not entirely clear. The most probable explanation is that the Yugoslavs lacked Soviet support and thought it inadvisable to risk an armed clash with the British and Americans. Indeed, the British ambassador in Belgrade advised London on 27 May that, after a conversation with his Soviet counterpart concerning Trieste, he was convinced that "although the Soviet [sic] is in full sympathy with Yugoslav aspirations she will not intervene actively." In retrospect it is clear that Tito's action in Trieste up to that point had been an expression of the nationalistic animus of the Yugoslav Communist movement that would later precipitate a complete break with Moscow. The Soviet Union, for its part, was not really interested in such reckless adventurism and gave only pro forma support to the Yugoslav position on Trieste while probably trying privately to curb Tito's zeal. Such action was perfectly consistent with Stalin's faith in spheres of influence. As long as he could exercise a free hand in Eastern Europe, the Soviet leader had little desire to risk confrontation with the British and Americans in Italy. This relatively indifferent Soviet attitude revealed, of course, that Churchill and the State Department were somewhat misguided in suspecting Yugoslav actions in Trieste to be a manifestation of Soviet expansionism.[27]

The State Department was greatly heartened by the news from Belgrade. Having secured a victory in principle, Washington left Alexander to work out the details of a settlement. The field marshal announced that he would not accept Yugoslav participation in AMG, but would permit Yugoslav observers at his headquarters. He was prepared to work through Yugoslav civil authorities if "they were functioning satisfactorily" but stressed that "my AMG must be empowered to use whatever civil authority they deem best in any particular place and to change administrative personnel at their discretion." Finally, Alexander informed his superiors that he did not "consider it desirable to take over Pola or the lines of communication from Trieste to Pola."[28]

The question of Pula now became the major source of delay in presenting a draft agreement to Belgrade, sparking a debate between military and political desiderata. The State Department feared Alexander was making too many concessions. Grew urged Truman on 26 May to demand that Pula be included within the AMG zone in the draft agreement. Alexander immediately protested to the CCS that, from a military perspective, "this will be a most unwelcome commitment for me." The American Joint Chiefs of Staff agreed with him. Meeting with Truman on 29 May, Grew acknowledged the military disadvantages of extending AMG to Pula but declared that if the city were left to the Yugoslavs, "it would mean a recession from the principles which we have enunciated for the orderly and just settlement of territorial disputes." The president accepted the State Department's advice. Churchill was of the same opinion. He drafted two sharply worded telegrams to Alexander, criticizing his attitude and pointing out how crucial American support was for the British. Despite Alexander's misgivings Pula was included in the draft terms of the military agreement presented to Belgrade—an example of the political impetus undergirding the military veneer of proposed Allied administration of part of the Julian Region.[29]

The draft agreement was presented to Tito on 2 June. The Soviet Union was informed of Anglo-American policy and expressed hope that a peaceful settlement could be concluded that safeguarded Yugoslav interests in the area. Moscow, however, did not seek an active role. After a delay that caused momentary alarm in Washington and London, Tito accepted the Anglo-American terms. The most important effect of the subsequent agreement, signed in Belgrade on 9 June, was the partition of the Julian Region into two temporary zones of military occupation along a demarcation line—soon dubbed the Morgan line in recognition of the leading role played by Alexander's chief of staff in the negotiations with Tito. In conformity with the Belgrade agreement, AMG was set up in "Zone A" on 12 June 1945 and Yugoslav forces withdrew into "Zone B" to the west of the Morgan Line.[30]

## Conclusion

After nearing the brink of armed conflict, the Julian problem had been resolved temporarily to Washington's satisfaction. Close examination of the Western Allies' "victory" in this dispute reveals some significant trends in the development of immediate postwar American policies in Europe. To a certain extent actions taken by the United States during the Trieste crisis may be seen as part of an emerging but as yet indistinct pattern of early Cold War policymaking.

After the occupation of Trieste began in early May American policy on the Julian Region shifted in two almost contradictory directions. On the one hand, Washington's earlier caution and the desire to avoid military conflict with the Yugoslavs at all costs steadily diminished. By mid-May the United States appeared willing to risk that possibility and Truman even ordered a show of force. On the other hand, the long-standing policy of AMG over the whole Julian Region was quietly set aside with barely a murmur of protest from the State Department officials who had consistently championed it. When "victory" was achieved over the Yugoslavs AMG was only extended to areas west of the Morgan Line and Pula—not the whole Julian Region.

The first shift in American policy may be attributed to several factors. In a sense it amounted to the continuation of a wartime commitment to the Atlantic Charter principle of orderly territorial settlement, which was the public justification for American firmness. Washington presumably felt more confident about toughening its stance against the Yugoslav challenge to that principle because the importance of maintaining a common front against the Nazis had ended. Beyond the question of principle, the hardening of American policy may be seen as part of a nascent "Cold War consciousness" among high-level American policymakers influenced by their subordinates in Washington and in the field. From their perspective, Tito's actions in Trieste exemplified an emerging pattern of Soviet-directed aggression throughout Europe. It was important to counter that expansion in this instance not only for reasons of principle but also because of the area's possible strategic significance and the implications for Italian political stability.

Yet the other important change in American policy requires qualifications to these explanations. If the United States was now basing its policy on the defense of Atlantic Charter principles, concern for Italian political stability, or anticommunist objectives, why did Truman not insist on extension of AMG to all the Julian Region as originally contemplated? That goal was, in fact, pragmatically abandoned. With the minor exception of Pula, the United States challenged only Yugoslav occupation of the areas supposedly required by Alexander for military purposes.

Was the United States merely seeking the fulfillment of "military requirements"? Although the outcome of the dispute appears to suggest this motivation, these areas were not really essential for Anglo-American military needs once the war ended; Alexander's occupation forces in Austria could have been supplied through Venice if necessary. Moreover, records of the internal discussions among American decisionmakers reveal a significant political component in Washington's stance that went beyond rhetoric. The symbolic inclusion of Pula in the AMG zone at the State Department's insistence—despite Alexander's disagreement on military grounds—was an example of this political dimension. Neither the rationale of military necessity nor that of political motivation in themselves offer a comprehensible explanation for the course of American policymaking on Trieste.

Having traced the unfolding of the Trieste crisis in these first weeks of the Truman administration, it is possible to discern a more complex picture. American policy was in reality a curious mélange of tentativeness and confrontation, of military pragmatism and political principle. Although some State Department officials may have wished to insist on AMG over the whole Julian Region, they realized that Anglo-American policy was circumscribed by the field position of Alexander's troops and his limited demands on Tito for fulfillment of military requirements. Truman and the American military were also reluctant to risk conflict with an ally. Once Tito politicized the issue by rejecting even Alexander's limited demands, State Department officers considered a compromise had already been made. By not deviating from those terms thereafter, the United States, with one stroke, could (1) appear to stand firm on principle for the benefit of public opinion, especially in Italy; (2) offer Tito a reasonable compromise in lieu of the original AMG policy; (3) step into line with British policy and fulfill Alexander's military requirements; and (4) offer terms which it was capable of obtaining by military force if necessary, as Anglo-American forces already were present in the areas in question.

The "success" of American policy on the issue in immediate terms was no longer defined by the amount of territory which came under AMG (for it fell far short of original American intentions) but by the fact that the Yugoslavs had backed down and accepted the Anglo-American terms. Washington's wartime commitment to abstract Atlantic Charter principles had given way to a realistic spheres-of-influence approach to European international politics. In part, American policy during the Trieste crisis may be interpreted as an early attempt by the Truman administration to prevent encroachment on one of the boundaries of the Western sphere of influence.

The general impact of the Trieste imbroglio on postwar American policymaking is difficult to ascertain precisely. It is significant, however, that the incident represented the first case of direct East-West military confrontation faced by the Truman administration. Its timing was crucial, unfolding just as the war in Europe ended and only weeks after the new president assumed office. Under those circumstances State Department officials, led by Joseph Grew, were able to describe Tito's actions as communist aggression and they eventually convinced Truman of the efficacy of a firm but restrained response.[31] During the ensuing showdown with Yugoslavia the United States attained its immediate aims by the application of incremental diplomatic pressure visibly backed by the determination to use military force if necessary. By responding to the Trieste crisis in that fashion, the Truman administration succeeded in tailoring its policy objectives to match available resources, thereby securing a realistic compromise in which the United States achieved its most pressing goals without armed conflict.

Given this successful outcome, the Trieste case would seem to fall into a category similar to the policymaking "model" described in Bruce Kuniholm's study of the origins of the Cold War in the Near East:

> After World War II, a negative model of international behavior— of how *not* to act when confronted by a totalitarian adversary— was reinforced by what happened in Poland and led the administration to adopt policies which later served as the antithesis of the Munich analogy. Positive models—models of how one *should* act when confronted by what the administration regarded as a totalitarian regime—were created by events along the Northern Tier [Iran, Turkey, Greece] in 1946–47. If Eastern Europe served the Truman administration as an example of how not to deal with the Soviet Union, the countries of the Northern Tier provided a different kind of example, and verified the viability of a firm and determined response to Soviet pressures.

Although on a more limited scale, the Trieste episode seemed to offer the same sort of positive example for dealing with "totalitarian" pressure, whether it emanated from Moscow or from Belgrade. Indeed, during a 1950 interview President Truman explicitly linked the Trieste and Iran crises as the two occasions when he had successfully resisted a perceived threat from the Soviet Union.[32]

Truman's comment suggests that American policymakers may have unwittingly taken some of their first stumbling steps on the road to containment during the Trieste crisis of mid-1945. After all, had they not successfully "contained" communist pressure on one periphery of the postwar Western sphere of influence? That successful outcome provided a tangible demonstration of the viability of a slightly modified quid pro quo approach to postwar relations between East and West. American policymakers could therefore have drawn on their experience in the Trieste crisis to fashion a relatively flexible and restrained policy of "containment" which realistically matched means with ends. There is little evidence, however, that they consciously absorbed any general lessons from this early postwar incident, despite the State Department's contemporary insistence on the broader implications of the problem. The Trieste episode proved to be the exception rather than the rule, and there were precious few other successes for the Truman administration's experimentation with a quid pro quo policy toward the Soviet Union and its allies. The Trieste case was thus quickly forgotten, except perhaps in the vague and selective sense that Truman recalled it as a rationalization for firmness against communist aggression. Indeed, instead of serving as a possible alternative model for a more general containment strategy, the Truman administration's policy toward Trieste after the May crisis would itself be increasingly subordinated to the dictates of the rigid and monolithic containment doctrine which American policymakers eventually adopted as the Cold War unfolded in the following eighteen months.

# 4

The Cold War Sets in:
Trieste in the Balance,
June 1945 to
September 1947

⊙ THE United States cannot accept Yugoslav sovereignty over the Trieste area. I recognize that the Soviet Union cannot accept Italian sovereignty. — James F. Byrnes, *Speaking Frankly*

For the United States, the establishment of Allied Military Government in Trieste on 12 June 1945 opened a new phase in the development of the Italo-Yugoslav boundary dispute that would transform it into a Cold War problem. The immediate postwar crisis was over and a direct military clash with Yugoslavia had been averted. During the following two years American involvement would occur on two levels: locally, as one of the two powers responsible for military administration in Zone A of the Julian Region; and internationally, as one of the architects of a proposed long-term solution for the Trieste dispute as part of the peace settlement with Italy.

The steady escalation of Cold War tensions during this period would influence American policy on both levels. On the international front Trieste became one of many pawns in that East-West confrontation. On the local level American AMG officials had to work within the broad parameters of Washington's evolving Cold War strategies, though they exercised considerable administrative autonomy and sought to tailor their mode of governance to suit local conditions. In general, American policy on both levels would become explicitly more anticommunist in thrust during these two years.

This process, however, was by no means inexorable and did not unfold according to any preconceived plan. To explain how and why American policymakers at all levels came to view the Trieste issue largely in Cold War terms, it is necessary to examine in some detail their actual experience in administering Trieste and in seeking a long-term solution for its problems during this period. As had occurred during the war, American policy would emerge in response to an interplay between the local dimensions of the problem and developments on the international scene.

## Setting up AMG in Zone A

The initial task confronting AMG officials in Zone A was that of finding a model of administrative control that could respond adequately to the area's problems. Those problems were daunting. As elsewhere in Europe, there was a need for extensive reconstruction efforts in the wake of a war which had not only wreaked massive physical destruction but had toppled political and social structures. In addition, Trieste was a focal point of bitter doctrinal and nationalistic struggles on both the local and international levels. The AMG officers who began operating in Zone A on 12 June were charged with the responsibility not only of exercising military control but also of bringing stable, impartial administration to this troubled setting until its final disposition was determined in the peace treaty with Italy.

The precise character AMG would assume in Zone A was unclear. Precedents established during Allied occupation of other parts of Italy were not necessarily appropriate—especially since a communist-dominated civil administration, installed during the Yugoslav occupation, was still in place in Trieste and nearby localities. Moreover, the Belgrade agreement of 9 June provided few guidelines for the specific implementation of AMG control in the disputed territory. The reason for this lacuna was that the agreement had been primarily a political-military accord, hastily engineered to avoid a crisis in inter-Allied relations, rather than an administrative brief. Consequently, the operational structure of AMG in Zone A of the Julian Region was determined in the field over the next few months. That process would reveal the central objectives of Anglo-American military administrators in the Trieste area and the extent to which the burgeoning Cold War impinged on their actions.¹

In the absence of other guidelines, AMG officials could at first rely only on earlier experiences in Italy. They recognized, however, that local conditions were unusual and proceeded with caution. Their first formal act was to publish a proclamation on 12 June establishing military government in Zone A under the overall command of SACMED, temporarily recognizing Italian laws in effect on 8 September 1943, and describing the jurisdiction of the AMG judicial system. Since Alexander's headquarters were in Italy, he appointed Lieutenant General John Harding, commander of the Thirteenth Corps of the British Eighth Army, as his local representative and the highest authority in Zone A. A Senior Civil Affairs Officer [SCAO] was to direct AMG itself and serve as Harding's principal staff officer and adviser on all matters concerning civil administration. The administration of Zone A was to be conducted separately from AMG in Italy and to be known as AMG, Thirteenth Corps (later AMG – Venezia Giulia [AMG-VG]), a special unit subject only to technical direction from the Allied Commission. Having introduced AMG, the Anglo-American officials in Zone A did not immediately dismantle the Yugoslav civil administration recently established there, but awaited further guidance regarding implementation of the Belgrade agreement before creating any alternative system of local government.²

Both Yugoslav and Anglo-American military officials realized that the vague Belgrade understanding left various practical problems unresolved and required amendment for operational purposes. For that reason Morgan met with General Arso Jovanović, Tito's chief of staff, in Duino (Devin) on 20 June to conclude a supplementary accord arranging the detailed implementation of parts of the Belgrade agreement. This technical document principally concerned human and economic movements between the two zones of the Julian Region and established joint committees to supervise those movements. In effect, the supplementary agreement represented a realistic acknowledgment by both sides that some economic collaboration between the two zones would be essential if normal life in the Julian Region were not to be disrupted unduly.³

These negotiations failed to settle the more controversial question of political collaboration raised by the Belgrade agreement. Although that understanding accorded the Supreme Allied Commander "command and control" of Zone A, its third article included an ambiguous provision inserted as part of the compromise with the Yugoslavs: "Use will be made of any Yugoslav civil administration which is already set up and which in the view of the Supreme Allied Commander is working satisfactorily. The Allied Military Government will, however, be empowered to use whatever civil authorities they deem best in any particular place and to change administrative personnel at their discretion." At Duino the Yugoslavs asserted that the organs of local government installed during the "forty days" were an expression of the wishes of a majority of the population of Trieste and its environs. They contended that AMG was obliged to work through those institutions and to reject the allegedly fascist-tainted system of Italian civil administration. The Anglo-American negotiators refused to accept this interpretation of article 3 and stated categorically that SACMED could not accept any limitations on its authority. A joint note was subsequently appended to the Duino accord recording the disagreement and noting Yugoslav intentions to raise the matter again at a diplomatic level. The Duino discussions thus offered little guidance for AMG officials pondering what sorts of mechanisms of civil administration would best fulfill their objectives in Zone A.[4]

The differing interpretations of article 3 at Duino precipitated a flurry of diplomatic correspondence. Despite Yugoslav and Soviet protests, Anglo-American political decisionmakers firmly backed their military representatives. The State Department, in particular, insisted that the previous Italian administrative system be reintroduced in Zone A, "both for practical administrative reasons and because establishment of purely Yugo system would prejudice final settlement even in Allied occupied territory." From Rome Kirk added a characteristically anticommunist viewpoint and even suggested that Morgan had not been firm enough with the Yugoslavs.[5]

Two weeks after entering Zone A, AMG officials still remained uncertain about how to organize local government there. Consequently, Alexander decided to provide the necessary guidance. As a first step, he advised the CCS of his own interpretation of article 3 of the Belgrade agreement. Rejecting the Yugoslav view, the field marshal argued that any commitment implicit therein applied not to the pro-Yugoslav system of administration but only to personnel. He added that "we have also maintained (a) that the Italian system of administration must be continued in its essentials since the basic law of this area is Italian and must continue to be so, and (b) that we cannot recognize the [Yugoslav] system of committees as an executive instrument of local government, although we will use committees in an advisory capacity, where they are useful, as we do in other parts of Italy." Alexander also noted that even if the existing civil administration were functioning "satisfactorily" in some parts of Zone A, the situation would still be unworkable as AMG might be faced with the anomaly of an "Italian system of government operating in one locality and a committee system functioning in the neighboring one." He did not believe that further negotiations with the Yugoslavs were necessary.[6]

The next day AFHQ sent a directive to Thirteenth Corps headquarters outlining the form of local government to be established in accordance with Alexander's views. AMG was to operate through organs of local government based on an Italian model, though "adjustments and modifications" were permitted if expedient for administrative reasons. The directive explicitly reiterated Alexander's views on the Yugoslav civil administration:

> You will utilize whatever civil authorities you deem best in any particular place and administrative personnel will be changed at your discretion. Subject to the above, use will be made of any Jugoslav civil administration which you find on entry to be already set up and which in your view is working satisfactorily. In interpreting the term "civil administration" you should consider the term relates to personnel employed rather than the system of administration itself.

This directive established the guidelines that AMG officials in Zone A had been awaiting but still allowed them considerable discretion in adapting its provisions to the area's particular circumstances.[7]

AMG–Venezia Giulia gradually assumed definitive shape over the next six weeks. During this period it became clear that the fundamental objectives guiding local AMG officials until ratification of an Italian peace treaty would be twofold. The first aim was to project an image of AMG as a scrupulously impartial arbiter between rival national groups in the area. The other objective—considered an indispensable corequisite for fulfillment of the first—was to secure complete and autonomous control of the situation in Zone A to ensure efficient administration and stability.

The goal of impartiality was a cornerstone of AMG activity from the outset. For instance, AMG officials in Zone A had promptly disbanded the Special People's Court and People's Militia created during the period of Yugoslav administration because they viewed them as unabashedly pro-Yugoslav (and communist) institutions. But they did not strictly follow precedents set during the Allied occupation of Italy in establishing alternative judicial authorities and a police force. Although the pre-1943 Italian system of civil courts was reintroduced alongside AMG military courts, there was no power of appeal to higher courts in Italy. The judicial system in Zone A also differed from Italy's in that Slovenes had the right to be heard in their own language. The question of a civil police force was considered even more delicate and the normal AMG practice of using regular Italian police was deemed inappropriate. Instead Alexander proposed to the CCS that the necessity for impartiality required formation of a special civil police to be "equipped, maintained, administered and commanded, as a combined US-UK commitment exercised through the military chain of command." A police force of 3,500 men was set up along these lines to meet the conditions prevailing in Zone A. Another significant departure from AMG practice in Italy was a decision on 3 July not to adopt "the policy of implementing Italian Governmental and Ministerial Directives . . . in this region." Moreover, the pre-1943 laws applicable in the territory were promptly purged of fascist measures. As a directive of 29 July reiterated, the central guiding principle for all AMG actions in Zone A was that "no steps will be taken which support or may appear to support or prepare for any ultimate disposition of the area to any claimant nation."[8]

An important corollary of the desire to create an impression of impartiality was the autonomy AMG–Venezia Giulia came to enjoy within Allied policymaking circles in matters pertaining to local administration. There was a conscious effort to distance AMG in Zone A from the influence of the Allied Commission and Anglo-American diplomats in Italy. After repeated protests from Admiral Stone that the Allied Commission was being excluded from the administration of the area, the Civil Affairs Division of AFHQ declared in July that it was inadvisable to involve the commission in this question because of its close links with the Italian government. Toward the end of August Kirk advised General Morgan that there was concern in Washington "with what seemed to be a tendency at AFHQ to take political decisions regarding Venezia Giulia without reference to our two governments." Though perhaps exaggerated, Kirk's observation was not completely unfounded. By that time military officials in AFHQ and Thirteenth Corps had clearly concluded that AMG–Venezia Giulia required a high degree of autonomous authority over the local situation in Zone A. They feared that if AMG were not granted such authority it would never be able to discharge its duties of interim trusteeship.[9]

The most significant challenge perceived by AMG officials to their goal of total control over the local situation emanated from the procommunist institutions erected during the forty days of Yugoslav rule. During the first six weeks or so of AMG, the Anglo-American authorities eliminated some of those institutions and effectively by-passed the Yugoslav-installed National Liberation Committees in the daily administration of areas with Italian majorities. Nevertheless, this committee system was not immediately dismantled and was allowed to continue administering Slovenian localities. After Alexander's directive of 26 June, AMG officers carefully studied the question of a suitable model of local government and actively sought the cooperation of local Italians and Slovenes in its evolution, hoping to involve all national and political groupings. They soon concluded that the Communist bloc would not cooperate and that the communist organs of civil administration formed a rival system which detracted from AMG's undisputed authority and compromised its image of impartiality.

At the end of July the American senior civil affairs officer, Colonel Alfred Connor Bowman, warned that "the time is approaching when our policy must be applied in a stronger manner." On 11 August he published General Order No. 11 providing for a system of local government designed to meet AMG criteria for stable and effective administration. The general effect of this edict was to introduce a system of civil administration based on a slightly modified form of Italian local government and to abolish the Yugoslav committees. As Bowman himself observed later, "the real heart and most important part of the order . . . was compressed into two pregnant sentences" in sections 10 and 11 of the order:

> No committee, council or group other than those herein created and provided for, except those previously constituted by a Proclamation or order of the Allied Military Government, shall possess any of the administrative, legislative, executive or other powers of government.
>
> Allied Military Government is the only government in those parts of Venezia Giulia occupied by the Allied forces and it is the only authority empowered to issue orders and decrees and to make appointments to public or other offices.

General Order No. 11 was drafted in accordance with Alexander's general directive, but its specific terms were formulated in the field to meet local conditions and were not dictated from outside Zone A—as Bowman has confirmed in his memoirs. The rejection of communist institutions in Zone A may be best explained not as pro-Italian or a purely anticommunist move in an ideological sense but as the consummation of AMG's quest for total control of the local situation.[10]

Anglo-American military administrators certainly appeared to view it primarily in terms of a practical administrative problem. For instance, a message from AFHQ to the Combined Chiefs of Staff on 25 August explained that the Yugoslav administrative machinery had been progressively dismantled by AMG because it was "incapable of functioning in practice" and "no other course was possible if the area was to be administered impartially." Colonel Bowman, as senior administrative officer, also took this view and maintained that the Yugoslav civil administration was "incapable of effectively conducting [the] routine, essential business of government." Despite Yugoslav protests that the Belgrade agreement was being violated, the CCS, on 29 August, approved the actions taken by AMG: "You should as far as possible administer that area on the following lines: Jugoslav system of natural committees should in general be discontinued in whole area and Italian system reinstalled. In predominantly Jugoslav towns and villages, token Jugoslav administration might be retained and national committee used in advisory capacity." At the same time, the CCS asked SACMED to assure the Yugoslavs that AMG would "take no action which will prejudice the position of either of the disputing parties." The basic structures of the AMG regime in Zone A had now been defined, but it remained to put it into effect.[11]

AMG administrators attempted to implement the provisions of General Order No. 11 with impartiality. Both communist and "democratic" groups were invited to nominate candidates for positions in the new system of local government. In particular there was a conscious attempt to staff positions in the local civil administration with Italian and Slovenian personnel in accordance with their respective proportions in the population. In predominantly Yugoslav areas AMG officers attempted to carry out the suggestions of the CCS to work through Yugoslav officials. These actions were in keeping with the belief of Anglo-American military administrators that they had rejected a specific *system* of administration because it was incompatible with the effective and impartial functioning of AMG, not because its personnel were of a particular nationality or espoused leftist political beliefs.[12]

The communist groups in Zone A did not share this interpretation of AMG action and responded to General Order No. 11 with protests and demonstrations. They viewed the civil administration established in May as a true expression of the will of the "popular forces" of Zone A and believed their committees constituted more advanced "democratic" institutions than those operating in Italy. They interpreted AMG's rejection of the committee system of local administration primarily in class terms and saw it as a blow directed against socialism and democracy. Consequently, the Communist parties—Yugoslav and Italian—refused to cooperate with AMG in staffing the new organs of local government. Their attitude was much as Bowman summarized it in his monthly report for August: "We will willingly cooperate if the Allied Military Government will govern in accordance with our views and through our institutions but we will not cooperate otherwise, as any other form of government is considered to be Fascist and non-democratic." As AMG would not sanction the continuation of communist institutions of civil administration, the Communists saw no advantage in serving as impotent functionaries in an AMG-controlled system which they regarded as reactionary. Their political strategy was to boycott the new system entirely. The Communist bloc in Zone A became the major local source of opposition to AMG activity while the area's final disposition was being determined. This development was hardly surprising, for the Communists had the most to lose from AMG's insistence on asserting total control over the local situation.[13]

At first AMG officials sought to ensure compliance with General Order No. 11 by patient persuasion and repeated offers to consider nominations for the new positions. For instance, during a meeting at AMG Headquarters on 8 September, Bowman remarked that "while we shall eventually have to comply with the letter as well as the spirit . . . of our directives, it is assumed that higher headquarters do not want us to force this issue too precipitately. General Order No. 11, wherever it can, will be implemented and we shall force the errant children into the mold later." AMG officials soon discovered, however, that in some areas (generally small, rural Slovenian communes or communist-dominated Italian localities) they could find no one willing to serve in the new administrative positions. Direct military government under civil affairs officers was imposed in those places. Moreover, in the larger communes, where 85 percent of the population of Zone A lived, the new civil administration was staffed mainly by noncommunist Italians, many of whom had served in similar roles during the Fascist period. Nevertheless, AMG was in firm control and could administer the area as it saw fit. This administrative system would remain substantially unchanged until ratification of the Italian peace treaty.[14]

Inevitably the emerging Cold War cast its shadow on the process of defining the character of AMG in Zone A. Anglo-American soldiers were there, after all, because of one of the first postwar confrontations between East and West, which had effectively been resolved on the basis of a spheres-of-influence agreement. As Zone A fell within the Western sphere of influence, AMG–Venezia Giulia was, almost by definition, an expression of broader Anglo-American policies based on liberal democratic principles. Thus a "Central Directive for Venezia Giulia" produced by AMG officials in October 1945 stressed as one of the aims of AMG "to project Great Britain and the U.S.A."[15] Similarly, the Anglo-American interpretation of article 3 of the Belgrade agreement might be viewed as complementary to an anticommunist policy. The AMG's subsequent quest for a suitable administrative regime resulted in the removal of all communist institutions in Zone A and the imposition of an Anglo-American system of direct rule. For the Left in the Trieste area the administrative scheme inaugurated by General Order No. 11 implied a restoration of the bourgeois order. Even the great care taken by AMG not to appear to discriminate between local nationalistic or political groups could be interpreted as a means of countering Yugoslav and Soviet protests and of projecting a favorable Anglo-American image for the benefit of international public opinion. Given the recent history and location of the area assigned to them, AMG officials in Trieste could not avoid being sensitive to rising Cold War tensions, especially when the most immediate threats to stable AMG rule in Zone A took the form of internal "subversion" by local communist groups and external military pressure by Yugoslavia—a communist state.

Although unavoidably buffeted by the Cold War sweeping across Europe, AMG administrators sought nevertheless to insulate the local situation from some of its effects. AMG actions in Trieste demonstrated, in fact, that American military and political decisionmakers in the Mediterranean were out of step with each other and had not yet refined the integrated politicomilitary strategy for countering communism which both groups would embrace at the height of the Cold War. AMG administrators in Zone A enjoyed relative autonomy and consciously sought to distance themselves from Allied political agencies in Italy. They conceived of their task in primarily local terms: AMG was in the area to provide impartial and efficient military administration for a disputed frontier zone so that stability would be maintained until its final disposition was decided. It was primarily to this end that they demanded total control of the local situation—not because they wished to initiate a local offensive against a universal communist threat. For instance, despite repeated complaints by British and American diplomats that the failure to hold early administrative elections in Zone A was a constant source of communist propaganda against the British and Americans, military officials declined to hold them because they feared such elections would exacerbate local tensions and stimulate disruptive activities and would not improve the quality of administration.[16] Moreover, as pro-Italian groups in the area grew more confident after 1945 and began criticizing AMG as an impediment to the restoration of Italian sovereignty, AMG officials grew more conscious of being embattled arbiters. The apparent impossibility of reconciling local national and political forces would be a major reason why those officials eventually came to favor internationalization of the area rather than its restoration to Italy. They believed such a solution was the only practical one to safeguard the interests of the area itself.

Although the character of the Anglo-American presence in Trieste was obviously influenced by the early stages of the Cold War, the process of establishing an AMG regime in Zone A was not a crude manifestation of some conscious, larger Cold War strategy. It was a complex response to local conditions.

## Trieste on the International Front

British and American representatives engaged in the drawn-out negotiations for an Italian peace settlement were not as concerned with local issues as the AMG officials in Trieste. They debated the area's long-term future in a framework influenced strongly by Cold War concerns. Winston Churchill dramatized this connection between Trieste and the Cold War during his now famous speech of 6 March 1946 at Fulton, Missouri: "from Stettin in the Baltic to Trieste in the Adriatic, an iron curtain has descended across the continent." Trieste had become a place of importance in the Cold War because it was a disputed area located at a strategic point on the dividing line between the rival politicoeconomic systems of East and West. A very real question for American policymakers during the Italian treaty discussions was whether or not Trieste would remain on their side of the line, thus saving "democracy's vital outpost in Venezia Giulia." On the international diplomatic level, between mid-1945 and early 1947, Trieste became yet another counter in the larger game played by the great powers on a board that would eventually encompass the whole world.[17]

The negotiations concerning peacemaking in Europe were one arena in which this East-West competition was played out in 1945 and 1946. At the Potsdam Conference Truman, Stalin, and Clement Attlee, the new British prime minister, agreed to establish a Council of Foreign Ministers (CFM) of the three great powers, in conjunction with France and China, to draft the treaties of peace with Italy, the Balkan nations, Finland and, later, Germany. Though intended to determine the fate of the vanquished, these deliberations became part of a new struggle between the victors for dominant influence in Europe. As historian Patricia Ward has noted, Secretary of State James F. Byrnes had the "benevolently arrogant expectation" that American military and economic power would enable his nation to shape the peace as it saw fit. He soon discovered, however, that "the Soviet Union wanted its status as a victorious power acknowledged in treaties giving it control of the Balkans, reparations with which to rebuild, bases in the Mediterranean, a share in the control of Japan, and benefits for Yugoslavia. These explicit Russian demands directly conflicted with the American peace expectations of collective security, representative governments, and equal trade rights." The council's meetings from September 1945 to December 1946 made explicit the broad divergence in American and Soviet postwar objectives in Europe. These differences meant painfully slow progress, but at least the major powers were still talking and in that sense the sessions of the Council of Foreign Ministers represented an opportunity to avoid the ideological rigidification of the Cold War. The foreign ministers failed to achieve that but they did produce some treaties which realistically reflected the postwar balance of international power in Europe. Despite concessions to the Soviet Union and Yugoslavia, the Italian settlement would confirm American and British dominance there, while the Balkan treaties did not weaken Soviet control of that region.[18]

The question of Trieste's future loomed large in the CFM's verbal sparring matches and was problematical precisely because the area fell on the boundary between these emerging Western and Eastern spheres of influence. Dean Acheson, later secretary of state, accurately summarized the discussions concerning Italy's northeastern frontier as "a prestige battle between the Russian and the Anglo-American position, the former backing the Yugoslav claim to the whole eastern coast of the Adriatic, the latter supporting retention by Italy of the Northeastern littoral which included the city of Trieste." Similarly, John Campbell, who advised Secretary of State James Byrnes on the issue during the negotiations, later accepted that by  the time it reached the Council of Foreign Ministers, "the Trieste thing was important because it had become, in world opinion, a test place for East-West relations, a U.S.-Soviet confrontation over the issues. Ethnic composition of the precise boundaries were [sic] not so important as one side or the other being able to claim some kind of victory." As a result, the Trieste question became one of the most intractable problems associated with the Italian peace settlement and assumed a prominence in CFM discussions which the small amount of territory at stake did not justify in itself.[19]

The council first considered the Trieste problem in September 1945 while meeting in London. Italy and Yugoslavia were permitted to submit rival territorial claims and the foreign ministers then discussed the matter. There was general agreement that Trieste should be a free port, but the Soviet Union backed Yugoslavia's claims to the city while the Western powers agreed that it should remain under Italian sovereignty. In view of the disagreement it was decided to accept a suggestion by Byrnes to appoint a four-power commission of experts to recommend a new Italo-Yugoslav border based primarily on ethnic criteria but also taking economic considerations into account. As on previous occasions, the United States had succeeded in conveniently postponing this contentious issue—but only temporarily.[20]

When the experts reported back in April 1946, each representative of the four powers recommended a different boundary. The American proposal was closest to the Italian claim, while the Soviet suggestion was virtually identical to that of the Yugoslavs. A long series of debates followed, during which the Americans were consistently frustrated by Soviet obstructionist tactics—a practice with which American policymakers would become familiar in this period. The frontier line proposed by the French appeared to offer the most acceptable compromise solution, but the council was deadlocked for months on the future of Trieste itself. Trieste became the key element in a logjam of issues (such as reparations and disposition of Italy's colonies), preventing progress on an Italian settlement. All attempts to break the logjam were frustrated by the Soviet Union's insistence on Trieste being ceded to Yugoslavia and the Western powers' refusal to accept that proposal.[21]

It is not possible to provide a complete, verifiable explanation of Soviet policy on Trieste during these discussions, for relevant Soviet and Yugoslav documents are inaccessible. It may be assumed with some certainty, however, that this action was largely a quid pro quo for Yugoslav support of Soviet foreign policy. Moreover, once the Russians had made a public stand on the issue in favor of the Yugoslavs, they could not easily concede the return of Trieste to Italy, even if such a concession might strengthen the Italian Communist party. As a British official noted at the time, "the Russians can scarcely compromise now, at any rate as far as sovereignty over Trieste itself is concerned, without discrediting themselves seriously with their satellites and striking a shattering blow to the Tito regime." In retrospect it has become clear that the Soviet Union—even less than the United States—had little direct interest in the issue but was obliged to support the Yugoslavs because of its own perception of broader Cold War exigencies. Nevertheless, although the Trieste problem offered an opportunity to confound the West, the Soviet Union did not consider it sufficiently important to justify refusing any solution short of Yugoslav sovereignty—as Tito would discover to his chagrin.[22]

The interests of the United States in the matter can be explained in more detail. American support for Italian claims to Trieste was not based simply on impartial application of the principle of self-determination, although this factor was of considerable importance. In part it was also an outgrowth of general American postwar policy toward Italy, whose central objectives were the achievement of political and economic stability on the domestic front and integration into a community of Western nations. The prompt conclusion of a mild Italian peace treaty was an indispensable part of this policy. As Campbell recalled, "for Italy, we had to get a peace treaty which preserved our position, which preserved the position of the Italian noncommunist parties, and which didn't give the Soviets a handle ... to dominate the future of Italy." Similarly, in a memorandum for the president on 18 April 1946, Ellery Stone of the Allied Commission urged that favorable peace terms were essential "if Italy were to be preserved as a 'bastion of democracy' in the Mediterranean."[23]

Consequently, Trieste was a key issue at stake in the Italian settlement because it had considerable emotional significance for Italians and represented a test of American support (against Soviet and Yugoslav pressure) for the Italian government on the international level. Another concern of the United States was that the loss of Trieste might precipitate a resurgence of fanatical nationalism, whose impact would undermine liberal government in Italy, creating a climate of instability in which the far Right or Left could advance. Italian political leaders, such as Prime Minister Alcide De Gasperi, further exaggerated these concerns. He repeatedly advised the Americans and British that "unjust peace terms" (meaning in this instance the cession of Trieste) would strengthen the extreme Right in Italy and debilitate the centrist, democratic parties. De Gasperi charged that this outcome would constitute an international victory for the Soviet bloc. Many American officials concurred in this assessment. For example, David Key, the American chargé in Rome, criticized American acceptance of the French line as the Italo-Yugoslav border during the CFM meetings and warned that "failure to recognize legitimate Italian ethnic and economic interests (Venezia Giulia) climaxing a series of Italian disappointments in other clauses of the treaty will create [a] national atmosphere so unhealthy that possibilities of [the] young republic developing in [a] normal and democratic manner will indeed be slight." American diplomats were under great pressure not to hand Trieste to Yugoslavia and viewed the issue as one whose repercussions might frustrate their general Italian policy.[24]

The pro-Italian position of American policymakers on Trieste was reinforced by a growing conviction that Yugoslavia was a mere Soviet satellite. Angered by the confrontation over Trieste in the spring of 1945, American officials had grown increasingly hostile toward Yugoslavia because of Tito's active support of Soviet foreign policy and the Communist party's total domination of national life. Washington made no attempt to conceal its displeasure. When Yugoslavia asked for economic assistance the American government turned down its appeal on the grounds that the Trieste imbroglio had had an adverse effect on congressional opinion. In early 1946 the State Department declared that the United States was unwilling to make any postwar loans to Yugoslavia, not only because of developments in the Trieste area but, more important, because of its disapproval of "the general tactics of the Tito regime." In April 1946 Secretary of War Robert Patterson secured State Department cooperation in limiting the shipment of potential military items amongst United Nations Relief and Rehabilitation Administration (UNRRA) supplies to Yugoslavia, arguing that Tito might use such items against American forces stationed in the Julian Region. Throughout 1945 and 1946, the American ambassador in Belgrade, Richard C. Patterson, Jr., directed a steady stream of reports to Washington critical of the Yugoslav government and its links to the Soviet Union. By the time of the Italian peace treaty discussions Campbell recalled that, "We [the United States] regarded them [the Yugoslavs] as worse than the Russians, as being more anti-American and tougher, even though we regarded them as servants for the Russians and really just as pushing Soviet interests." Similarly, Charles Bohlen, one of the State Department's most important Soviet experts and adviser to Byrnes at the CFM meetings, wrote in his memoirs that "in those days, the Soviets and the Yugoslavs were as one." Thus the United States firmly resisted Yugoslav claims to Trieste as another example of the systematic communist territorial expansion—ultimately directed from Moscow—which seemed to have engulfed Eastern Europe.[25]

A further factor influencing American opinion on Trieste was the high level of tension prevailing in the area throughout this period. Within Zone A, local Italian and Slavic nationalist groups held rival demonstrations to influence the CFM deliberations. A number of people were killed in confrontations in the Allied and Yugoslav zones during 1946. Rumors arose in both zones that the other side was planning military action, and frequent frontier incidents involving Anglo-American and Yugoslav troops developed into an especially sensitive issue. AMG officials were worried that a Yugoslav invasion of Zone A was imminent. General Harding became so concerned by Yugoslav troop movements that he obtained permission from the British and American governments to issue a public statement in March reaffirming that "public order will be enforced with justice, and in our zone we shall tolerate no attempt to prejudice in any way the final disposition of the territory. To this end the American and British Governments have authorized me to declare that it is their firm intention to maintain their present position in Venezia Giulia until an agreed settlement of the territorial disputes has been reached and put into effect." The fact that Harding was given approval to make this announcement indicated that the possibility of a Yugoslav attack was not just a local concern.[26]

When the CFM resumed its meetings at Paris in June, after a brief recess, American delegates seriously feared that the Soviet Union was seeking to pave the way for the Yugoslav seizure of Trieste by force if the council did not soon reach a favorable decision on the city's future. No Yugoslav military action was actually taken against Zone A, but two serious incidents occurred in August when the Yugoslavs, who had long protested American violations of their airspace, forced down and fired upon American transport planes flying over the Julian Region. In response the Americans used armed fighter bombers for transport missions in the area, reinforced their troops along the Morgan line, and strengthened their air force in northern Italy. These incidents helped turn public opinion in the West against the Yugoslavs. Local Italian-Yugoslav tension and the specter of Yugoslav aggression against Trieste—whether illusory or real—also combined to persuade AMG officials and Anglo-American policymakers of the efficacy of internationalization guaranteed by the great powers as a possible solution for the territory's problems.[27]

The idea of internationalization also offered the opportunity to break the deadlock in the Council of Foreign Ministers. After months of impasse, Georges Bidault, the French foreign minister, suggested "without enthusiasm" on 21 June that the council consider setting up a temporary international regime for Trieste under the auspices of the United Nations. According to Byrnes, the suggestion was received with caution by the other members of the CFM. Over the next few days the Soviet delegation made "what apparently was a final effort to obtain Trieste for Yugoslavia" and, on 24 June, Vyacheslav Molotov, the Soviet foreign minister, proposed privately to Byrnes that an autonomous state of Trieste be created, but under Yugoslav sovereignty. The American secretary of state rejected this proposal categorically, stating to his Soviet counterpart: "The United States cannot accept Yugoslav sovereignty over the Trieste area. I recognize that the Soviet Union cannot accept Italian sovereignty." Given those circumstances, Byrnes explained that the United States was willing "to consider any proposal that offers a way—either United Nations' administration . . . or leaving the issue to the peace conference for decision." Apparently ready to bargain, Molotov asked whether the problem of reparations from Italy could be "disposed of in a positive fashion" if the Trieste issue was resolved. Byrnes replied that was indeed possible and later added that "if the Soviet Delegation could accept the French line in Venezia Giulia we would be prepared to settle all other questions [concerning the Italian and Balkan treaties]." Though Molotov continued to stall for a time the way was clear for a compromise. Progress on Trieste, after all, promised to break the general stalemate in the council.

After further unsuccessful attempts to modify the border in favor of Yugoslavia, the Soviet delegation accepted a French proposal on 1 July that Yugoslavia receive all the area east of the French line and that the region west of the French line south of Duino to Novigrad (Cittanova d'Istria) constitute an international territory of Trieste. The American position on internationalization was later summed up by Byrnes: "We didn't like the free territory idea, but since this was the only way out of the dilemma, we were determined that the regime would be set up so that it had a chance to work." For that reason the American delegation persuaded the CFM on 3 July to agree to the principle of establishing an autonomous Free Territory of Trieste [FTT] to be administered by the Security Council of the United Nations. In order to assure that "a really good international plan of action be worked out," the details of provisional and permanent statutes for this new international entity were to be based on recommendations made by the full peace conference of twenty-one nations.[28]

The Julian question was discussed at length during that conference in Paris, with Italy and Yugoslavia each striving in vain to amend the frontier compromise to its own advantage. Both nations denounced the idea of internationalizing Trieste as unsatisfactory. But the compromise had been largely dictated by the new logic of Cold War summitry—an arena wherein local interests were invariably subordinated to the imperatives of Soviet-American confrontation. Despite the submission of various alternative proposals concerning the Italo-Yugoslav frontier, a plenary session of the conference on 10 October approved the CFM recommendations concerning the idea of a Free Territory of Trieste within the boundaries originally proposed by the French foreign minister.

The conference also made detailed recommendations to guide the drafting of a constitutional statute for the proposed free territory. The CFM had appointed a commission to prepare such an instrument, but East-West rivalries again resulted in divergent proposals by each of the powers, as well as a fifth scheme suggested by the Yugoslavs. The Western nations advocated a powerful governor and a weak popular assembly for the FTT. The Soviet Union wanted the exact opposite. Byrnes's memoirs demonstrate that the Western position was not as puzzling as might appear:

> We were determined that the Governor of Trieste should be invested with such powers. This created the anomaly of the western democracies advocating appointment by the Security Council of a governor having almost dictatorial powers, while the eastern dictatorship sought to place control in a popularly elected legislature. We were determined, however, to do our utmost to protect the area from infiltration and similar tactics that would pave the way for a coup aimed at delivering Trieste to Yugoslavia, as Danzig had been delivered to Germany.

Similarly, John C. Campbell has recalled that, although American diplomats "were not enamored of the FTT idea . . . we tried very hard in the peace treaty negotiations to get provisions that would make it work." When the proposals were considered at the plenary session of 9-10 October, the conference adopted a compromise plan suggested by the French that was closer to the Anglo-American proposals than to the Soviet draft statute. It only remained for the CFM to act on the peace conference's recommendations.[29]

When the Council of Foreign Ministers met for the final time at New York, one of the major tasks before them was to finalize the constitutional structure of the Free Territory of Trieste. The Western powers assumed the issue had been decided by the Paris peace conference's majority approval of the French compromise proposal on the statute, but the Soviet Union suggested extensive amendments that would favor Yugoslavia. In particular, Molotov continued to strive to weaken the powers of the governor vis-à-vis the legislature. The members of the council were able to reach compromises on specific amendments, but progress was agonizingly slow. Eventually Byrnes suggested to Molotov that the United States and Soviet Union merely agree to disagree and proposed maintaining the status quo in Trieste as "the more attractive alternative." Faced with that prospect, the Soviet Union accepted the essential features of the French proposal for the FTT, suggesting only minor amendments which were readily accepted by the United States. Byrnes had succeeded in maintaining the governor's status as the most powerful element in the FTT's constitutional structure. In general, American diplomats could take satisfaction in the fact that they had probably obtained as much as was realistically possible from the Trieste negotiations. As John Campbell has noted, "the Soviets in the end gave way on many points in order to get the negotiations finished, and we thought we had constitutional and economic arrangements for the FTT sufficient to keep the Yugoslavs from subverting it." The Soviet Union, for its part, was willing to compromise because, as Charles Bohlen has pointed out, "if the Trieste situation was left as it was, with most of the area occupied by the West, the Yugoslavs might lose all chance of winning control over the area. Internationalization always held open the possibility that a more favorable conclusion [for Yugoslavia and the Soviet Union] could be reached within that framework." Despite protests by the Italians and Yugoslavs, the decisions on Trieste and the Italo-Yugoslav frontier were formally incorporated into the peace treaty with Italy, signed in Paris on 10 February 1947.[30]

In view of the overbearing East-West antagonisms that had further complicated the ethnic and economic problems of Trieste, the compromise embodied in the concept of the FTT seemed wise in theory. It recognized that no strictly ethnic line could be drawn around Trieste which would also meet the economic needs of a port whose hinterlands lay in Yugoslavia and Central Europe. Furthermore, the administration of the FTT by the Security Council of the United Nations, rather than by a combination of powers favorable to either Italy or Yugoslavia, was intended to guarantee the independence and security of the area—thereby eliminating many of the sources of international tension there. The success of the FTT, however, was predicated on harmony in the Security Council. In fact, the same Cold War pressures which had necessitated this seemingly exemplary compromise were also present in the Security Council and would prove to be the nemesis of the FTT scheme.

### Preparing for the FTT

The provisions of the Italian peace treaty relating to the Italo-Yugoslav boundary remained a source of confrontation even after the document was signed. Both Italy and Yugoslavia continued to protest the proposed Trieste settlement and it was unclear whether they would ratify the treaty. That threat was neutralized by the decision that the peace treaty would become operative regardless of Italian or Yugoslav signature as soon as all four great powers had ratified it. For a time Soviet ratification was uncertain, but Moscow finally added its signature to those of the three Western powers. The Italian peace treaty came into force as expected on 15 September 1947.

It had been assumed that the new Italo-Yugoslav frontier would also be established at that time and the FTT would come into existence. According to the permanent statute of the FTT attached to the treaty, the new free state was to be governed by a constituent assembly, a council of government, and an independent governor. The governor's position was crucial, for he was the only official with power to organize elections for the two governing bodies and thereby set in motion the full mechanisms of FTT government. The Italian peace treaty also included an Instrument for the Provisional Regime of the

Free Territory of Trieste (the provisional statute), which briefly outlined the system under which the governor would rule during the transitional period from military government to permanent FTT civil administration. The provisional statute provided few guidelines for that interim phase, as the great powers had assumed a governor would already be appointed and that the transition period would be of short duration. It was stipulated that the governor should take office as soon as possible after the treaty came into force, but article 1 of the provisional statute added that, "pending assumption of office by the Governor, the Free Territory shall continue to be administered by the Allied military commands within their respective zones." British and American officials dealing with Trieste policy spent much of 1947 preparing for the establishment of the FTT as envisaged in these various provisions; but it became clear to them long before September 15 that the birth pains of the FTT would be more arduous and prolonged than had been anticipated by the framers of the Italian peace treaty.[31]

As it happened, this period of preparation for the FTT coincided with further intensification of the Cold War. The East-West tensions evinced during the drafting of the Italian peace treaty grew more pronounced after General George Marshall became secretary of state and the United States began to take an even stronger stand against the Soviet Union's actions to tighten its grip on Eastern Europe. On 12 March 1947 President Truman requested a congressional appropriation of $400 million in military and economic aid to counter perceived communist threats to Greece and Turkey. Advocating an American commitment to assist "free peoples" and to oppose "totalitarian regimes," the president announced the "Truman Doctrine"—a policy which has been dubbed as the American "declaration of Cold War" by a leading American diplomatic historian. A few months later, in his famous address at Harvard University, Secretary Marshall announced the more general economic recovery program that would become known as the Marshall Plan and that was directed at stabilizing Western Europe. In July 1947 George Kennan's "X" article appeared in *Foreign Affairs* as a public rationalization for the doctrine of containment that was coming to underpin American foreign policy throughout the world.

The Soviet Union, for its part, grew more hostile and intransigent in its dealings with the West. Moscow set about increasing its control over the Eastern bloc politically and economically. In July 1947 the Soviet Union established a Communist Information Bureau (Cominform) and initiated a program of bilateral trade agreements with Eastern European states (the Molotov Plan), which would eventually culminate in the Council of Mutual Economic Assistance (COMECON)—the Soviet answer to the Marshall Plan.[32]

This consolidation of two distinct Cold War blocs directly impeded implementation of the FTT concept. The immediate stumbling block was the governorship. At first there appeared to be some effort by the parties concerned to find an appropriate and impartial candidate. It rapidly became apparent, however, that the Soviet Union and Yugoslavia would not accept any of the candidates suggested by Britain, the United States, and Italy, who in turn were equally hostile toward the Soviet and Yugoslav nominees. As the disagreement wore on, the Americans and British grew less concerned to secure appointment of a governor before 15 September than to ensure that any proposed candidate fully met their criteria for impartiality (which included a definite stipulation that the individual could have no leftist sympathies). Without a governor the mechanism for establishing a civil government in the FTT could not be set in motion. Underlying the governorship issue was a specific fear among policymakers in Washington and London, and AMG officials in Trieste, that if the FTT were established in 1947 the Soviet Union and Yugoslavia would soon find a means of destroying it in order to introduce Yugoslav control of the area. This concern had been evident among American officials even during the CFM negotiations on the Trieste settlement. It grew more marked during 1947 and led many Anglo-American policymakers to conclude that maintaining the status quo would be the best means of preventing a Yugoslav takeover of Trieste. Consequently, the United States and Britain were not perturbed when the Security Council had failed to agree on a generally acceptable candidate by 15 September 1947.[33]

This deadlock affected local planning for the termination of AMG–Venezia Giulia. Despite having to work in a tense atmosphere of nationalistic and doctrinal resentments at the outcome of the peace treaty, AMG officials had been making reasonable progress on local preparations for "R" day (15 September), such as the demarcation of boundaries for the FTT and supervision of the evacuation of thousands of Italians from parts of the Julian Region assigned to Yugoslavia (mainly from Pula). By mid-1947 they came to realize that appointment of a governor for the new FTT before "R" day was highly unlikely. In June General Terence Airey, the British commander of AMG–Venezia Giulia, had already asked the British and American governments for approval to issue a proclamation on 15 September prolonging AMG in the Anglo-American zone of the FTT until a governor assumed office. The CCS sent that approval in July, with an amendment added by the State Department "to link responsibility for the integrity and independence of the Free Territory with the Security Council."[34]

Earlier in the year AFHQ had also requested continuation of funds for civilian relief in Zone A, which were due to expire on 30 June. The British government had responded that, in view of their general economic difficulties, they would no longer be able to provide funds. But, as in the somewhat analogous case of Greece earlier in the year, the Americans considered it vital to continue economic assistance to Trieste. Policymakers in Washington agreed in July that the United States would continue to provide relief assistance to Trieste under Public Law 84 of the Eightieth Congress "until AFHQ is dissolved and thereafter until the Governor of the Free Territory of Trieste assumes office." Responding in the spirit of the Truman Doctrine, the United States had assumed a greater economic responsibility for another area in the Mediterranean where the British could no longer afford to do so. This decision was part of a much broader historical development wherein Britain was painfully acknowledging the very severe limitations on its international power in the postwar world, while the United States was taking over the influential role Britain had played in many parts of the world for centuries.[35]

Thanks to these high-level decisions and their own planning efforts, AMG officials were well prepared when the Italian peace treaty came into force without the appointment of a governor. AMG–Venezia Giulia was duly terminated and the new Italo-Yugoslav frontier came into existence. But the Anglo-American military administration continued to operate in those parts of Zone A of the Julian Region assigned to the FTT. Similarly, those parts of Zone B to be included in the FTT remained under Yugoslav military government. The free territory had been stillborn and it remained to be seen if it could be brought to life in the coming months.

## Conclusion

During the two years after the conclusion of the Second World War the Trieste problem had become inextricably entangled in the developing Cold War. Lying on the fracture line between the increasingly antagonistic blocs of East and West, Trieste's future came to depend on more general developments in that struggle.

The heightening of Cold War tensions directly affected the direction and tone of international deliberations concerning the disputed territory's final disposition. The United States strongly backed Italian claims to Trieste on the grounds of self-determination. Washington's stand was influenced by its desire to strengthen Italy as a liberal democratic state within the Western sphere of influence and by the fact that Yugoslavia seemed to be a compliant Soviet client-state, with a totalitarian domestic system and an aggressively anti-American foreign policy. The Soviet Union, for its part, supported Yugoslav claims to Trieste largely on economic and historic grounds. The motives for that support, though undocumented, appear to have been a mirror image of those of the United States: Yugoslavia was a communist state that Stalin hoped to control, while Italy, despite a strong domestic Left, seemed firmly ensconced within the Western camp. Consequently, the Trieste question became a matter of direct East-West confrontation and, like many other issues discussed at the CFM talks, illustrated the extent of Soviet-American disagreement about Europe's future. At the same time it is significant that, despite the growing tensions of the immediate postwar period, negotiations were still possible and there was some hope of compromise on matters such as the Trieste dispute. For that reason the spectacle of the foreign ministers of the world's great powers haggling ad nauseum over the minutest details in each others' proposals for a Trieste settlement was a measure not only of the gulf separating the Western nations from the Soviet Union but also of the fact that rigid politicomilitary confrontation had not yet become the only method of responding to that divergence of views.

On the local level the interim administration of Trieste by an Anglo-American Allied Military Government was also affected by the general deterioration in East-West relations, but in a rather complicated way. The aims and character of AMG rule necessarily reflected certain Anglo-American liberal principles and thereby encountered intense ideological opposition from the forces of the Left in Zone A. The institutions of government introduced by AMG officials were purposefully designed to replace the communist-dominated system of committees. The severe restrictions the AMG placed on local political activities were also directed primarily against the well-organized communist groups in Zone A. The local situation was thus in many ways a microcosm of a much broader ideological conflict between liberalism and communism in the early postwar era. Indeed, Colonel Bowman, the senior civil affairs officer in AMG during most of the 1945–1947 period, has argued in his memoirs that "the political and doctrinal confrontation at Trieste" was a key focal point of the early Cold War.[36]

Nevertheless, as the main body of Bowman's own book demonstrates, AMG officials were not primarily concerned about pursuing Cold War objectives in their everyday administration of Zone A. In fact, they usually resisted what little pressure their superiors placed on them to adjust local methods of government to advance more general Anglo-American aims in the Cold War. Enjoying considerable local autonomy, AMG officials developed mechanisms of local government in the field to suit local conditions, and their administration of Zone A—up to mid-1947, at least—was not consciously intended to serve as the local embodiment of a systematic anticommunist policy. Their most pressing concern was to maintain total control of the *local* situation so as to ensure order and stability in an area whose inhabitants were divided by intense national and ideological antagonisms (of which the former posed the more serious problem for AMG officials).

In 1946 Anglo-American policymakers reluctantly concluded that internationalization of the disputed territory appeared the most fitting solution to the Trieste problem from both the international and local perspectives. On the international level it seemed to offer a means of bypassing the East-West deadlock on the question. Locally, internationalization represented a mechanism for transcending bitter national rivalries. The Americans and British also hoped initially that the creation of a Free Territory of Trieste under Security Council protection would prevent Yugoslav seizure of the area.

Ironically, this "ideal" solution proved bankrupt almost as soon as it was agreed upon. Both of the nations directly concerned opposed the idea, and the sustained vigor of Italian and Yugoslav nationalism among the inhabitants of the proposed Free Territory of Trieste threw into doubt the viability of the concept. Moreover, American and British officials eventually came to fear that if the FTT were established the Yugoslavs would soon take it over. They therefore favored maintaining the status quo—unsatisfactory as it was. Most important, the worsening of the Cold War in 1946 generated a climate of intense suspicion and implacable hostility in which neither international bloc was willing to risk the possibility of the FTT being incorporated in toto into the other camp. The Western powers and the Soviet Union would fail to agree on a suitable governor, and internationalization of the Trieste area would prove impossible to implement as planned. Trieste would remain an object of East-West confrontation.

As a result of these developments, the United States found itself with an indefinite military, political, and economic commitment in Trieste when the Italian peace treaty came into effect in September 1947. That situation had evolved primarily as a consequence of the Cold War and, in particular, was a direct outgrowth of American postwar policies toward Italy and Yugoslavia. Having willingly accepted such a commitment, the United States would now be less interested in seeking immediate activation of the FTT than in ensuring that its policies did indeed further its general Cold War objectives in the region.

# 5

## Cold War Pawn: Trieste and American Policy, September 1947 to December 1949

> [The] FTT has symbolic as well as intrinsic importance. Trieste represents today the continuing concern of [the] US in Eastern Europe. [Our] troops there are [a] stabilizing influence throughout this whole region. It has been and remains a proving ground for both American and Soviet intentions.—Cavendish Cannon to the State Department, 8 November 1947, *FRUS, 1947,* 4

The postwar division of Europe had almost crystallized when the Italian peace treaty came into effect. If the Free Territory of Trieste had become a fully autonomous political entity, as envisaged in the provisions of that settlement, it would have been poised precariously between two Cold War blocs. Instead, its anticipated birth on 15 September 1947 was abortive and the territory in question remained divided into two zones, each associated with one of the rival camps.

In view of this situation the United States would shortly thereafter reject outright the very concept of the free territory that it had helped formulate. The major goal of its Trieste policy would be to ensure that at least Zone A remained firmly in the Western sphere of influence. Since that would be the case as long as the area remained under Anglo-American military administration, the United States ceased to be anxious for a long-term solution to the problem. The more pressing concern for policymakers in Washington would be to ensure that their Trieste policies conformed with broader American objectives in the Cold War—especially in Italy and Yugoslavia.

## The Cold War in Zone A

As no governor had been selected for the FTT by 15 September 1947, General Airey, commander of the Anglo-American forces in Zone A, proceeded with the plan approved by the American and British governments. In accordance with their interpretation of article 1 of the provisional statute for the FTT, he issued a public declaration that, until a governor was appointed, AMG would continue to govern under his authority in those parts of the former Zone A of the Julian Region now included in the FTT. Ten thousand American and British troops would remain in the area for this purpose, and AMG–Venezia Giulia would give way to AMG-FTT. Airey's action clarified Anglo-American intentions. The two powers would insist on exclusive AMG control of the parts of the FTT that they had hitherto administered until a suitable governor was found—or, perhaps, until some other permanent solution was suggested.[1]

The Yugoslavs took a different view. According to them, article 1 of the provisional statute meant that, until appointment of a governor, the whole FTT should be administered jointly under Anglo-American *and* Yugoslav military government. They hoped to realize this objective immediately by presenting the Anglo-Americans with a fait accompli the moment the Italian peace treaty came into force. On 15 September, they took a bold step. Yugoslav military authorities sent Airey a note stating that, at midnight, a Yugoslav detachment would "move on the city of Trieste and take up positions therein."[2]

The note caused great alarm at AMG headquarters in Trieste, for it seemed that the worst fear of Anglo-American officials was about to materialize. General Airey met at once with General John H. Lee, the acting supreme Allied commander in the Mediterranean, William Sullivan, the British political adviser, and Robert P. Joyce, the recently appointed U.S. political adviser. Airey told them that the Yugoslavs were clearly determined to take over the FTT in violation of the Italian peace treaty. He believed this last-minute ploy was "in accordance with a well thought-out plan to destroy the Free Territory at the same moment it came into existence." The four men agreed that Anglo-American forces should resist any Yugoslav armed entry into Zone A. Joyce believed that the Yugoslav move was probably a bluff that could be easily dissipated by Anglo-American firmness, but Airey cautioned that "if this matter were not handled very carefully a third World War might start here." They decided, therefore, to seek further instructions from higher authorities. Sullivan met with communications difficulties in reaching his superiors, but Joyce was able to contact the American ambassador in Rome, James Dunn, who agreed that the Yugoslavs should not be permitted to enter the Anglo-American zone. By 11:30 that night Dunn telephoned back to say that Washington concurred strongly in this judgment.[3]

Airey thereupon warned the Yugoslavs that if they sent troops into Trieste he would respond with force. The State Department also sent a strong note of protest to Belgrade describing the planned Yugoslav action as contrary to the terms of the Italian peace treaty. To the satisfaction of Anglo-American policymakers, this firm stand dissuaded the Yugoslavs from moving into Trieste. On 16 September, the Yugoslav government instructed local military commanders not to enter the city and informed the British and Americans that it would pursue the matter through diplomatic channels. The immediate crisis was over.[4]

Reactions in Washington to the Yugoslav note had been dramatic. Admiral Leahy, Truman's chief of staff, recorded in his diary on 15 September that the Yugoslav threat was probably a bluff "but it may very possibly be the beginning of Soviet [sic] military action that will start the third world war with only America among the democracies capable of providing an effective army." Truman himself ordered the secretary of defense to be ready to reinforce Trieste if necessary, using available American forces in Europe. This brief Yugoslav attempt to secure participation in the administration of Trieste strengthened American policymakers' tendency to view the Trieste problem in Cold War terms and furnished further reasons for hostility toward Yugoslavia.[5]

At the same time four congressmen from the Herter Committee (established to investigate European recovery needs) had been visiting Trieste. Officials in Trieste were intent on persuading these congressmen of the continuing need for a firm American political and military stand and for American economic assistance. When briefing them on 17 September, Joyce stressed that Trieste was a crucial testing ground in the "conflict between Communism and Western Democracy." The effect of his address was heightened visibly by the Yugoslav note of 15 September and by the vigorous Anglo-American reaction, which the congressmen witnessed at first hand. Sullivan reported to the Foreign Office that the American politicians left, "professing their determination to back financial support for the Free Territory, events of the last few days having aroused in them a crusading fervour to resist communist encroachment on Trieste."[6]

The events of 15–16 September also influenced local Anglo-American thinking concerning the problems of continued AMG control of Zone A of the FTT. Joyce reported to Washington that he, Airey, and Sullivan now believed that the Yugoslavs were determined to seize Trieste using whatever means they could and that, therefore, ". . . we are constrained to base our local day to day policy on the hypothesis that we are dealing with potential enemies and not with the forces of a friendly or associated power." While the attempted Yugoslav coup de main had failed, the three men anticipated "a carefully planned and executed war of nerves against Allied Military Government in our zone calculated to undermine the authority of the zone commander, the morale of the Italian majority and the slender chances of economic recovery." Joyce also mentioned the problems created by the "foolish" and "irresponsible" activities of pro-Italian elements but was concerned about this behavior largely because it afforded a pretext for demanding Yugoslav and communist involvement in local government. Finally, Joyce pointed out that Airey considered the central responsibility of AMG to be the maintenance of order and the prevention of all threats to the Anglo-American zone of the FTT, whether external or internal. The State Department concurred in this analysis of the situation, underlining the necessity to check "not only overt Yugoslav moves, but actions by subversive elements [in the] Anglo–United States zone." The department added approvingly that a serious situation had thus far been averted only by a firm AMG stance, which should be vigorously maintained.[7]

After 17 September the Cold War affected AMG methods of governance to an extent not hitherto experienced. The sense of impartiality that had formerly informed AMG activities gave way to a siege mentality with a distinct anticommunist thrust, thereby paralleling general American containment policy in Europe. AMG officials in Trieste had no doubt that Yugoslavia posed the greatest threat to the external security and internal stability of the Anglo-American zone of the FTT. Determined to resist that perceived threat on both fronts, AMG officials maintained unyielding opposition to Yugoslav attempts to influence the administration of Zone A and also sought to curb internal "subversion" by local communist parties. For instance, they now viewed reconstruction measures as important not only for their intrinsic benefits but as a means of defusing local political support for the Left.

The strong anticommunist attitudes manifested by AMG administrators after 15 September were summarized quite candidly in a report on morale and confidence in the FTT prepared in October by Colonel H. P. P. Robertson, the deputy senior civil affairs officer. Identifying communism as the main source of instability in the Anglo-American zone of the FTT, Robertson questioned whether or not the AMG policy of "rigid impartiality" which had alienated both Italians and Slovenes should be continued. His recommendations for improving local morale and confidence hinged on an explicit anticommunist strategy:

> (a) Adopt the theory that every person in the Free Territory, British–United States Zone is a Triestine and there is no distinction between Italians and Slovenes. On the other hand, however, there are two main groups, Communist and anti-Communist.
>
> (b) As Communism is anti-law-and-order it must be opposed whenever and however it is met. Communism flourishes on discontentment, unemployment, bad living conditions and when wages are below the cost of living. The Allied Military Government must therefore do everything possible to alleviate these conditions and hit back at the leaders, whose leadership is based on these conditions existing.
>
> (c) Endeavour to diminish fear of the future by ourselves adopting an attitude of faith in the future of the Western Powers and

as long as the Free Territory lines itself up with the Western Powers and opposes Communism there should be no fear of the future.

Robertson added that noncommunist organizations (Italian and Slovene) should be encouraged, but AMG should seek "the gradual liquidation of all Communist organizations." During the months after the Italian peace treaty came into effect, AMG officials began moving in this general direction. In doing so, their administrative policy took on a somewhat more pro-Italian hue. This development was not due to any innate preference for Italians over Yugoslavs but was more a consequence of Italy's close association with the Western powers.[8]

Another important factor distinguishing AMG–FTT from its predecessor was that AMG administrators were no longer as concerned to preserve as much autonomy as possible from the influence of other Anglo-American decisionmaking centers. If anything, they took the opposite view. During the final months of 1947 AMG officials repeatedly depicted the Trieste problem in terms of a broader struggle against communism and urged their superiors not to consider the issue solely as a localized one. In effect, they were seeking to apply the universal tenets of Washington's recently unveiled containment strategy to the local Trieste situation. Joyce's briefing of the visiting American congressmen in mid-September can be viewed in this context. In a similar vein Airey stressed in early November that

> Trieste cannot be dealt with on its own merits and the problem must be seen against the whole European background. It is comparable to Greece, for example. It is a stronghold to be firmly held until the tide of the political battle now being fought in Europe turns our way. I believe that the tide is slowly turning. This winter will be crucial and in any case we must not give up vital ground at the very moment when the U.S.A. is likely to make its influence felt so decisively with Interim Aid and the Marshall Plan.

The policy recommendation that invariably accompanied such interpretations was that, above all, exclusive Anglo-American control of

Zone A of the FTT should be continued until the international situation was clarified.⁹

These gradual shifts in tenor of AMG administration after 15 September were in part a consequence of the growing conviction among AMG officials that the FTT scheme would never be implemented in the form envisaged in the Italian peace treaty. Their reasoning was based not only on reactions to the Cold War impasse blocking the selection of a governor but also stemmed directly from observations of the local situation. AMG officials believed that even if a governor were found, the Yugoslavs would constantly seek to destabilize the FTT and would eventually annex it after British and American troops had left. Two weeks before the Italian peace treaty came into effect Joyce had already reported that AMG officials "consider that part of Zone B which will become part of the FTT gone with the wind" and effectively absorbed into Yugoslavia. Thereafter they grew increasingly skeptical of the FTT concept and governed their zone with the intention of containing communist influence until an alternative solution to the problem could be found which safeguarded Western interests in the area.¹⁰

Local factors notwithstanding, the continuation of Anglo-American administration in Zone A was only possible because of the failure on the international diplomatic level to agree on a governor. That search effectively halted after the Italian peace treaty came into force. For a time policymakers in Washington did not fully share the pessimism of AMG officials about the FTT's prospects. They still appeared somewhat interested in finding a suitable candidate but saw no need for haste. The rationale for Washington's strategy was summarized in the State Department's instructions to its representatives at the United Nations on 19 September: "We feel that in this case time plays on our side. We believe that if the Allied Military Command in Trieste is sedulous in resisting every Yugoslav attempt at encroachment, the Yugoslavs and their Soviet masters will realize that no advantage is to be gained by prolonging a stalemate in finding a suitable and impartial governor." The British held similar views. Though still committed publicly to establishing the FTT, Britain and the United States were not averse to maintaining the status quo until the West's criteria for a "suitable and impartial" governor were met.¹¹

Only six weeks later the British appeared to have a change of heart. On 31 October, Foreign Secretary Ernest Bevin advised Washington that, in view of the apparent Yugoslav threat to the FTT, "I have come to the conclusion that no Governor, no matter how strong, will be able to ensure the long lasting independence of the Free Territory, far less its prosperity; and I would therefore favour a partition of the Territory by which the Italians would regain sovereignty over what is now the Anglo-American zone." He recommended that the British and Americans should "stall on the appointment of a Governor (even in the event of the Russians suddenly showing a disposition to agree on a suitable candidate) and thus facilitate the possible discussion of partition at the appropriate moment." Bevin's action was not merely of local interest but appeared to be part of an ongoing general disengagement by Britain from traditional areas of prewar influence in the Mediterranean—as had been similarly evidenced in mid-1947 when the United States had been obliged to accept most of the financial burden for maintaining AMG in Trieste. Only days later Joyce cabled Washington that Sullivan had just completed a draft study entitled "British/U.S. Zone of the Free Territory of Trieste and the Problem of its Administration in the Immediate Future." The British political adviser thought the FTT was unworkable. He recommended direct Italo-Yugoslav talks to arrange an eventual partition, thereby relieving the British and American governments of their commitments. Sullivan concluded that it was probably not worth a grave international crisis to insist upon all Western demands. He surmised that "perhaps there is no alternative to the eventual absorption of Trieste by Yugoslavia and that we are merely fighting a rearguard action to delay this inevitable consummation." This study had not yet been forwarded to the Foreign Office but its conclusions influenced American reactions to the British proposal for partition.[12]

American diplomats in the field were alarmed at the "defeatism" of Sullivan's proposal and urged the State Department to reject it. Joyce emphatically recommended consolidation of the Anglo-American position in Trieste, arguing that it was "in the long range vital interests of both the US and UK Governments to continue to enforce the treaty here." Cavendish Cannon, who was now American ambassador to Yugoslavia, reported with dismay that British embassy sources had informed him that Sullivan's conclusions reflected Foreign Office views and that the "British have thrown up their hands in despair." His own comments on the importance of Trieste and its psychological significance for general American containment strategy were even more pointed than Joyce's:

> [The] FTT has symbolic as well as intrinsic importance. Trieste represents today the continuing concern of [the] US in Eastern Europe. [Our] troops there are [a] stabilizing influence throughout this whole region. It has been and remains a proving ground for both American and Soviet intentions. Our withdrawal under whatever guise would not mean [the] loss only of Trieste but would be [an] encouragement [of] incalculable proportions to [the] Soviet purpose in [the] world's troubled regions.

Like Joyce, he believed that the time was not ripe for revising the Italian peace treaty and that the United States should stand firm. From Rome Ambassador James Dunn added that any immediate Anglo-American initiative in proposing partition, "would be detrimental to our position vis-à-vis [the] Yugoslavs and extremely harmful to our prestige in Italy." These diplomats had not rejected the idea of *eventual* partition of the FTT, but were arguing that if the Trieste policy of the United States was to reflect broader Cold War objectives, then the time was not yet propitious for such action.[13]

In replying to Bevin the State Department adopted a similar line. Walter C. Dowling of the department's European division prepared a memorandum for the secretary of state on 14 November. Analyzing the merits and disadvantages of London's proposal, he agreed that "the eventual restoration of Trieste to Italy may be the best situation," but recommended that partition should not be attempted "at the present time." His reason was that it seemed unlikely there would be a preemptive Yugoslav or Soviet move to suggest partition in the near future (as the British feared) and that any Anglo-American proposal to this effect might be interpreted as "indicative of anxiety to remove our military forces from the area without due regard for the consequences." Like Dunn, Dowling suggested the question might be more usefully reevaluated in the light of future international developments. In the interim he recommended telling the British orally that the United States preferred the status quo and thought it unwise to press "unduly" in the Security Council for appointment of a governor. Surprisingly, he added that "at the same time, we should continue to make it clear to the Soviet member that we are prepared to accept any Governor who, in our opinion, is qualified for the responsibilities of the office." This final point caused further misunderstanding between London and Washington concerning their respective policies on the future of the FTT.[14]

Lord Inverchapel, the British ambassador in Washington, advised the Foreign Office of the American reply on 24 November. Geoffrey Wallinger, head of the Foreign Office's Southern Department, viewed the response as "rather woolly." He asked the ambassador to express British concern about the State Department's apparent desire to continue seeking "a really acceptable Governor," even though Bevin's message of 31 October had stressed that "no Governor, no matter how strong, will be able to assure the lasting independence of the Free Territory, and that we should therefore stall on the appointment of any (repeat any) Governor." Inverchapel replied that the State Department believed the situation required great caution and that it was not yet appropriate to declare that "our ultimate objective should be partition." The Americans were clearly concerned about international public opinion, he reported, and in order to avoid premature charges of violating the Italian peace treaty, the "State Department would prefer to define our joint position as being that we continue to hold out for a 'good' Governor, knowing as we do that there is little or no chance of agreement being secured to the appointment of such a person." In the meantime the Americans intended to support fully General Airey's efforts to maintain a barrier between the two zones of the FTT and to prevent Communist subversion in Zone A. This time London was satisfied. Wallinger believed that the exchange had cleared the air and that the British and American policies were essentially the same.[15]

He was correct. In reality the Anglo-American debate had merely concerned tactics and timing. Both governments lacked confidence in the viability of the FTT and hoped for an alternative long-term solution favorable to the West. As Dowling had noted on 14 November, the principal criteria to be considered in reaching such a solution were "the degree of stability and security which Italy may attain and the policy towards Italy and the West which Yugoslavia may pursue." By the end of November the British and Americans were in agreement about the tactics to adopt in pursuing these objectives. The Americans had persuaded the British that a demand for partition would be premature even though they agreed that returning Trieste to Italy would probably be the most satisfactory ultimate solution. On the governorship issue, Washington did not think it advisable to announce publicly that no candidate would be suitable and quickly adopted the British ploy of frustrating the selection of a candidate. The State Department, in January 1948, informed the American representative at the United Nations that the

> Dept's policy has consistently been that we will accept no less than an absolute top-notch governor for Trieste and that unless and until such a man is found we are content to maintain the *status quo.* . . . For your secret info we feel that in this critical juncture of affairs in Europe it would be dangerous to alter [the] current situation in Trieste where [the] presence of 10,000 US-UK troops serve as [a] decided stabilizing influence at a key point.

By early 1948 the United States and Great Britain had clearly rejected the FTT concept—for international and local reasons—but were content to await further developments in the Cold War before proposing an alternative solution. In effect their commitment to Trieste (especially that of the United States) had become indefinite, and the ultimate settlement of the question had been thrust into limbo.[16]

### The Tripartite Proposal

In early 1948 Cold War confrontation in Europe worsened. A communist government took power in Czechoslovakia in February. The next month the Soviet Union began interfering with the flow of American military supplies to Berlin after four-power discussions on the issue broke down. The United States meanwhile was preparing to implement the Marshall Plan and promoted the formation of a formal Western alliance system. Some American policymakers feared that war might be imminent in Europe.

In this context of heightened Cold War tensions the Italian elections to be held in April took on particular significance for American policymakers. They were concerned that an electoral victory by the Italian Left would thrust a strategically important nation into the Soviet orbit and would have disastrous repercussions for American prestige throughout Western Europe. As historian James Miller has observed, "these elections thus became an apocalyptic test of strength between communism and democracy for the leaders of the U.S. government." According to opinion polls in early 1948, there was a distinct possibility that "communism" (in the form of the powerful Italian Communist and Socialist parties) would prevail in the April elections. To forestall such an outcome the United States mounted a deliberate campaign of intervention in Italy's internal politics.[17]

A key stratagem in that campaign concerned Trieste. While the Americans and British had been content since late 1947 to delay implementation of the FTT concept, the Italian elections provided an occasion for reconsideration of Trieste policy. Joyce cabled Washington on 2 March 1948 to suggest that the Anglo-American commitment "should now be considered on a high political level in relation [to the] forthcoming Italian election." A day earlier Ambassador James Dunn in Rome had reported that Italian Foreign Minister Carlo Sforza had suggested that "from the tactical point of view in relation to the electoral campaign," the United States and Britain should recommend publicly the return to Italy of that part of the FTT under AMG. Despite "recognizable difficulties" Dunn felt that such a statement would "serve [the] interests of Italian democracy and therefore [those of the] US." The British were also reviewing their Trieste policy, as a Foreign Office minute of 1 March shows: "The Italian elections are of such vital importance to the future of Western Europe that we are at present considering whether we might not have to alter our Trieste policy if by doing so we can substantially assist the non-Communist parties during the next two months." Having favored partition of the FTT for some time, the Foreign Office viewed the elections as an opportunity to secure American support for an announcement to that effect. Unaware of Sforza's discussion with Dunn, Wallinger suggested on 1 March that the British consult the Italian government to ensure that a declaration favoring a division of the FTT, with Trieste reverting to Italy, would indeed help defeat the Italian Communists on 18 April. The scene appeared set for public confirmation of a policy which many Anglo-American officials had already assumed privately would be the most realistic solution to the Trieste problem on a long-term basis.[18]

Washington, however, now sought a more drastic revision of Anglo-American policy. The State Department, on 6 March, asked for London's views on "the tentative idea that the French, United Kingdom and United States Governments might shortly declare their support for the return to Italy of the whole of the Free Territory of Trieste." Unlike the partition idea, such an action could not be anything more than an electoral ploy, for the Yugoslavs, and probably the Soviet Union, were certain to oppose it. Yet the British responded favorably. They thought it advisable, nevertheless, to ask Italian Prime Minister Alcide de Gasperi to assess which proposal would have the greatest electoral benefits for the nonleftist parties: a tripartite statement favoring the return of the whole FTT to Italy or one supporting the return of the Anglo-American zone only. The State Department agreed and began consultations in London and Paris concerning a joint approach to De Gasperi. The department also solicited the views of its representatives in Europe.[19]

Even before these responses arrived the United States had decided in effect that a statement on Trieste would be part of its strategy for securing a "democratic" victory in the Italian elections. On 8 March the recently formed National Security Council considered NSC 1/3, "The Position of the United States with Respect to Communist Participation in the Government of Italy by Legal Means." The report opened with a dramatic warning:

> United States security interests in the Mediterranean are immediately and gravely threatened by the possibility that the Italian Communist-dominated People's Bloc will win participation in the government in the April national elections and that the Communists will thereafter, following a pattern made familiar in Eastern Europe, take over complete control of the government

and transform Italy into a totalitarian state subservient to Moscow. Such a development would have [a] demoralizing effect throughout Western Europe, the Mediterranean, and the Middle East.

Stating that the United States had only six weeks to prevent a possible victory by the Italian Left, the report recommended a series of actions to assist the Italian moderate parties, ranging from covert funding of those groups (through the Central Intelligence Agency) to a campaign of public statements stressing the critical importance of the elections. Among the suggested measures was a proposal to "announce without delay, after informing the British and French governments, that the United States supports an immediate return of Trieste to Italy." Approved on 11 March, NSC 1/3 underscored Washington's willingness to take the initiative on this issue and to subordinate the Trieste question to the more immediate necessity of strengthening the noncommunist forces in Italy.[20]

State Department officials now sought British and French approval for a statement to be issued on 18 March supporting the return of the whole FTT to Italy. Both governments agreed to the American proposal in principle and suggested only minor modifications. When informed, Airey also favored the idea. American diplomats in Europe did not foresee serious objections as long as the desired electoral impact of the proposal was assured. When Dunn approached De Gasperi for that purpose the Italian premier "immediately" indicated his preference for a statement recommending the return of all of the FTT to Italy, rather than just the Anglo-American zone. Having secured Italian approval, the Americans wished to announce the declaration as planned on 18 March—in part because they feared a possible preemptive statement on the same subject by the Soviet Union. There was a delay, however, in obtaining French approval. Foreign Minister Georges Bidault wished to announce the proposal personally during an official visit to Italy the next week. Fearing that such an action would lessen the impact of the maneuver, the Americans eventually obtained French agreement to a simultaneous declaration by all three governments on 20 March.[21]

A striking feature of the press statement issued on that date was that it made no reference to the imminent elections that had actually motivated it. In this so-called Tripartite Proposal the three powers asked the Soviet Union and Italy to join them in formulating an additional protocol to the Italian peace treaty whereby the FTT would be returned to Italy. They had supposedly reached this decision because "discussions in the Security Council have already shown that agreement on the selection of a governor is impossible and because they have received abundant evidence to show that the Yugoslav zone had been completely transformed in character and has been virtually incorporated into Yugoslavia by procedures which do not respect the desire expressed by the powers to give an independent and democratic status to the Territory." In separate notes to the Soviet and Italian governments the United States argued, moreover, that it had always maintained that both zones of the FTT were "ethnically and historically Italian territory" and that it had agreed reluctantly to the area's separation from Italy "only on the condition that it [the FTT] was really independent and that the human rights of the population were completely protected." Announced less than a month before the Italian elections, these arguments were a flimsy disguise for the Tripartite Proposal's underlying intent.[22]

Not surprisingly, the Yugoslav government protested immediately, denouncing the "propagandistic character" of the proposal. The Italian Communists complained that the tripartite statement was merely an opportunistic electoral stratagem. They contended that the Anglo-American powers were deliberately frustrating the selection of a governor so as to prolong their military presence in Trieste. The Soviet Union delayed its response until 13 April and then avoided any reference to the substantive thrust of the Western declaration. Moscow chose instead to reject the Tripartite Proposal on procedural grounds, arguing that any revision of the Italian peace treaty "by means of correspondence or the organization of private conferences is considered unacceptable by the Soviet Government as violating the elementary principles of democracy."[23]

Protests from the Communist bloc were of little interest to the Western powers. Their attention was riveted on the Tripartite Proposal's impact on the Italian electoral race. They seemed to have ample cause for satisfaction on that front. Dunn reported from Rome on 4 April that the "tripartite proposal on Trieste was dramatically effective in encouraging democratic parties, leaders and placing [the] communist front on [the] defensive in [the] electoral campaign." Ambassador Jefferson Caffery in Paris informed the State Department that "the French believe that while the individual gestures made thus far by France and the U.S. to Italy have been of importance, they have not left the great impact of the tripartite Trieste proposal." Carlo Sforza expressed the Italian government's gratitude for the Western action even before the elections were held. The precise effect of the three-power declaration cannot be isolated from that of other external influences on the election, but it did appear to assist the Italian Christian Democrats in winning a surprisingly high 48.5 percent of the votes on 18 April. Anthony Eden concluded confidently in his memoirs that the Tripartite Proposal was highly successful as a measure "calculated to embarrass Communists everywhere" and "contributed to a sweeping victory won by the Christian Democrats."[24]

Eden noted nonetheless that "juridically it did not mean so much, because any revision [of the Italian peace treaty] required the agreement of Soviet Russia, which would not be forthcoming." The problem of Trieste thus remained unsolved. The initial suggestion by the United States of returning all the FTT to Italy had been motivated solely by its interest in the outcome of the Italian election. Former State Department officials have readily confirmed that winning the election was the overriding consideration and the long-term implications of the proposal were given little thought when the idea was first conceived. Indeed, John Campbell has observed that "by including Zone B the declaration entered the realm of political propaganda. It seemed fairly cheap, because at that time we had no reason to take account of Yugoslav concerns. And in a way it was dishonest, since we had no means of delivering Zone B to Italy." It was hardly surprising, therefore, that after the Italian election there was no consideration of whether such a proposal could possibly provide a realistic basis for the solution of the FTT stalemate. When the Soviet government delayed its reply to the original proposal, the three Western powers submitted a second note to that government, on 9 April, suggesting a preliminary meeting of the powers interested in the

Trieste question to negotiate the necessary revision of the Italian peace treaty. This note was intended to give a semblance of public authenticity to the Tripartite Proposal so that it did not appear a "mere electoral move." When the Soviet Union tersely rejected the idea on procedural grounds, the United States formally expressed regret but did not press the issue further. The Tripartite Proposal was the most egregious example up to that point of the way in which the United States and Great Britain had subordinated the question of Trieste's long-term future to more pressing Cold War exigencies.[25]

### The Local Impact of the Tripartite Proposal

Although conceived as an electoral gesture, the declaration of 20 March had important implications for American and British policies toward Trieste. It served as definite confirmation of their intent to repudiate the FTT concept and to seek revision of the Italian peace treaty. The Tripartite Proposal also created a public commitment for the United States and Britain to support the return of the whole FTT to Italy, thereby compromising their earlier expectation of an eventual de facto partition. The two powers would be obliged to maintain this position as their official policy on Trieste for some years.

After the Italian election, however, there soon emerged a tacit acknowledgment that the Tripartite Proposal was unworkable. Since Soviet or Yugoslav cooperation was not forthcoming, the return of the whole FTT to Italy presumably could only be secured by force. In these circumstances the State Department cabled Trieste on 7 May to advise that

> Position stated [in the] Mar 20 Proposal . . . remains [the] basis [of the] US Government's policy vis-a-vis FTT, but until further development [of the] situation we feel AMG must continue [its] administration [of] Zone A in accord [with] Treaty obligations insofar as practicable in [the] face [of] existing difficulties. Within these limits, however, it is expected that steps may nevertheless be taken to facilitate eventual restoration [of the] area to Italy.

Foreign Office officials were of a similar mind. They recommended in an important memorandum of 19 May that the tenets of subsequent British policy on Trieste should be:

> (a) To retain Allied Military Government and troops in our Zone until we are satisfied that the position can be held against Communist subversion by AMG's successors.
> (b) To prepare to negotiate an arrangement whereby the city and port of Trieste, and as much of the remainder of the Free Territory as possible, revert to Italy.
> (c) Until such an arrangement is arrived at, so to administer the Zone with the Americans that the anticipated handover to the Italian Government will eventually be as simple as possible.

The postelectoral policy of the United States and Britain on Trieste's future was emerging. Cognizant of Yugoslav and Soviet opposition, neither Washington nor London wished to risk military conflict by forcing prompt implementation of the 20 March declaration. Both were content to maintain the status quo for the immediate future. The United States and Britain thus intended to maintain firm control of Zone A, but they were now also prepared to sanction a slightly more pro-Italian policy on the local level in anticipation of the eventual return of this portion of the FTT to Italy.[26]

After March 1948, AMG reached several financial and economic agreements with the Italian government which increased Italy's influence on Zone A. Shortly before the Tripartite Proposal was announced, three agreements were signed on 9 March according to which Italy would provide and regulate the currency supply and foreign exchange needs of the zone. In a related accord of 16 April, the Italian government received the power to regulate export and import activities in Zone A. Moreover, when preparations were being made for Trieste's inclusion in the European Recovery Program (ERP), the State Department agreed to a suggestion from Rome that "the proposal for membership [of the] US-UK Zone, FTT, in OEEC [Organization for European Economic Cooperation] should come from [the] Italian Govt and that [the] Italian desire [to] assist Trieste should be emphasized and reference made to [the] close economic relations [of]

Italy and Trieste, to [the] extent [that] there is no conflict with peace treaty terms." The latter qualification was somewhat fatuous in that the Department also assured the Italians that the United States would take every opportunity to emphasize that Zone A's inclusion in the OEEC implied no change in the policy advocated in the Tripartite Proposal—itself a direct repudiation of the Italian peace treaty. In late September, only a few weeks before the OEEC formally admitted Zone A into the ERP, AMG and the Italian government concluded a further agreement whose effect was to extend Italian control of the local currency supply and foreign exchange requirements. A mixed commission was also created to meet monthly in Rome to discuss financial and economic questions of common concern and to coordinate ERP programs in Italy and Zone A. By the end of 1948 Trieste's economy had definitely become more closely integrated with that of Italy.[27]

There were, however, clear limits to the extent of Italian economic influence which AMG officals were prepared to sanction. While accepting the necessity for close economic cooperation with Italy, they had no intention of giving up overall control of Zone A's economy to Rome. In fact, the AMG's Financial and Economic Division insisted —contrary to Italy's demands—that Trieste participate directly in ERP as an independent member of the OEEC rather than be represented by Italy. The American and British governments agreed with AMG rather than Italy. This decision was not surprising for, as the State Department informed the American embassy in Rome on 23 April 1948, the major objective of American economic policy in Zone A was "to integrate Trieste in [the] Western European economy and enable [the] US [to] broaden assistance from present relief to ECA recovery basis." In view of Trieste's location and the fact that Yugoslavia, unlike Italy, was not part of that Western European economy, it was almost inevitable that the fulfillment of ERP objectives in Trieste would require close involvement with the neighboring Italian economy. But AMG officials and their superiors in Washington and London still wanted to maintain independent control of the Triestine economy so that they could pursue their own objectives. The main political goal of Zone A's participation in the Marshall Plan, as was true elsewhere in Western Europe, was to weaken the appeal of communism—not to further Italian national interests.²⁸

This fact was also evident in AMG policies of local administration after announcement of the Tripartite Proposal. To some extent AMG officials appeared to take a more pro-Italian line in their administration of Zone A. Several actions were taken to reorganize the structure of AMG in 1948, the most important of which were embodied in Order No. 259 of 25 June (replacing General Order No. 11 of 11 August 1945) and Order No. 308 of 26 July. These measures served to increase the autonomy of the local administration and cast the AMG into a role analogous to that of a central government. The immediate effect of these changes was to bolster the pro-Italian groups in Zone A and bring local government more closely into line with Italian administrative models, largely because Italian personnel dominated the positions of significant power within the system. There was nevertheless a strict insistence on continued overall control by AMG, and Order No. 259 reiterated firmly that AMG was the supreme authority in Zone A. By instituting these measures, AMG officials were trying to adjust to the policy implications of the Tripartite Proposal while still fulfilling their obligations under the Italian peace treaty. In his 1948 quarterly reports to the Security Council of the United Nations, General Airey repeatedly recommended that the whole FTT be returned to Italy on ethnic grounds. But until international developments created that possibility, he would govern cautiously and maintain the autonomous status of Zone A under AMG.²⁹

After the failure of the FTT to come into being and the announcement of the Tripartite Proposal, the United States and Britain had modified their Trieste policies, giving the distinct appearance of a more openly pro-Italian demeanor. But the two Western powers knew that neither Yugoslavia nor the Soviet Union was likely to agree to the Tripartite Proposal. Zone B, moreover, remained under firm Yugoslav control and impervious to Anglo-American influence. Their continued commitment to the statement of 20 March was therefore merely rhetorical and was maintained only for the sake of public consistency. The real importance of the actions taken in the aftermath of the Tripartite Proposal was to confirm that the United States and Britain had rejected the FTT concept but were content to mark time until international developments made it advantageous to pursue some alternative solution— probably de facto partition between Italy and Yugoslavia along the lines of the existing zones.

## The Soviet-Yugoslav Break and its Effects

Only a few months after the announcement of the Tripartite Proposal a major new development occurred in the Cold War which would put the Trieste question into a very different context for the United States. On 28 June 1948 Yugoslavia was expelled from the Cominform after an angry exchange of letters between the Yugoslav and Soviet Communist parties. During the following months this rift led Yugoslavia steadily out of the Soviet orbit.[30]

News of this controversy within the Communist world came as a surprise to most American policymakers. There had been tensions between Yugoslavia and the Soviet Union for some time, but only a few Americans in the Belgrade embassy had hitherto taken note of them. Now that open antagonism had erupted between the two nations, Washington did not delay in evaluating the potential ramifications for its own Cold War policies. By 30 June, the Policy Planning Staff of the State Department had already drafted NSC 18, "The Attitude of This Government toward Events in Yugoslavia" for consideration by the National Security Council. The report observed that "the defiance of the Kremlin by the leaders of the Yugoslav Communist Party creates an entirely new problem of foreign policy for this Government. For the first time in history we may now have within the international community a communist state existing on the basis of Soviet organizational principles and [for] the most part on Soviet ideology, and yet independent of Moscow." NSC 18 cautioned that Yugoslavia remained a communist state and that Tito's defiance of the Soviet Union did not imply Yugoslavia had "come over" to the West. The depth and duration of the Soviet-Yugoslav rift remained uncertain. In these circumstances the Policy Planning Staff advocated a noncommittal policy of extreme circumspection until a clearer picture emerged. Heeding this advice, the United States government was cautious in its response to the Stalin-Tito schism over the coming months.[31]

The repercussions of this split in communist ranks were of great potential significance for the future of Trieste. Local Anglo-American officials realized the possible implications from the outset and sought to prevent opportunistic changes in policy by their superiors. On 3 July, Joyce advised Washington that "General Airey desires to point out that any change in Anglo-American policy for reasons of expediency and in view of [the] Belgrade-Moscow conflict might place his administration in [a] most embarrassing position and that in particular, any concessions to Yugoslavia which might be considered a weakening [of the] tripartite decision, would be bound to have [an] unfortunate effect here." In replying to this cable and other expressions of local concern, the State Department maintained that its Trieste policy was still based on the Tripartite Proposal and stated firmly that no change was contemplated. Similar assurances were given to the Italian government throughout 1948, and Anglo-American policy remained somewhat pro-Italian in its impact insofar as the administration of Zone A was concerned.[32]

Even at this time some officials in Washington believed that future policy on Trieste would have to be modified to take account of the Soviet-Yugoslav dispute. This view became apparent as a consequence of a British initiative. Before learning of the Cominform-Yugoslav disagreement, Britain, France, and the United States had planned to issue a press statement backing up the Tripartite Proposal. The statement was intended to reiterate that the FTT concept was unworkable, to criticize Yugoslav administration of Zone B, and to make clear that Anglo-American forces would remain in Zone A until a just settlement was reached. On 5 July, G. T. C. Campbell of the Foreign Office suggested a reconsideration of this proposed move, pointing out that

> it is possible that one of the causes of the present breach between Soviet and Yugoslav Communists was [a] divergence of aims regarding Trieste. While the Soviet Government were in all probability most concerned with achieving the removal of our troops, Yugoslav plans have undoubtedly been animated by territorial ambitions. It would now therefore seem wiser to do nothing for the time being and to see whether the Soviet Government reply to our proposals during the next three weeks.

Other British officials approved this suggestion and informed Washington that nothing was to be gained from further pressing the matter of the Tripartite Proposal at that time.[33]

Interestingly, the State Department also concurred. On 21 July — the same day Joyce had been assured of an undiminished American commitment to the Tripartite Proposal — the department cabled the American embassy in Paris to advise that Washington considered it desirable to await "clarification [of] developments and also repercussions [for the] Communist Party in [the] FTT" before taking further action on the statement of 20 March. The commitment to implement the three-power declaration had become merely nominal. Now that the sense of emergency precipitated by the Italian elections had passed, the Yugoslav situation became the critical variable in determining major changes in Anglo-American policy on Trieste.[34]

In view of their uncertainty about the precise course the Soviet-Yugoslav rift would take, American policymakers remained circumspect in their approach to the Trieste question over the next year or so. There were several imponderables to consider. Would Yugoslavia move into the Western camp? Would Tito prove more flexible on the Trieste question? Would the Soviet Union continue to press for nomination of a governor for the FTT? Would the Soviet Union perhaps even support the Tripartite Proposal? Definitive answers to these questions long eluded American policymakers and they continued to play a waiting game in Trieste.

In early 1949 the State Department maintained that an indefinite commitment to the status quo in Trieste was "entirely satisfactory to the United States" and that the Anglo-American military presence there represented an important stabilizing force in a potentially volatile region. The new U.S. political adviser in Trieste summarized the advantages of this position in a dispatch of 29 March 1949: "Such a policy seems to be an essential part of the general plan of the Western Powers to resist any further open or concealed Russian moves to the West. The policy would also appear to have at least psychological value in furthering U.S. policies vis-a-vis Yugoslavia by providing a 'cooling-off' period during which the best means of solving the troublesome problem of the Yugoslav zone might become more apparent than it is today." When General Airey visited Washington in May, State Department officials articulated a similar view. In accordance with this "wait-and-see" policy the United States deliberately stalled debates on Trieste in the United Nations and sought to frustrate Soviet efforts to secure appointment of a governor. Washington clearly judged it advisable for political and strategic reasons to maintain a visible Anglo-American military and economic presence in Trieste as long as the Yugoslav situation remained uncertain.[35]

This decision meant that the Soviet-Yugoslav break would have little immediate effect on local AMG administration of Zone A. Maintaining the status quo, however, left local Anglo-American officials in a somewhat contradictory position. As Charles Baldwin reported in March 1949: "One of the most difficult problems which AMG has experienced has resulted from the obligation of the Zone Command to recognize its trusteeship responsibilities under the Security Council and the Italian Peace Treaty and the desire to avoid any action which would be counter to the Allied policy to return Trieste to Italy." Since their superiors took no steps to clarify the situation after the Soviet-Yugoslav rift developed, AMG officials continued to work on the assumption that Zone A, at least, would eventually revert to Italy. They therefore maintained the tacitly pro-Italian policy they had embraced in the wake of the Tripartite Proposal. This policy was perhaps most blatantly evidenced in the preparations for the first local elections of the postwar period in Zone A. The timing of the elections was carefully selected to favor the Italian centrist parties and to exploit the deep split in the local communist forces that the Soviet-Yugoslav dispute had precipitated. Anglo-American officials in Zone A were most concerned about the apparent disarray in the Italian parties before the elections and did all they could to strengthen them. Elections were eventually held on 13 June 1949 and the pro-Italian parties gained a substantial victory, taking 64 percent of the votes in Trieste. On the Communist side the pro-Cominform groups prevailed resoundingly over the Titoist parties. There were no major pro-Italian initiatives by AMG thereafter in 1949.[36]

It had become obvious by then that the Soviet-Yugoslav split was not ephemeral. After the initial break the Cominform applied economic pressure to force the recalcitrant Yugoslavs back into the Soviet camp, but with little effect. Consequently, in 1949 the Soviet Union and its satellites denounced Tito's regime as an enemy and revoked their treaties with Yugoslavia. To the surprise of many Yugoslavia succeeded in retaining its independence of action and began to move into a "non-aligned" position in the Cold War between East and West.[37]

During 1949 American policymakers gradually abandoned their initial skepticism and began considering how to exploit the Soviet-Yugoslav animosity to their own advantage. After several reports from the Belgrade embassy stressed that the rift was indeed real, the State Department began to review the Yugoslav situation in early 1949. One of the officers involved in that process has recalled that "there was at that time a beginning of the concept that the United States did have a role to play in the Yugoslav-Soviet dispute and it must be economic." The Yugoslavs had already requested American economic assistance and Washington now responded. In June 1949 the State Department persuaded the Commerce Department that political considerations required the removal of export restrictions to allow shipments of machinery to Yugoslavia. In September similar advice by the State Department was instrumental in securing a loan of $20 million from the Export-Import Bank. More extensive economic aid followed with no strings attached, for the United States was careful to play down anything of political significance so as not to embarrass Yugoslavia. By late 1949 the United States had demonstrated that it was willing to be flexible in its relations with Tito's regime in order to keep Yugoslavia out of the Soviet bloc.[38]

This gradual thawing in the Truman administration's policy also stimulated reassessments of the Trieste question in the latter half of 1949. The British moved first. Talking with Italian and Yugoslav officials in June, British representatives indicated that their government would not oppose direct Italo-Yugoslav negotiations leading to a compromise settlement. Reporting the British initiative in Belgrade, the American chargé, Robert Reams, recommended that the United States should also reexamine its position and should pressure Italy to accept a realistic compromise solution in lieu of the Tripartite Proposal. The chargé in Moscow agreed. But the State Department demurred, informing its London embassy on 29 June that the

United States wished to stand by the status quo and believed the Italians were not anxious for immediate changes in the situation. The message did state, however, that Washington considered "Yugo agreement on [a] formula which wld [would] save face for Tito and have his support [is an] indispensable element [for] any solution." The department also intimated that it might not be averse to a compromise settlement resulting from a Yugoslav approach to the Italians. In short, while not yet judging the time propitious for any Anglo-American initiatives to modify the status quo, the State Department had hinted that it was open to a permanent resolution to the FTT impasse outside the framework of the Tripartite Proposal, which it still supported officially.[39]

The major reason for the State Department to contemplate any changes in the status quo at this time appears to have been the fear of a possible Soviet move to exploit the Trieste issue to embarrass both Yugoslavia and the West. This concern had featured prominently in the cables from the chargés in Belgrade and Moscow as the major justification for promoting a compromise settlement. The State Department had also expressed its own anxiety about such a possibility. On 18 July, Leonard Unger, the assistant chief of the Division of Southeastern European Affairs, informed a British official that because of the danger of Soviet acceptance of the Tripartite Proposal, the department was now reevaluating whether the advantages of a conclusive settlement might outweigh the usefulness of maintaining an Anglo-American military presence in Trieste. Over the next few months the United States came to adopt the position that "the best hope for progress is in Italy and Yugoslavia working out an agreement themselves," as one official put it on 19 October. American policymakers realized, however, that such a policy raised formidable difficulties, including securing Italo-Yugoslav agreement on a realistic compromise, renouncing the Tripartite Proposal, bypassing the Italian peace treaty, and arousing likely Soviet opposition. The United States took no initiatives to seek implementation of its new policy objective.[40]

As it happened, Yugoslavia also changed its policy toward the FTT in mid-1949 by deciding to favor some sort of partition as the only basis for a realistic settlement. In late November the Yugoslavs sounded out the Americans. Dr. Aleš Bebler, the Yugoslav deputy foreign minister, met with State Department officials in Washington and asked "that the U.S. Government approach the Italian Government, urging the latter to accept a compromise solution." He argued —with good reason—that "so long as the Italian Government believes they have the support of the U.S. Government on the proposal made by the three Western powers on March 20, 1948, they will not budge from claiming return of the entire Free Territory to Italy." The American officials declined to put pressure on Italy, though the department informed the Italian government of these discussions with Bebler.[41]

In fact the United States was growing increasingly receptive to the idea of an Italo-Yugoslav compromise on the FTT. On 1 December, Reams again cabled Washington to emphasize the advantages of an early settlement of the Trieste problem:

> Such [a] settlement would make possible much closer relations between Italians and Yugoslavs in both political and economic fields and would eliminate one of Europe's sore spots. Finally, it would avert the danger which to some of us seems more possible than it did in June of Soviet adherence to [the] March 20 declaration. . . . Considerations above appear to us [the Belgrade embassy] greatly to outweigh advantages derived from [the] continued presence [of] US-UK troops in Trieste. Factors which made troops important have altered since [the] Cominform resolution and could only be restored to [their] former value by Soviet conquest of Yugoslavia.

While realizing the need to maintain a public stand on the Tripartite Proposal, Reams recommended "private intimations" to the Italian and Yugoslav governments that "the United States should welcome a peaceful compromise solution of this question." Baldwin had expressed similar views when he left Trieste in November. The department now appeared to agree with its diplomats in the field and sought out military opinion on the advantages of maintaining troops in Zone A. The Joint Chiefs of Staff responded that there were "no overriding strategic or military objections" to the removal of Anglo-American forces from Trieste. As the decade of the 1940s closed, the

United States was ready to support—at least privately—a negotiated, bilateral solution to the Trieste question.[42]

## Conclusion

In his final report from Trieste, on 11 November 1949, Baldwin reflected that "the real Trieste problem involves external factors and necessitates careful determination of the over-all objective which appears to be most beneficial to United States interests."[43] This statement effectively described the leitmotif of American policy toward Trieste in the period from the coming into effect of the Italian peace treaty to 1950. Washington consistently subordinated the FTT problem to the exigencies of its general Cold War policy of containment in Europe, displaying limited concern for the long-term future of the disputed area. Even its reconstruction efforts and administrative procedures in Zone A were perceived to be part of a broader anticommunist policy. In short, the United States had virtually ignored the local dimensions of the Trieste question for more than two years.

This fact was illustrated glaringly by the most dramatic American action with respect to Trieste in this period: the Tripartite Proposal. The suggestion that the whole FTT be returned to Italy was obviously not an earnest effort to solve the Trieste problem. It was a blatantly opportunistic ploy to gain a short-term advantage in the Cold War by preventing a leftist victory in the Italian national election of 1948. The Christian Democrats prevailed in those elections, but it is difficult to assess the degree to which the Tripartite Proposal helped them to secure a convincing win. In terms of American Trieste policy, the statement of 20 March proved to be an unnecessary and costly liability in the long run. The United States could as easily have suggested partition in early 1948 (with Zone A going to Italy) rather than proposing outright cession of the whole FTT to Italy. Although such a suggestion would not have been as immediately appealing to many Italian voters as the Tripartite Proposal, it might have been just as effective because it might not have been seen as merely a crude electoral maneuver. It would also have provided a realistic basis for later Italo-Yugoslav negotiations and would not have limited American freedom of action to the extent that the Tripartite Proposal did. Such a policy, moreover, might have facilitated a quicker resolution of the Trieste dispute after the Soviet-Yugoslav split transformed the complexion of the problem in Cold War terms.

After 1949 American policymakers would discover that the issues at stake in this longstanding dispute could not, in fact, be analyzed solely from a Cold War perspective. It appeared by then that the front lines of East-West confrontation had moved far to the east of Trieste as a consequence of the Soviet-Yugoslav quarrel. Concluding that the FTT problem now only represented an issue for the Soviet Union to exploit, American policymakers gradually decided that their overall interests in the Cold War would be better served by supporting a resolution of the dispute on the basis of an Italo-Yugoslav compromise. Yet the local clash of Italian and Yugoslav nationalisms created a powerful obstacle preventing a prompt solution along those lines. As a new decade opened, the Trieste problem was entering a final phase for the United States, but it would be a difficult and protracted one which promised to yield few advantages for broader American strategy in the Cold War.

# 6

## From Paralysis to Partition: Steps toward a Settlement, 1950–1954

⊙ I could recall the hours and months on end in which my associates, principally Foster Dulles, and I, had focused our concern . . . on such things as a tiny patch of land at the head of the Adriatic, . . . on those bits of geography and the handfuls of people within them in those years, war and peace could have hung in the balance.
—Dwight D. Eisenhower, *Mandate for Change*

The United States began to work in earnest for a conclusive settlement of the Trieste question after 1949. Shifting American objectives in Italy and Yugoslavia had eliminated Trieste's usefulness as an instrument of Cold War policy for the United States. By the early 1950s Italy had become firmly integrated into the Western camp and was a member of the North Atlantic Treaty Organization (NATO), while Yugoslavia remained outside the Soviet bloc. The unresolved problem of the FTT's future was thus a needless source of tension between two countries the United States considered important. Trieste was obviously no longer a Cold War problem in the sense that it had been before the Soviet-Yugoslav break. American policymakers justifiably concluded that it was pointless to maintain indefinitely a military and economic commitment which now held few strategic or political advantages for their country.

Beginning in 1950, there was a series of direct Anglo-American initiatives to terminate this commitment. These efforts led to lengthy and tedious negotiations but were invariably aborted by Italo-Yugoslav disagreement. The United States discovered that it was a prisoner of its own earlier actions in the 1940s, when it had accepted an indefinite commitment and had manipulated the issue to its own short-term advantage in the Cold War. The final five years of Anglo-American occupation of Trieste were a period of frustrating paralysis. Italy and Yugoslavia became the crucial actors in the Trieste drama, with the United States and Britain trying in vain to play a secondary role as "honest brokers." The Anglo-American powers would be unable to secure Italo-Yugoslav agreement to a final resolution of the Trieste dispute until late 1954—and then only after applying considerable political and economic pressure.

### Early Attempts to Secure a Negotiated Settlement

It was evident from the outset that a solution of the Trieste problem would not be easily attained. On 18 January 1950 the Foreign Office sent the State Department an aide-mémoire outlining the reasons why a prompt negotiated settlement of the Trieste question would serve common Anglo-American interests. The British declared their readiness to encourage both Italy and Yugoslavia to reach an agreement and inquired if the United States concurred.[1]

State Department officials immediately pointed out the obstacles likely to impede an Italo-Yugoslav compromise. Despite some enthusiasm for the British suggestion, the prevailing view in Washington was one of extreme caution. The State Department proceeded to seek advice from its officers in the field before responding to London. R. Borden Reams, the chargé in Belgrade supported the British proposal, adding that the Yugoslavs appeared ready to reach a realistic compromise. In contrast, Ambassador Dunn in Rome asserted that the status quo was satisfactory for the moment and that Anglo-American pressure on Italy to negotiate would be premature. Their divergent responses reflected the respective positions of the countries to which the two men had been posted.[2]

The Yugoslavs were probably ready to open direct negotiations with Italy because they realized they would hold the upper hand in bilateral talks. They already controlled Zone B and hoped to secure further concessions in Zone A in return for restoration of Italian sovereignty over the city of Trieste. Tito could be confident that the British and Americans would not pressure him unduly to make major concessions for fear of nudging his country back into the Soviet fold. For the same reasons Italy was reluctant to engage in serious bilateral discussions and clung to the Tripartite Proposal of 1948 as its only trump card.

While the British awaited Washington's reply to their aide-mémoire the prospects of securing an Italo-Yugoslav compromise in the near future grew even dimmer. When British Foreign Secretary Ernest Bevin raised the subject with his Italian counterpart, Carlo Sforza, in early February, he was accorded a cool reception. After their own tentative approaches to Italy failed, Yugoslav officials took a more openly intransigent stand on the future of the FTT. By early March frustrated American diplomats in Belgrade concluded that "in view of Italian insistence on substantial implementation of [the] tripartite declaration . . . and Yugoslav reluctance to surrender any Zone B territory," further consideration of the matter was fruitless for the moment.[3]

Officials in Washington agreed and deemed it unwise to press the issue in the circumstances. On 11 March, the State Department specifically directed Ambassador George Allen in Belgrade not to raise the Trieste question in conversations with Tito and other Yugoslav officials. A few days later the department indicated in its tardy reply to the British aide-mémoire of 18 January that the United States certainly desired a "lasting solution for the Trieste problem," but cautioned that, "despite the possible sources of conflict inherent in the continued existence of the Free Territory, great care must be exercised, lest in the search for a permanent settlement new frictions and animosities are generated which revive certain difficulties now dormant." Citing evidence of both Italian and Yugoslav intransigence, the Americans concluded that "it would be unwise for any outside party to inject itself into this situation at this time beyond taking any appropriate opportunity to remind both parties of the advantages of a settlement, which would take ethnic factors into account, and the necessity for both sides to make substantial concessions from the position they have publicly adopted if a settlement is to be reached."[4]

The United States maintained this cautious position for about a year. Believing that prevailing circumstances made a bilateral settlement highly improbable, American policymakers hoped to put Trieste on the back burner until either Italy or Yugoslavia became more accommodating. In the interim their major goal was to prevent the issue from flaring up as a cause of direct confrontation between the two countries.

This task was complicated by Moscow's efforts to exploit the FTT problem to embarrass the Western powers. There had been some concern in London and Washington that the Soviet Union might do so by endorsing the Tripartite Proposal. In the event, the Russians chose a different plan of attack. On 20 April 1950 the Soviet government sent a note to the American, British, and French governments accusing them of violating the Italian peace treaty and obstructing the selection of a governor of the FTT for three years. The Soviet Union demanded that the permanent statute of the FTT be put into effect as soon as possible.[5]

The Kremlin's policy had been consistent in this respect since 1948. Without access to Soviet records it is not possible to verify the reasons for this policy. It is highly likely, however, that Anglo-American officials were correct in assuming that Moscow's interest in Trieste after the Tito-Stalin break was limited principally to its usefulness as a source of anti-Western propaganda and as a means of impairing American relations with both Italy and Yugoslavia. Though realizing that the FTT was unlikely to be established in the immediate future, Soviet policymakers probably considered that it would serve their interests to advocate that development. After all, as Leonard Unger, the American political adviser in Trieste, observed at the time of the Soviet note, "full establishment [of the] FTT would keep alive discord between Yugoslavs and Italians, prevent three Western powers fulfilling [the] March 20 proposal even to [the] extent of returning Trieste city to Italy, secure withdrawal of allied troops and open [the] possibility [of] Cominform control [of a] strategic area beyond [the] present limits [of the] Soviet orbit." Not surprisingly, local pro-Cominform communist forces in Zone A, led by Vittorio Vidali, adhered strongly to this Soviet line on Trieste and campaigned actively for establishment of the FTT.[6]

Whatever Moscow's motives were, the immediate problem for Anglo-American policymakers was to determine how to respond to the Soviet note. The British favored issuing a detailed refutation and defense of the Western position on Trieste, but the Americans argued that, to avoid the risk of offending either Italy or Yugoslavia, no reply should be sent. The Soviets forced the issue by indicating in May that they would not sign an Austrian peace treaty until the Western powers had replied to the note of 20 April. Anglo-American representatives refused to accept any connection between the two issues. After further debate the American and British governments dispatched a terse response rejecting Moscow's original accusations. The Soviet Union evidently concluded its ploy would not work and rejoined the deliberations on Austria. Although unsuccessful on this occasion, the Soviet maneuver was a pointed reminder to the Anglo-American powers that Trieste had become an unnecessary sore spot which brought them little advantage in the Cold War.[7]

British policymakers were particularly eager to find "a way out of the Trieste commitment" but the Americans remained pessimistic about a quick settlement of the question. The State Department again rejected a British proposal in August that the two powers actively urge Italy and Yugoslavia to negotiate directly. In an official policy statement prepared in late 1950 the State Department made clear its commitment to an Italo-Yugoslav settlement of the Trieste dispute but believed the political conditions necessary for such an agreement had not yet been established. The parameters of the Trieste situation had not altered at all in 1950.[8]

By 1951 this lack of progress appeared to be working to Yugoslavia's advantage as the Western rapprochement with Tito gained momentum. The United States Congress had appropriated $50 million for food relief to Yugoslavia in 1950. Fearful of a Soviet attack on the former satellite, the Americans began supplying military assistance to Yugoslavia in 1951 and hoped to integrate the nation, at least partially, into the Western defense system in Europe. The very precariousness of Tito's position made the Anglo-American powers unlikely to press the Yugoslavs to yield on Trieste. Policymakers in Rome, on the other hand, were now seeking revision of the Italian peace treaty to enable Italy to commence extensive rearmament.

Consequently they could not afford to antagonize their Western allies by adopting too rigid a position on Trieste. Italy, moreover, appeared securely entrenched in the Western alliance and could no longer invoke the specter of domestic instability as effectively as in 1948 to stimulate favorable Anglo-American responses on Trieste. In these circumstances the United States and Britain moved progressively from the officially pro-Italian stance of the Tripartite Proposal to a more openly neutral position toward the Trieste dispute.[9]

Italian leaders realized the adverse implications of the new international context for the Italian claims to the FTT and tried to hold the Western powers to the Tripartite Proposal—in large part for domestic political reasons. To Belgrade's dismay, the Italians succeeded in obtaining nominal reaffirmation of that declaration by the United States and Britain early in 1951, but both countries made clear privately that they were no longer prepared to back Italy's claims to the whole FTT and were anxious for direct Italo-Yugoslav talks leading to a compromise solution. In fact, by early 1951 State Department officials had begun to reconsider their earlier view that direct Italo-Yugoslav talks would be premature.[10]

The Italians, however, remained reluctant to pursue serious talks with the Yugoslavs because they feared that, without Anglo-American pressure on Tito, they would be unable to regain more than Zone A at best. The Italian government still hoped for more than a partition along existing zonal lines and was under domestic pressure—especially from the Right—to obtain at least Zone A *and* the coastal towns of Zone B. Consequently, Rome sought to convince Britain and the United States that prospects of an unsatisfactory settlement of the Trieste problem were provoking domestic instability and would undermine Italy's contribution to the Western alliance.[11] Washington's responses to the Italian campaign for more active Western support for their position would make clear that American thinking was continuing to move in another direction as 1951 wore on. Thus the State Department was quick to reject an Italian request in July that the Italian electoral law of linked party lists be adopted by AMG for the planned October communal elections in the FTT. Although the Italians argued that "this system had proved its value in combating communism in Italy," the State Department advised its Rome embassy that "acceding to [the] Italian request although perhaps having desirable short term consequences [in] Italy would in long run hinder rather than help [the] possibility [of an] Italo-Yugo agreement on Trieste question." When the Italian government then asked that the communal elections be postponed for six months or a year, State Department officials sought to exploit the election issue as a means of pressing the Italians to begin serious talks with the Yugoslavs, who at the time were indicating a willingness to consider a compromise settlement of the Trieste problem. Despite initial British reservations, the State Department and Foreign Office advised the Italian government at the end of August that they were willing to postpone the Trieste elections for two months if the Italian government would give assurances to enter into serious negotiations with the Yugoslavs concerning Trieste. The ploy only generated resentment in Rome and the elections were eventually postponed without any corresponding Italian guarantees to negotiate. Despite its failure this application of "pressure" on the Italians made clear that the United States was willing to consider new tactics to break the frustrating Trieste stalemate.[12]

The fact that such tactics required jettisoning the tripartite declaration was made plain to the Italians at the highest government levels when Prime Minister De Gasperi visited Washington in September 1951. He had indicated earlier that Trieste was the most important issue he wished to discuss and that even the proposed revision of the Italian peace treaty "did not have [the] importance that Trieste had." In discussions with Secretary of State Dean Acheson and President Truman, De Gasperi repeatedly linked a favorable resolution of the Trieste dispute to the effectiveness of Italy's participation in the Atlantic pact. The prime minister appealed for American influence on Tito to ensure that all ethnically Italian parts of Zone B be restored to his country and he insisted that any negotiations be conducted within "the framework" of the Tripartite Proposal. He went so far as to suggest to the president "that without a satisfactory settlement of the Trieste question no democratic government in Italy could get parliamentary support for a joint defense effort. If Italians should think that their allies could not save Trieste for Italy, the result would be a dangerous trend toward neutralism. His coalition would lose votes to the left and right." Acheson and Truman expressed sympathy for the Italian government's position but emphasized that the United States was now adopting a neutral stance on the issue. In his memoirs Acheson recalled telling De Gasperi that

> the March 20, 1948 declaration could not possibly be the basis of a settlement because of the intensity of Yugoslav opposition to it and the immense harm that would result to all Western interests, especially Italian, should Tito be driven to make his peace with Stalin. . . . the declaration of March 20, 1948 had been overtaken by events and . . . the basis of settlement had to be founded on the ethnic principle, helped if necessary by the exchange of populations in stubborn situations.

Acheson also told De Gasperi that he was certain the Yugoslavs were now ready for realistic negotiations and "the important thing" was to begin them. The United States was willing to help facilitate those talks but, Acheson added, "we could not attempt to mediate in the question." Eager to see the removal of "this troublesome source of controversy" (as Truman called it), the Americans had made clear that they believed their objective would best be achieved by bilateral negotiations without direct Western influence on either party. Having laid their cards on the table, they hoped Italy would become more accommodating.[13]

Direct Italo-Yugoslav negotiations began shortly thereafter in November, after much prodding from Washington and London. These talks continued intermittently for several months with little success. The problem was that the Yugoslavs refused to accept the Italian proposal for partition of the FTT according to a continuous ethnic line because such a solution definitely favored Italy. As the Anglo-American powers had also indicated a preference for a settlement based on the "ethnic principle," Italy pressed vigorously for their support. The State Department responded in January 1952 by sending Philip Mosely to "persuade the Yugoslavs to take a more constructive attitude." That effort failed and the talks broke down in March. A frustrated Acheson told his department to give closer consideration to the issue and ordered a study made "as to whether we are better off in Trieste or out." The renewed Italo-Yugoslav impasse led the State Department to reconsider its options, including the possibility of allowing greater Italian control of or even annexation of Zone A. In the following months local developments in Trieste would intensify the pressure for such action, and the focus of attention on the FTT problem would shift from the international diplomatic level to the administration of Zone A itself.[14]

## Developments on the Local Front

The changes in British and American policy toward Trieste on the international level between 1949 and 1952 had not been without repercussions inside Zone A, though their impact came in indirect fashion. Initially, Anglo-American policymakers saw little reason to modify the mildly pro-Italian effect of some AMG administrative methods, for they assumed most of Zone A would eventually be assigned to Italy by a compromise settlement based on ethnic criteria. As a result, however, of growing pressures from the Italian government and local Italian nationalist forces, AMG officials found themselves obliged to assert more forcefully the autonomy of Zone A of the FTT and their authority over that area. When combined with a more "neutral" Anglo-American policy on the international level, these AMG actions would intensify protests from the Italian government and trigger violent local reactions by Italian groups. The eventual outcome of this process would oblige the United States and Britain to accept even closer Italian involvement in the governance of Zone A.

The difficulties the changing Anglo-American policy created for AMG control of Trieste are illustrated pointedly by some of General Airey's experiences. From his perspective the most important factors to consider in administering Zone A continued to be that 80 percent of the population was Italian and that most opposition to AMG emanated from communist (usually Yugoslav) sources. As zone commander, he continued to base AMG administration on a moderately pro-Italian and rigidly anticommunist policy. Airey considered that he was responding realistically to local conditions but he found himself in an increasingly awkward position after London and Washington adopted a more "neutral" stance on the international level. For instance, he complained to Sullivan in July 1950 that, during a visit to Trieste, George Allen, the American ambassador to Yugoslavia, had indirectly criticized AMG—and by implication Airey—for not falling into line with the new American policy of reconciliation toward Yugoslavia. Visibly irritated, Airey reminded Sullivan that "in Trieste we had to consider other factors in addition to the important one of Allied/Yugoslav relations, for example, Allied-Italian relations, and the stated policy of our two governments with regard to the future of the Free Territory, to say nothing of the problems inherent in governing an historically irredentist Italian population." A month later Airey protested to the Foreign Office that he was often being bypassed on significant issues by his American deputy, General William Hoge. The Foreign Office thought it advisable to support Airey from the viewpoint of maintaining British prestige vis-à-vis the United States, but was also sensitive to criticisms that he was too pro-Italian and not attuned to the "new American pro-Tito policy."[15]

One of the reasons for Airey's irritation with remarks like Allen's was that by mid-1950 AMG was being increasingly criticized by local Italian groups and the Italian government for allegedly undermining the essential *italianità* of Trieste. The major sources of Italian concern were summarized by Ambassador Dunn in a message from Rome to the State Department at the end of 1950:

> Italians fear that [the] time may come when they will be called upon to sacrifice their recognized interests in FTT in [the] cause of increased solidarity with Tito. They have interpreted numerous recent incidents such as removal [of the] Italian flag from City Hall, our insistence on [the] establishment [of a] separate court of cassation in Trieste, regulations requiring Trieste ships [to] fly [the] FTT, rather than [the] Italian flag; all as evidence of a change in our attitude, if not in our official position.

While it was true that AMG had taken these actions, they had been implemented largely in response to a direct Italian challenge to AMG's continued authority over Zone A. Since the end of 1949 the Italian government had sought a greater role in the administration of Zone

A on the basis of the so-called Cammarata thesis—an idea put forward by the rector of the University of Trieste that Italian sovereignty over Trieste had never legally ended because the statute of the FTT had not come into operation as provided for in the Italian peace treaty. A particular bone of contention—which former AMG officials still recall with frustration—was whether the jurisdiction of the Italian Court of Cassation could be extended to Zone A. This Italian campaign was viewed by AMG officials from Airey down as an unacceptable challenge to their control of Zone A and prompted actions such as those mentioned by Dunn in order to reassert their authority. Though Anglo-American policy toward Zone A thus remained little changed in spirit, these AMG actions generated tensions and were seen by Italian observers as further evidence of a changing Anglo-American disposition in favor of Yugoslavia.[16]

The replacement of General Airey in March 1951 by General John Winterton seemed to provide the Italians with additional confirmation of such a stance. And, in fact, his arrival in Trieste did appear to coincide with the inauguration of an administrative policy that was more in line with Anglo-American policy on the international level. AMG policies had previously accepted integration of Zone A into Italy to a certain extent. But AMG officials were now required to treat the area as a fully autonomous territory as originally envisaged in the Italian peace treaty. There were changes in some administrative practices and there was an attempt to improve relations with the Yugoslav military administration in Zone B. In actuality the substantive impact of the new policy was slight, for its main purpose was not to sever the close relationship between Italy and Zone A but merely to demonstrate that AMG remained firmly in control. As an internal American policy statement in late 1950 had made clear: "whereas it is our policy to preserve the cultural, psychological, and economic ties existing between Zone A and Italy, we should make it clear to these [Italian] officials in appropriate instances that until the Italian Peace Treaty is modified, Allied Military Government continues to exercise jurisdiction over Zone A." This modest objective unleashed unexpected consequences.[17]

The perceived shift away from a pro-Italian posture precipitated outbursts of irredentist protest in Zone A and Italy. The unrest culminated in a general strike in Trieste and violent riots against AMG—in particular its British elements—in late March 1952. Winterton stood firm against what he saw as an officially supported Italian threat to AMG authority, and tensions ran high in the city. Large demonstrations were held in sympathy throughout Italy and the Italian Foreign Office advised Washington that "it fears for the life of the present government and for Italy's position in NATO if this question is not handled properly." Though there was evidence that these unsettling events were at least partially inspired by Italian officials, the Italian government seized upon the incidents to elicit some "gesture" from the United States and Britain and to press them to modify their internal policies in Zone A.[18]

The British and Americans agreed to meet with the Italians in London to discuss the issue of "closer collaboration in the Zone amongst themselves with the local authorities." The talks resulted in a memorandum of understanding issued on 9 May which involved some modification of internal administration in Zone A. Supreme authority was left in Winterton's hands, but a representative of the Italian government was to join the British and American political advisers in providing guidance to the zone commander. The Italian government, moreover, was to have direct control of various branches of the civil government in Zone A. The State Department hoped these measures would create "a convincing facade of Italian participation in FTT but in such a way as not to give Yugos serious ground for complaint." These cosmetic changes for the benefit of Italian public opinion were nevertheless of significance insofar as they represented the first real devolution—albeit partial—of AMG authority since the establishment of the AMG administrative system in mid-1945. The Yugoslavs did not heed Anglo-American explanations that the changes were insubstantial and, after heated protests at the new arrangements, proceeded with similar steps to integrate Zone B more closely into Yugoslavia.[19]

These developments on the local level highlighted the depth of Italian and Yugoslav intransigence on the issue and helped foreclose certain options for a settlement of the FTT problem. They led Anglo-American policymakers to realize that any realistic solution would have to be based essentially on a partition along existing zonal lines.

From Paralysis to Partition | 143

Moreover, the introduction of the changes embodied in the London memorandum of understanding did not remove the real source of tension in Zone A but only plastered over the underlying conflict between the authority of AMG and Italian groups in Trieste. In this situation the idea of immediate Anglo-American withdrawal from Zone A—already mooted by some in AMG circles in March 1952 as the best option—began to have increasing appeal in Washington and London.[20]

In effect, a de facto settlement had already been suggested on the local level by the end of 1952. It remained the task of Anglo-American diplomacy to make Italy and Yugoslavia acknowledge that reality, for this solution could not be made permanent without diplomatic agreement on the international level.

## The Continuing Quest for a Bilateral Settlement

In mid-1952 the Americans remained hopeful that bilateral Italo-Yugoslav talks could be restarted and might yield a compromise settlement. The Italians indicated they were willing to resume negotiations on the basis of a continuous ethnic line but, as Ambassador Allen noted, the "Yugo[slav] position had hardened following [the] London agreement." When the United States, France and Britain made a joint approach to Italy and Yugoslavia to reopen talks on the basis of the ethnic principle, Belgrade declined outright and expressed irritation that the Tripartite Proposal had still not been openly rejected. After more than a year of sporadic diplomatic activity, a solution seemed no closer.[21]

By late 1952 the British were especially anxious to be rid of the problem. Like the Americans, they considered Trieste an unnecessary irritant in Italo-Yugoslav relations which might flare up to the detriment of Western interests. Unlike their more prosperous Atlantic ally, the British were also highly conscious of "a more prosaic consideration." As Foreign Secretary Anthony Eden recalled: "the cost and trouble of maintaining the Allied occupation of Zone A could not be endured indefinitely, while we received little for our pains but abuse from both sides." After meeting personally with De

Gasperi and Tito in September, Eden became convinced that the best prospect for early settlement of the Trieste question lay in partition of the FTT along the existing zonal lines. The Americans agreed with him that it was very difficult to prevail on the Yugoslavs "to accept a solution of the Trieste question unless it is based on the present demarcation line between Zone A and Zone B," but they were reluctant to apply "pressure" on De Gasperi to modify the Italian position of a division based on a continuous ethnic line. Eden believed that the Americans were deluding themselves if they thought a Trieste settlement could emerge from Italo-Yugoslav talks without Western pressure. He realized that for internal political reasons "neither side could take the political risk of accepting a proposal from the other." Eden concluded that the only realistic course was for the United States and Britain to urge the Italian government to accept a settlement whereby Zone A would be assigned to Italy and Zone B to Yugoslavia, with minor adjustments if necessary.[22]

Although American policymakers were not averse to such a settlement, they remained unwilling to put "pressure on the Italians to accept a solution likely to be greatly disappointing to them." National elections were planned in Italy and the Americans did not wish to harm the Christian Democrats, who were not reticent in pointing out that the Trieste problem would have "an important bearing" on those elections. Washington, moreover, was anxiously awaiting the Italian parliament's ratification of an agreement signed in 1952 to join the proposed European Defense Community (EDC), a military alliance of Western European states complementary to NATO. The State Department recommended that "the best course would be for Mr. Eden to proceed independently," which he did. Like preceding initiatives, Eden's came to nought but it was significant in revealing a divergence in British and American thinking on Trieste. The greater sense of urgency on London's part to be rid of an unnecessary financial and military burden was obvious, while Washington remained less perturbed by those costs of the Anglo-American commitment in Trieste and more sensitive to Italian domestic considerations.[23]

In the final months of 1952 the British continued to believe that the only realistically possible settlement was a Zone A–Zone B partition, but the State Department sensed "signs of wavering in

Tito's position." It was now the turn of the Americans to move unilaterally by seeking to devise an alternative compromise solution that might meet Italian objections to partition of the FTT along existing zonal lines. Washington also wished to mitigate Italian concerns after recent Yugoslav-American talks concerning military cooperation. In December the United States submitted a new proposal that was more favorable to Italy: Zone A and the commune of Koper (Capodistria) in Zone B would go to Italy, while Yugoslavia would have the rest of Zone B and a few Slovene villages in Zone A. But the Italians rejected this plan, reiterating their demands for other coastal towns in Zone B.[24]

By December a new Republican administration was preparing to take office in Washington. The Trieste dispute had been one of the first problems to confront Truman in 1945, prompting one of the earliest American postwar commitments in Europe. His administration left office with that problem far from resolved.

The inauguration of a new Republican administration did not mark any change in United States policy toward the Trieste problem but it did coincide with news of a new challenge to that policy. The State Department learned on 23 January from its Rome embassy that the United States might soon have to deal with an Italo-British proposal "to allow [the] Italians [to] take over full administration [of] Zone A with British American troops pulling out to be replaced by Italian troops." As the State Department realized, this "provisional" solution appealed to the Christian Democrats as national elections drew closer because it was a move by which they could "present their electorate with [a] de facto return [of] Zone A to Italy plus [the] propaganda that [a] 'provisional solution' [in] Zone A in no way jeopardizes Italian rights to Zone B." There were "very deep misgivings about such a proposal" in Washington. The Americans thought it would only "accentuate rather than diminish [the] strain imposed on Italo-Yugoslav relations by [the] Trieste question." They also suspected that the British would support it as a definitive solution and would acquiesce in Yugoslav annexation of Zone B, which would in turn trigger a negative public reaction in Italy. While not rejecting outright the idea of a provisional solution, State Department officials sought to think of some way of dissuading the Italians from supporting such an approach.[25]

American policymakers thus decided to "make one last attempt to reach an agreed solution between Italy and Yugoslavia before giving final consideration to [the] alternative of [a] provisional solution." Once again they acted unilaterally. In February 1953 the United States secretly proposed a north-south division of the FTT, giving Italy Trieste and the coastal towns in Zone B south to Piran (Pirano) and assigning most of the interior of the two zones to Yugoslavia.  Although this scheme had first been proposed to the Americans by Alberto Tarchiani, the Italian ambassador to the United States, and was more favorable to Italy than the Truman administration's final proposal, De Gasperi believed he could not accept it unless Italy received the coastline to Umag (Umago). Secret Italo-American discussions continued until early May, and the Italians eventually agreed that the Americans test Tito's response to their proposal; but the Yugoslav reply was "completely negative."[26]

Despite this lack of progress, the State Department concluded in the wake of the Italian elections in June that "all in all, the best we can do is to urge Italy and Yugoslavia to resume their direct negotiations." Pressure from Italy, however, would oblige the United States to take more decisive action later in the year. Though remaining the strongest individual party in the Italian parliament, the Christian Democrats suffered considerable losses in the June elections and De Gasperi fell from power shortly thereafter. Another Christian Democrat, Giuseppe Pella, took over in August as caretaker prime minister until the ruling coalition of parties (dominated by the Christian Democrats but including the Liberals, Republicans, and moderate Socialists) could reach a more enduring agreement. Pella's government was weak and dependent in part on support from the nationalistic Right, leading him to take an uncompromising stand on the FTT. Strongly worded rhetoric on the Trieste dispute poured out of Italy in the following months and the Yugoslavs responded with equally inflammatory statements. Italian leaders chose to interpret the Yugoslav reactions as a threat to annex Zone B and responded by sending troops to the frontier of the FTT in late August. Arguing that Trieste now had "an absolute priority over all other Italian foreign matters," the Pella government put pressure on the United States and Britain to support Italy by continuing to refuse to ratify the EDC treaty and even threatening to withdraw from NATO.[27]

State Department officials were alarmed at what they considered a dangerous overreaction and tried to remedy the situation. Their principal aim, as indicated in instructions to the Rome embassy, was "to relieve [the] tension which however artificially created by both governments for their internal purposes has resulted in [a] threatening situation." They expressed surprise at Italy's drastic actions, indicating that they did not believe Tito was seriously contemplating annexation of Zone B. Livingston Merchant, of the European division of the State Department, also asked Mario Luciolli, the chargé at the Italian embassy in Washington, on 1 September "whether the Italian government still favored a provisional solution of Trieste." He received a noncommital reply. Given the sudden deterioration in the previously "manageable" Trieste situation, policymakers in Washington were obviously reconsidering their previous objections to the British idea of imposing a provisional settlement.[28]

## The Crisis of October 1953

This new Trieste crisis was of particular concern to Clare Boothe Luce, the outspoken American ambassador to Italy and a woman of influence in the Eisenhower administration. She had been a prominent Republican congresswoman and was married to Henry Luce, the wealthy publisher of *Time, Life,* and *Fortune.* She also had a direct line to the president through C. D. Jackson, a former vice president in her husband's Time-Life organization who had become Eisenhower's special assistant for psychological warfare. This quintessential "iron lady" of Cold War politics was determined to use all the resources at her disposal to ensure that communist influence in Italy declined during her time in that country.[29]

Upon arriving in Rome Luce had immersed herself in Italian politics. She caused much controversy during the 1953 election campaign by implying that the United States would apply economic sanctions if Italians elected a government of the Left. Ironically, her efforts probably hindered the Italian government at the polls. Luce, however, echoed some Italian officials in attributing the Christian Democrats' losses to an unfavorable American stance on Trieste—an issue she considered the "key log in the Italian foreign policy jam." She also seriously questioned the Eisenhower administration's policy of supporting Tito. As the Trieste issue began taking on crisis proportions in early September, the ambassador resolved to elicit a more favorable response from Washington.[30]

Luce's perceptions of the seriousness of the crisis were heightened by a meeting with Pella on 3 September in which the prime minister told her that the "settlement of Trieste question overshadows any other problem in Italian policy." By chance, Secretary of State John Foster Dulles stated in a press conference on the same day that American policy on Trieste was no longer necessarily bound by the Tripartite Proposal and that the United States had been "exploring other alternatives." His statement caused a furor in Italy and Luce was called into the Italian Foreign Office on 4 September to be told that failure to clarify the secretary's statement would heighten tension over Trieste, increase anti-American sentiment in Italy, and possibly trigger the fall of the Pella government. Luce believed this "estimate of Italian public reaction" was not greatly exaggerated. She advised the State Department that failure to find a "rapid solution of [the] question, will result in great harm to USA-Italian relations and prolong a tension that will endanger not only [the] future of [a] moderate pro-American government in Italy, but might crack wide open [the] NATO system in Europe."[31]

Luce also sought to use her high-level contacts in the Eisenhower administration to get action. She personally telephoned Dulles on 4 September to tell him how "jittery" the Trieste situation was. A few days later she wrote to Jackson explaining in detail why an adverse outcome of the Trieste dispute for Italy would also be a moral, diplomatic, strategic, and political blow for the United States. She appended an intriguing note for the president's information, which she had penned in June after the Italian elections but had not sent because she realized "the Korean pot was boiling" at the time. This letter included a "brief if unorthodoxly phrased estimate of the situation in Italy:"

> For the want of Trieste, an Issue was lost.
> For the want of an Issue, the Election was lost.
> For the want of an Election, De Gasperi was lost.
> For the want of De Gasperi, his NATO policies were lost.
> For the want of his NATO policies, Italy was lost.
> For the want of Italy, Europe was lost.
> For the want of Europe, America . . . . . . . ?
> All for the want of a two-penny town.

Luce believed her evaluation in verse was now even more valid. She argued that the fall of the Pella government over the issue of Trieste was a distinct possibility and would set in motion that same disastrous concatenation of consequences. Even allowing for the usual tendency for ambassadors to sympathize with the interests of the country where they are serving, Luce's assessment was extreme and somewhat farfetched.[32]

Yet her admonitions did have some impact in Washington. In late September, as Italo-Yugoslav tensions persisted, C. D. Jackson passed on Luce's message and a memorandum to the president backing her arguments:

> I am sure that you agree that the solution of the Trieste problem rates the very highest priority. The situation, which in 1948 was soluble very easily, has already steadily deteriorated since then and is going to deteriorate still further as the months go by. . . . Necessary as it is to remain on working terms with Tito, I doubt if by any stretch of the imagination a Trieste solution which didn't give Tito everything he had asked for would drive him back into the arms of Moscow or into war with Italy. If he did fulminate a bit, we've been fulminated at by experts.

Jackson noted that high-level policymakers appreciated the urgency of the situation, but he suspected that the problem was being dragged out "down the line at the working level." He suggested that Eisenhower discuss the matter with Dulles and set a deadline for the State Department to bring about a solution. Jackson included a copy of Luce's poem in the memorandum. Eisenhower passed on the memorandum to the secretary of state querying, "What are we doing about the Trieste affair? Ever since I returned to Europe in January of '50, I have been expecting some kind of solution within a month. In spite of the fact that I was, of course, hopelessly optimistic, it does not lessen the importance of the subject to Italy—and consequently to Western Europe and to America." Dulles replied on 1 October that he hoped for a solution within the month.³³

The secretary thought he had good reason to be optimistic. State Department officials had been consulting with the British throughout September on the Trieste situation and were now proposing to London a variant of the plan for a Zone A–Zone B division which the British themselves had long advocated. Despite objections from both the American and British embassies in Belgrade, the State Department believed such a move was necessitated by the persistent failure of Italo-Yugoslav negotiations and by the recent tensions. It was thought such action would help save Pella's government and satisfy the Italians by "equalizing" their position in Zone A with that of the Yugoslavs in Zone B, while Belgrade would accept it because of Yugoslavia's need to "progress further with military cooperation with the West." After much debate about tactics and timing, the British and Americans eventually agreed to present Italy and Yugoslavia with a fait accompli by declaring that they had decided to withdraw their troops from Zone A and to allow Italy to take control of the area. Although both powers agreed to advise the Italians and Yugoslavs that they hoped this move would lead to a de facto settlement, they disagreed about whether to indicate publicly that the Anglo-American action would constitute a definitive solution. The United States successfully opposed such a statement because of the likelihood of a strong negative response in Italy. Consequently, on 8 October, the United States and Britain announced publicly only that they had decided to withdraw their troops from Zone A and hand over its administration to Italy. They also informed Tito secretly that they would not oppose Yugoslav annexation of Zone B and stressed that improved Western military relations with Yugoslavia rested on stabilization of the Trieste situation.³⁴

The solution appeared admirable from Washington's perspective. Eisenhower's diary notes for 8 October reveal clearly how this action would serve general American interests in the Cold War.

> Today ... the British and American governments made public a previously agreed upon position with respect to Trieste. Trieste has, of course, been for years a source of irritation and mutual recrimination between Italy and Yugoslavia. We need both nations as friends and we had therefore to try for some solution.... This is another step in a long series of things we have been attempting to do in order to strengthen America's political and security position vis a vis the Soviets. If this works—and I certainly can't think of any better solution of the problem because it is one of those that has no perfect answer—then we will vastly strengthen our position in the Adriatic and generate much greater confidence in all of Western Europe. As of now, the mutual hostility between these two countries has largely neutralized any help that Nato could expect from them in times of emergency. Obviously, if both accept this solution ... we will have the chance to plan confidently for the defense of the whole Alps region.

As Eisenhower did not often have to deal with the Trieste problem on a personal level, it is noteworthy that he stressed the issue's broader geopolitical and strategic implications in Cold War terms. The public declaration would not, however, have the general effect desired by the president.[35]

The Anglo-American statement only provoked a new crisis. The Italians were relatively satisfied, for they could regain Zone A without having to renounce formally their claims for Zone B. Thus the "provisional" nature of this settlement was stressed publicly in Italy and in some Italian circles it was even suggested that this move was merely a first step in implementing the Tripartite Proposal. The Yugoslavs, however, were outraged that they had not been consulted and appeared to regard the Anglo-American proposal as a "very great blow to [the] prestige of [the] regime and Tito personally." After sending a diplomatic note rejecting the proposal as an "unjust and dangerous act," Tito made a speech on 10 October in which he publicly denounced the Anglo-American plan and declared that "we would consider entry of Italian troops into Zone A as an act of aggression against our country." The Yugoslav leader even declared that if acceptance of the declaration of 8 October was a condition for continued economic and military assistance from Britain and the United States, then Yugoslavia would not seek further aid. Angry crowds demonstrated against Britain and the United States in Yugoslav cities, sometimes physically attacking American representatives. The Yugoslav government also sent additional forces to Zone B and the Italian frontier. Tito made clear that "the moment that the first Italian soldier enters Zone A we shall also enter it." The Italian government responded by reinforcing the units sent to the border earlier that year.[36]

The situation became increasingly dangerous. Observers feared that armed conflict was likely if the Anglo-American proposal was implemented. Indeed, as one scholar has pointed out, "there was the absurd possibility that two armies equipped by the Americans to defend themselves against a common enemy might fight each other." There was even a chance that Anglo-American forces might be involved and, fearing a "foolhardy movement on Tito's part," President Eisenhower ordered warships of the Sixth Fleet to move into the upper Adriatic. To use Luce's metaphor, it was now the Trieste pot that was boiling.[37] Paradoxically, the United States and Britain were now facing the very situation they had hoped to avoid by issuing their statement of 8 October. In the circumstances, the Anglo-American powers assured the Yugoslavs that there would be no immediate withdrawal of their troops from Zone A.[38]

Surprisingly, a possible means of reaching a permanent solution to the FTT problem emerged from the October crisis. The Yugoslavs suggested a conference of the governments of the United States, Britain, Italy, and Yugoslavia. It was significant that in the midst of a crisis one of the two most interested parties had expressed willingness to reach a negotiated compromise. The Yugoslav proposal set in motion the process which led to a final settlement.

In the short term, several obstacles stood in the way of serious four-power discussions on the future of the FTT. Italian and Yugoslav soldiers faced each other uneasily along the border near Trieste. Moreover, Italy insisted that the announcement of 8 October must be put into effect before a conference could take place, while Yugoslavia declared it would participate only if that proposal was not acted upon. To complicate matters further, the Soviet Union had immediately protested the declaration of 8 October, raising the matter in the Security Council on 13 October. As usual, the Soviets demanded the establishment of the FTT as specified in the permanent statute, but this time they proposed as governor a Swiss candidate who had originally been nominated by Britain in 1947.³⁹

American and British officials spent the final months of 1953 trying to clear those obstacles so that progress could be made toward an enduring settlement of the FTT problem. Their efforts took on added urgency after anti-AMG riots in Trieste resulted in the deaths of several Triestines in November. The Anglo-American powers successfully parried the Soviet maneuver in the Security Council by securing indefinite postponement of a debate on the FTT on the grounds that direct negotiations between the interested parties were imminent. They were also able to reduce Italo-Yugoslav tensions and persuade both nations to withdraw their forces from the border in December. The most intractable problem was that of finding an acceptable framework within which Italo-Yugoslav negotiations could be conducted effectively. Several proposals were submitted that might have allowed negotiations to begin but all were rejected either by Italy or Yugoslavia. As the year drew to a close, it became evident that Dulles had been wildly optimistic in October when he suggested to Eisenhower that the whole FTT problem might be resolved within a month.⁴⁰

## Final Steps toward a Solution

Early in 1954 American and British policymakers finally secured Yugoslav and Italian agreement to a formula for organizing negotiations in a manner which might yield a successful compromise settlement. Based on an adaptation of an American suggestion originally made in November 1953, this innovative plan was intended to diminish the influence of the many domestic pressures in both Italy and Yugoslavia that were impeding meaningful direct discussions between the two governments. The United States and Britain proposed, in effect, that they act as intermediaries in secret talks to be carried out in three stages at the ambassadorial level in London or

154 | Between East and West

Washington. The first phase involved negotiations between the three occupying powers of the FTT to determine the terms of a reasonable solution. The United States and Britain would then negotiate with Italy on the basis of those terms. During the final stage the two Western governments would mediate between Italy and Yugoslavia to eliminate outstanding points of disagreement. The Italians and Yugoslavs both indicated in January that they were willing to proceed within this format. The final movement toward a settlement of the FTT impasse had begun but it would be drawn out over nine months.[41]

Although the Trieste issue was recognized as an essentially Italo-Yugoslav problem, the objectives of the United States during this final phase were not unaffected by more general Cold War considerations. Indeed, the importance of viewing a Trieste settlement in a wider context was made most explicit in the State Department's letter of instructions to the American representative in the final negotiations:

> We want to put the Trieste problem in the larger context of an overall Italo-Yugoslav rapprochement.... the United States–United Kingdom should make clear at the outset that they are not thinking in terms of a local settlement, or even of Italo-Yugoslav relations alone, but rather of the political, military, and economic health of a key area which will have great significance for all of the free world and for the worldwide effort to throw back Soviet expansion. The implications of a failure to find a mutual accommodation between the powers which are or should be destined by geography and strategy to be close partners if Soviet expansion is to be successfully resisted in their parts of the world, are of a very serious character. On the other hand, the benefits of a successful settlement would be very great. There is no form of pressure against the Soviet system so powerful or so effective as the demonstration of unity among countries of the free world, and there is no part of the free world, except for the relations between France and Germany, where that demonstration would have more profound significance in the eyes of the Kremlin than in the area of Yugoslavia and Italy.... We are there-

fore seeking a 'package deal' which would put Italo-Yugoslav relations on a permanent sound basis.

The Eisenhower administration obviously hoped to transform an issue which had become an irritating liability for its European security policies into an asset. The allusion to a package deal indicated the United States was prepared to link a Trieste settlement to other issues of interest to Italy and Yugoslavia such as mutual trade and military cooperation. It implied, moreover, that the United States might offer political or economic concessions to the two countries to persuade them to achieve a satisfactory solution.[42]

The letter of instructions also stipulated the precise terms of the Trieste territorial settlement desired by the United States. The State Department told its negotiators to strive as far as possible for an ethnic line "which will give the Italians a continuous coastal strip including Capodistria, Isola, and Pirano." Such a partition of the FTT would have been more favorable to Italy than a division along existing zonal lines. Although American policymakers considered these terms the most desirable, they were not rigidly committed to them. Indeed, it soon became clear that the United States was more interested in securing any mutually acceptable settlement rather than in insisting on a pro-Italian line.[43]

The actual negotiating process began in February with meetings in London between the three states administering the FTT. The representatives of the United States, Britain, and Yugoslavia were Llewellyn Thompson, American ambassador to Austria; Geoffrey Harrison, assistant under-secretary of state in the Foreign Office; and Vladimir Velebit, the Yugoslav ambassador in London. Thompson soon decided that the State Department's territorial proposal was too pro-Italian and would never be accepted by the Yugoslavs. He persuaded the State Department to change his brief so that he could propose a permanent frontier based more or less on existing zonal boundaries —a formula also favored by the British. He also secured assurances from the State Department that, as American security interests "would be so greatly served" by a Trieste settlement, the United States government could probably make a "considerable contribution" toward the costs of any economic demands by Yugoslavia such as funds for port improvements in Zone B. The Anglo-American negotiating position was now a realistic one, but left little freedom to maneuver. As Eden recalled, "we could not present to the Italians anything that appeared less favourable than our proposals of October 8." The Yugoslavs would certainly not assent to territorial changes resulting in a less advantageous position than they already held, although they had long been reconciled to the loss of Trieste itself. Some tough bargaining ensued.[44]

The Anglo-American negotiators eventually hammered out an agreement with the Yugoslavs in May. There would be a partition substantially along existing zonal lines (with minor territorial exchanges between Zone A and Zone B), and minority rights would be mutually guaranteed by Italy and Yugoslavia. The Yugoslavs required considerable persuasion, but the Western powers were able to "sweeten the pill," as Eden put it, by promising economic aid (to the tune of $20 million from the United States and £2 million from Britain) to facilitate construction of a new port in Zone B and to fulfill other needs. This promise of economic assistance helped seal the bargain.[45]

In May Thompson and Harrison presented the draft terms to Manlio Brosio, the Italian representative. Now there was even less leeway for maneuver by the British and Americans, but there was some reason for hope. Italy had a new government headed by Mario Scelba, another Christian Democrat. Scelba was in a stronger position domestically than Pella had been and was prepared to take a more realistic position than his predecessors. After a month of negotiating and much American cajoling, the Italians accepted the proposed terms with only minor amendments. For reasons of prestige, however, they did not wish to be seen as accepting a dictated settlement. Consequently, Italy refused to sanction the proposed cession to Yugoslavia of Punta Sottile (Tenki Rtič). The area in question amounted to a few square miles of high ground overlooking Trieste that was to have been exchanged for some even more useless land in Zone B. Despite such Italian reservations the British and Americans were encouraged that Italy and Yugoslavia were in substantial agreement and "that what remains is now a matter of trading minutiae." Yet the trading of those "minutiae" proved more difficult than anticipated.[46]

In the third phase of the negotiating process, when Harrison and Thompson acted as intermediaries between Velebit and Brosio, the Italians and Yugoslavs eventually reached agreement on all points except control of Punta Sottile. Velebit later explained why the Yugoslavs were so obdurate on this point: "It was of face-saving importance.... The few square miles of territory were of no importance whatever, except to sweeten the deal a little bit in appearance to the Slovenes and to show that the solution was not a hundred percent imposed on the basis of the actual division between Zones A and B. It was just a token of the negotiations; the difference between an imposed settlement and a negotiated settlement." Similarly, Brosio admitted that Punta Sottile was "a tiny, almost insignificant, strip of land," but "from the psychological and political view its loss would have been an intolerable renunciation on our side and imposition by the other side, because it meant that Yugoslavia would always be at the point where they would be looking into the Trieste port." The Italian government even sought to bludgeon Washington into supporting them on the issue by linking the establishment of NATO bases in Italy and ratification of the EDC to a satisfactory Trieste settlement. The whole Trieste dispute had come down to two square miles of land and a question of prestige.[47]

After a few months American policymakers resolved to act unilaterally to break this exasperating stalemate. Once again a reminder from Luce of potential instability in Italy helped spur Washington into action. On 31 August, the ambassador sent Eisenhower a lengthy and somber analysis of the political situation in Italy, concluding that the Scelba government might soon collapse "*unless* we can produce a settlement of the Trieste question—and immediately." Eisenhower accepted Luce's view that the Yugoslavs were blocking progress on Trieste. He promptly informed Acting Secretary of State Walter Bedell Smith that he was "tremendously interested" in securing an agreement on the issue—"if for no other reason than to provide some counter-balance to the EDC flop."[48]

Typically, the indefatigable Mrs. Luce was already working on a method to persuade the Yugoslavs to yield on the minor territorial question. According to her biographer, Stephen Shadegg, a "mysterious stranger" had approached Luce in Rome late in August. Claiming to have worked for the CIA in Yugoslavia, the man noted that there had been a crop failure and that the Yugoslavs needed wheat to avoid famine. He informed Luce that "half a million tons of wheat would relieve the present shortage and unfreeze the situation in London [where the Trieste talks were being held]." The ambassador immediately left for Washington. She met with Dulles, who acknowledged that her anonymous informant may have been correct but observed that "Tito could never afford to admit to us or anyone that he would trade Trieste for a gift of wheat." Apparently, the secretary suggested that the problem might be resolved by finding an emissary who could negotiate with Tito in complete secrecy and whom Tito could trust to remain silent about the details of any deal concluded. Luce attended a dinner party a few days later at which she was seated next to Robert Murphy, a veteran diplomat who had established a personal rapport with Tito during wartime negotiations. They discussed the Trieste affair and, according to Murphy, Luce announced to him, "You are just the man we need to bring Tito around!" She suggested as much to the State Department the next day. As Murphy noted, "Ambassador Luce usually got what she wanted," and he was soon instructed to prepare for a visit to Yugoslavia and Italy.[49]

The United States was about to play out the final scene of the drawn-out Trieste drama. On 3 September, Walter Bedell Smith cabled Eisenhower to approve Murphy's special mission. The acting secretary of state added that, in Tito's case, Murphy "might wish to invoke your personal authority in warning of [a] future less sympathetic U.S. attitude toward their requests for economic and military aid if they refuse [the] concessions we seek." Eisenhower gave full approval. He also remarked that "I instinctively share your feeling the approach to Tito should take more the terms of warning, while in Scelba's case the proper term might be mild, even to the point of being encouraging." Smith informed the president on 10 September that Murphy was ready to depart and reiterated that economic pressure would be used, if necessary, to secure Yugoslav compliance:

> The Yugoslavs are in great need of wheat, which we can provide under our law. . . . In addition the Yugoslavs are greatly worried by their financial problem of converting their short-term liabili-

ties into long-term obligations. They would like our moral and political support in accomplishing this. . . . Both the wheat and the financial problem give us certain leverage on the Yugoslavs, which we intend to employ in reaching a Trieste settlement.

Eisenhower voiced no objection.[50]

Murphy first went to Yugoslavia, where he gave Tito a personal letter from the president. Eisenhower's message contained veiled references to American economic aid but primarily stressed Yugoslav-American friendship. It is unclear whether Tito was moved more by this personal appeal or by the prospect of continued American economic assistance. In any event, the Yugoslav leader proved accommodating and the mission was successful. Tito abandoned the claim to Punta Sottile and submitted two alternative proposals. These were conveyed to the Italian government, which accepted one of them in late September.[51]

After months of dogged negotiations the efforts of the Anglo-American negotiators had finally paid off. Their achievement was considerable given the seemingly irreconcilable positions of the Italians and Yugoslavs. Though helped by Washington's economic leverage in the final stages, Llewellyn Thompson in particular deserved credit for his patient, tough-minded, and skillful approach to those negotiations. Eisenhower sent him a personal letter of congratulation, stressing how important the Trieste settlement was "not only to the development of an adequate defense in Southeastern Europe, but as a symbol and an example in the whole free world." Luce, who ironically had often been a thorn in the side of the London negotiators, was even more effusive in congratulating Thompson on his achievement, describing the Trieste agreement as "one of the most important made in Western diplomacy since the end of the war." She added that "the agreement which you have made not only removes one of the most irksome and troublesome of the many problems confronting the free world, but it will also stand as a classic example of how diplomatic negotiations can be carried out." Those talks have in fact been recognized as such and are still studied by scholars of international relations as a classic triumph of the art of diplomatic negotiation.[52]

On 5 October 1954 representatives of the United States, Britain, Italy, and Yugoslavia signed the so-called memorandum of understanding in London. According to its terms military government was to cease in the two zones of the FTT, and Italy and Yugoslavia would assume governing authority on their respective sides of the new frontier. The agreement was ratified promptly by the governments concerned and came into effect a few weeks later.[53]

Interestingly, the Soviet Union accepted the Trieste settlement without protest. The American embassy in Moscow attributed this reaction to the Kremlin's "desire not to take sides in [the] matter or jeopardize its current efforts to 'normalize' relations with Yugoslavia." The issue also no longer held value as a source of anti-Western propaganda once an Italo-Yugoslav agreement had been secured. As there were no other potential objectors of any significance, implementation of the agreement proceeded smoothly.[54]

The departure of the Anglo-American garrison on 26 October 1954 ended almost a decade of direct United States involvement in Trieste. For various reasons. including bad weather and rumors of a plot to assassinate General Winterton, the formal ceremony to hand over authority from AMG to the Italians did not take place as planned. Winterton did, however, issue a public announcement on the morning of 26 October declaring that "the Allied Military government of the British and United States Zone of the Free Territory of Trieste is hereby terminated." In the afternoon thousands of Triestines crowded into Piazza Unità in pouring rain and a howling *bora* (the notorious Triestine gale) to see the Italian tricolor once again raised over their city. As far as American policymakers were concerned, the Trieste dispute had been conclusively resolved.[55]

In terms of international law the settlement was actually "provisional" in that a permanent, formal dismantling of the FTT would have necessitated revision of the Italian peace treaty—an act requiring the consent of all the signatory nations to that document. As a de facto solution, however, the London agreement was final because both the Italian and Yugoslav governments recognized it as a practical—if not ideal—compromise and they wanted it to endure. The two Western powers helped ensure the effective finality of the memorandum of understanding by making clear they would support neither Italian nor Yugoslav claims to the territory now under the other's sovereignty.

In the wake of a brief diplomatic flare-up of the dispute in 1974, Italy and Yugoslavia eventually decided to formalize the provisional solution by concluding the so-called Osimo accords of 10 November 1975. These agreements meant that Italy relinquished its claims to Zone B while Yugoslavia formally recognized that Trieste was Italian territory. There were also provisions for protection of national minorities and for local economic cooperation between Italy and Yugoslavia. The two governments duly advised the United Nations Security Council, the United States and Great Britain that "the 1954 London Memorandum which established the situation prior to the present agreement is now void." After more than two decades the "provisional" de facto settlement which had been so carefully engineered in 1954 had finally given rise to a permanent de jure solution of the Italo-Yugoslav boundary dispute. It is highly unlikely that the Trieste question will be reopened in the foreseeable future.[56]

## Conclusion

The United States had played a key role in the "provisional" resolution of the Trieste dispute, which had proved so frustrating for so many years. Speaking in New York after the signing of the London memorandum of understanding, Dulles recalled that "when I became secretary of state, I made a list of the more important problems which needed to be resolved in the interests of world peace and security. Trieste was in the top bracket of that list."[57] Of course, the "top bracket" also included more pressing and weighty problems such as Korea, Berlin, Germany, and the EDC. Alongside these issues the situation in Trieste did not seem to demand immediate attention and appeared "manageable." The Eisenhower administration did not really take meaningful action on its intention to resolve the Trieste problem until prompted to do so by the threat of local violence and Luce's forceful and melodramatic reports from Italy. Thereafter, however, the American government acted more vigorously. After several false starts the United States succeeded in initiating the three-phase negotiating process to bypass the domestic pressures which had prevented Italy and Yugoslavia from reaching a solution. It was the United States, moreover, which ensured the success of these talks by taking advantage of its political influence in both countries, supplemented by the economic leverage that had become a characteristic instrument of its Cold War policies in Western Europe.

American policymakers did not pursue a Trieste settlement merely for its own sake. It is true that after 1949 Trieste itself was no longer a focal point of direct confrontation between the Western and Soviet blocs. Indeed, it was this development which made a solution possible by removing the perceived need for a continuing Anglo-American presence in the area. The Trieste issue had thus become a specific problem in Washington's relations with Italy and Yugoslavia. Nevertheless, as had been the case since 1945, the interests of the United States in Trieste on the most general level were still expressed in terms of the Cold War. The only change was that the larger purposes of the United States in the Cold War were now served by terminating its commitment in Trieste. Eisenhower's own reaction to the resolution of the Trieste dispute exemplified this more general concern: "Now the way was open for Italian participation in the Western European Union and for success in negotiations for defense bases. The Communist threat to Italy had been averted, and that nation now trod on firmer ground. And the threat of an explosion had passed." Dulles was even more expansive in describing the implications of the Trieste settlement in October 1954: "A grave cause of dissension and unrest has been removed, so that all of South Europe can breathe more easily. Above all, a demonstration had been given of the capacity of the nations which are free of Soviet domination to resolve differences which weaken them and distract them from the greatest issue of our time." In short, the elimination of the Trieste problem was significant for the Eisenhower administration because it removed a needless distraction in Italo-Yugoslav relations, enabling both nations to stand more effectively alongside the United States in its global confrontation with the Soviet Union. In that sense the decisive role of the United States in ending the dispute in 1954 marked the consummation of its policy of approaching the Trieste issue as a part of a broader Cold War strategy.[58]

# 7
# Conclusion

⦿ The withdrawal of American troops from Trieste in October 1954 marked the conclusion of almost a decade of American participation alongside Great Britain in the "temporary" administration of the disputed city. During that period the United States became the dominant partner in the occupation and provided the lion's share of the funds needed to maintain AMG operations. Thousands of American soldiers spent some time in Trieste between 1945 and 1954, and a few even gave their lives while serving there. The United States, moreover, was the key actor in arranging a lasting resolution of the dispute.

This study has sought to explain why the United States became so intimately involved in a distant Italo-Yugoslav frontier dispute and to assess the significance of that involvement. Its central thesis has been that the United States was drawn into the Trieste dispute as a by-product of the more general process through which wartime intervention in Europe led to American entanglement in the Cold War with the Soviet Union. After 1945 American policymakers at all levels came to view the Trieste question in terms of broader Cold War objectives—especially with respect to Italy and Yugoslavia. In one sense American policy on this issue was dominated by essentially negative goals: preventing Yugoslav control of the city and thereby containing communism on the southeastern periphery of Western Europe. Yet the American presence in Trieste also represented the positive assertion of the principle of self-determination in accord with an underlying liberal internationalist ideology which predated the advent of the Cold War. This study has illustrated how those general policy concerns—positive and negative—were applied and adapted in Trieste to transform an issue of no apparent interest to Washington into a symbol of Cold War confrontation.

The story of the American experience in Trieste can be viewed basically as the conjuncture of two historical developments. The first of these was the continuation into the twentieth century of the Julian Region's historic function as a barometer of broader pressures in European international politics. After 1945 Trieste was not only a localized focal point of national and ideological conflict but also became a strategically important point on the edge of an increasingly sharp dividing line between two opposing systems of international order. If Trieste had not been a piece of disputed terrain on that demarcation line between East and West, there would have been little reason for a significant American presence there.

The other relevant historical development was, of course, the rise of the United States to global power and its willingness to exercise that power to promote a liberal, internationalist world order. Under Woodrow Wilson's leadership the United States first sought to employ its power to this end in Europe during and after World War I, but with little success. When the United States became embroiled in a second European war in the 1940s, it acted much more forcefully to achieve its wartime and postwar objectives, even though some of the latter were vaguely defined. On both occasions American policymaking was a direct outgrowth of more general American aims in Europe.

During World War II, however, there was a veritable gulf between Washington's general postwar aims as announced in the Atlantic Charter and its efforts at developing a viable policy mechanism to attain them in the Julian Region. American wartime policy toward the Julian problem was certainly based on the hope of solving it according to Atlantic Charter principles, but policymakers in Washington failed to define the United States' interests in the area and did not anticipate any significant postwar commitment there. Indeed, although American statesmen were anxious to avoid an armed clash with any of their allies, they made no realistic attempt to accommodate Yugoslav objections to Anglo-American plans for the occupation of the Julian Region. Until the crisis of May 1945 there was, quite simply, no coherent strategy for implementing American objectives in the Julian Region. When World War II ended Trieste was not yet a Cold War issue.

It was during the crisis of May 1945 that a conception of Trieste as such first really began to take hold among leading policymakers in Washington. Winston Churchill and Alexander Kirk had long been urging that Anglo-American policy on the Julian Region be viewed as part of a broader anticommunist strategy, but their exhortations had not been heeded by Roosevelt or the State Department. Indeed, the State Department had unrealistically continued to affirm its commitment to the policy of installing AMG throughout the Julian Region, while remaining cautious in practice and taking no practical steps to implement it. In the face of Yugoslav occupation of Trieste, the United States finally had to confront the fact that its existing policy was vague and unrealistic. Unable to rely on platitudes or to postpone the issue for reasons of "military necessity," policymakers in Washington chose to oppose the Yugoslav occupation of Trieste in the name of liberal principles. State Department officials, of whom Joseph Grew was the most influential, now began to see the issue in terms of broader communist aggression. The new American president, Harry S Truman, appeared to concur in their conclusion. Nevertheless, the Americans did not wish to be too aggressive and were satisfied to resolve the crisis with a working compromise: the Yugoslavs withdrew from Trieste, while the United States and Britain quietly put aside their official policy of imposing AMG on the whole Julian Region. That outcome represented a success for the tacit spheres-of-influence approach to East-West relations which the Truman administration would adopt in the immediate postwar period.

In itself, Trieste was not a central issue in the Cold War, and after the May crisis it had very little impact on the unfolding of the Cold War in general. It only came to prominence on occasions such as the discussions on the Italian peace treaty or the 1948 Italian elections, when the United States resurrected the issue for the opportunistic motive of assuring a victory for the Christian Democrats. Although not very important in itself, the Trieste case is of interest as an example of the way in which Cold War politics unfolded in an area where the United States and the Soviet Union were not directly in confrontation. The deadlock between the powers that prevented the establishment of the Free Territory of Trieste was a striking example of the way in which all kinds of issues were reduced to simplistic terms of direct East-West confrontation in the postwar world. For a time the problem of Trieste became a small pawn in the great game of Cold War politics and, in particular, was locked into the more general American strategy of containment.

Expendable in the long run, pawns can nonetheless serve important short-term functions. From the American perspective, Anglo-American control of Trieste was useful for several reasons: it prevented "communism" expanding into another part of Europe; it helped maintain Italy as a stable member of the Western alliance; it justified an Anglo-American military presence in a potentially important strategic point; it enabled the United States to appear as the champion of liberal principles; and, on the local level, it provided Trieste with an effective and relatively impartial administration. Whether laudable or self-serving, none of these American objectives was explicitly related to the task of achieving a lasting, long-term solution of the Trieste problem that Italy, Yugoslavia, and the Triestines could all accept. Ideally, the United States would have liked the return of the whole Free Territory of Trieste to Italy, but did not consider that goal to merit the risk of an armed clash with the Yugoslavs. Short of that outcome, Washington generally viewed Trieste as a manageable issue and seemed ready to maintain a military presence there indefinitely. In Cold War terms there was little reason for urgency in attempting to reach a permanent resolution of the dispute.

After the Soviet-Yugoslav split of 1948, however, the advantages of maintaining the status quo in Trieste gradually diminished. The United States now had an interest in keeping Tito out of the Soviet fold as well as supporting the Italian government. In the past Italy's Christian Democrats had successfully played on American fears of Italian domestic instability to ensure a relatively pro-Italian line on Trieste, because Washington viewed Italy as a Cold War ally while Yugoslavia seemed a stalwart member of the Soviet bloc. Once Yugoslavia's international status became more ambiguous, Belgrade was in a position to play a similar game. The United States found itself in an uneasy situation where, because of past commitments, it lacked the freedom to maneuver it would have liked on the Trieste issue.

In effect, Trieste's value as a pawn in the Cold War had been almost eliminated. It gradually became clear to American policymakers that the Trieste question was now merely an unnecessary source of tension between a valued ally and a would-be opponent of the Soviet Union. Though it remained manageable, the potential existed for an awkward crisis and the United States became increasingly eager to reach a compromise resolution. The pressures to be rid of this occasionally irritating problem were heightened by the local unrest and the Italo-Yugoslav tensions of 1952. By then the quest for a Trieste settlement had become an increasingly annoying challenge to Washington's skills in alliance management. Consequently, even if Clare Boothe Luce had not taken a strong personal interest in the matter, the Eisenhower administration would still have acted much as it did to ensure that a lasting settlement was reached in 1954 by initiating four-power negotiations and by using political and economic influence on Italy and Yugoslavia to bring about a final agreement. It is noteworthy that the United States ended its presence in Trieste only after the area had lost all usefulness as a Cold War pawn.

It is difficult to assess the success of United States policy in Trieste from World War II to 1954 because that policy was often unclear in its specific objectives. Yet there can be little doubt that American intervention "saved" Trieste for Italy—and, thus, for the West. The American presence served as a stabilizing force in the area and helped demonstrate the strength of the American commitment to Western Europe (and to the containment of communism on its borders). On the local level it helped ensure relatively impartial and efficient administration of the area until a permanent settlement could be agreed upon. Although the American stay in Trieste was unnecessarily prolonged, by 1954 the United States had resolved the problem permanently and at a minor cost. In Cold War terms American policy in Trieste might be termed a moderate success. That success did not necessarily attest to the astuteness of American Cold War policy in general but was in large measure due to circumstances peculiar to the Trieste case. The United States would certainly not be universally as successful in the Cold War.

Examined from today's perspective, over thirty years after its resolution, the Trieste dispute seems at first glance to be of little significance in that broader struggle. For the United States it had been merely one of the many skirmishes in the Cold War that did not involve direct American-Soviet military confrontation. Yet the Cold War has been an extended series of such skirmishes, and Soviet and American armies have not met in face-to-face combat in the postwar era. Basic strategies may have been conceived and approved in Washington and Moscow, but the key points at issue often concerned areas such as Trieste and involved third parties. Viewed from that perspective, the story of American involvement in the Trieste dispute from World War II to 1954 is indeed that of the Cold War in microcosm.

# Notes

## Preface

1. This point is echoed in Smith and Agarossi, *Operation Sunrise*, p. 220 n.
2. Rusinow, *Italy's Austrian Heritage*, also includes relevant material on the local struggle to 1946.
3. Cf. de Castro, *La Questione di Trieste*; de' Robertis, *Le grandi Potenze*.
4. Cf., for example, Valdevit, *Questione di Trieste*, pp. 89–109; and Rabel, "Prologue to Containment."
5. *Foreign Relations of the United States, 1947*, 4:123 [hereafter cited as *FRUS*, followed by the appropriate year].
6. The quoted phrase is borrowed from Campbell, *Successful Negotiation*, p. 3.
7. *FRUS, 1947*, 6:784–85.
8. For more detailed discussions of "post-revisionism" and "depolarization" see Gaddis, "The Emerging Post-Revisionist Synthesis on the Origins of the Cold War"; and Zeeman, "Britain and the Cold War: An Alternative Approach."
9. For an attempt to examine some of the human dimensions of the problem, see Columni, Ferrari, Nassisi, and Trani, *Storia di un esodo*. Cf. de Simone, *Memorie sull'Istria della Resistenza e dell'Esodo*.
10. See map 1.

## Chapter 1

1. See map 1. For similar definitions of the region, see Novak, *Trieste*, p. 3; Rusinow, *Italy's Austrian Heritage*, p. 11; Duroselle, *Conflit de Trieste*, p. 19. Cf. Moodie, *Italo-Yugoslav Boundary*, pp. 13–15.

   The principal distinction between the terms "Venezia Giulia" and "Julijska

Krajina" is that the former includes Rijeka and excludes the area known as Venetian Slovenia, which Italy gained from Austria-Hungary in 1866. The Yugoslav term excludes Rijeka and includes Venetian Slovenia. For further details concerning this nationalistic toponomy, see Novak, *Trieste*, pp. 4–5.

2 Semple, "Barrier Boundary," p. 32. For more detailed descriptions of the physical geography of the Julian Region, see Moodie, *Italo-Yugoslav Boundary*, pp. 13–43; Roglić, "Aperçu Géographique de la Marche Julienne," in *La Marche Julienne: Etude de Géographie Politique*, pp. 7–26; Duroselle, *Conflit de Trieste*, pp. 19–26.

3 The phrase "zone of strain" is borrowed from Moodie, *Italo-Yugoslav Boundary*, p. 9.

4 For the strategic significance of the Julian Region from Roman times to the nineteenth century, see Semple, "Barrier Boundary," pp. 36–43; Duroselle, *Conflit de Trieste*, pp. 52–59; Moodie, *Italo-Yugoslav Boundary*, pp. 46–60, 74–80, 83–104. Cf. de Castro, *La Questione di Trieste*, 1:3–10, 18–25; Rojnić, "L'Istrie," in *La Marche Julienne*, pp. 75–76.

5 For divergent Italian and Yugoslav accounts of Italian and Slavic influences on the Julian Region up to the nineteenth century, see de Castro, *La Questione di Trieste*, 1:3–21, Rojnić, "L'Istrie," pp. 75–118; Mihovilović, "Trieste," in *La Marche Julienne*, pp. 175–203; Kardelj, *Trieste and Yugoslav-Italian Relations*, pp. 6–7. Cf. Duroselle, *Conflit de Trieste*, pp. 61–69; Sestan, *Venezia Giulia*. Sestan succeeds in transcending the nationalistic biases which have characterized most Italian and Yugoslav studies of the Julian Region's ethnic history.

For Italian linguistic and cultural predominance in the Adriatic world to the eighteenth century, see Braudel, *The Mediterranean and the Mediterranean World in the Age of Philip II*, 2:131–32.

It is unnecessary for the purposes of the present study to enter the acrimonious debate over the precise size of the Italian and Slavic populations of the Julian Region. The problem with such debates, as noted by Eden, *Full Circle*, p. 196, is that "in nationalist controversy, everything depends upon where in the past you begin." In an area of such mixed population the criteria used to determine ethnic affiliation are also crucial, as is shown by the divergent results of the Austrian census of 1910 and the Italian census of 1921. Both censuses have been criticized for biases and inaccuracies in the tabulation of population data for the Julian Region. Yet, in the absence of more satisfactory censuses, they served as the basic points of reference for conflicting Italian and Yugoslav claims to the area for most of the twentieth century. Those census results are reproduced in Duroselle, *Conflit de Trieste*, pp. 28–29.

6 See the comments concerning ethnic intermingling in the Julian Region in Duroselle, *Conflit de Trieste*, pp. 60–61. The later intensity of nationalism in this area bears powerful testimony to the observation of Hans Kohn that, rather than being based on "objective" ethnic differences, "nationalism is first and foremost a state of mind, and an act of consciousness." *The Idea of Nationalism*, p. 10.

7   The growth of Italian irredentist aspirations for the Julian Region may be traced in Tergestinus, "Venezia Giulia," pp. 196–206; Rusinow, *Italy's Austrian Heritage*, pp. 16–20; Novak, *Trieste*, pp. 14–15; Duroselle, *Conflit de Trieste*, pp. 69–72; de Castro, *La Questione di Trieste*, 1:30–31; Vivante, *Irredentismo adriatico*, pp. 68–220, passim; Schiffrer, *Le origini dell'irredentismo triestino (1813–1860)*.

   Interestingly, even Dante had addressed the Italian boundary question centuries earlier when he wrote: ". . . Pola, presso del Quarnero/che Italia chiude e i suoi termini bagna" [Pola, near the Quarnero River, which marks the ends of Italy and washes its boundaries]. *L'Inferno*, canto 9, 11, 113–14.

8   This "ethnic" struggle in the Julian Region was often superimposed on a divergent pattern of "class" conflict. For instance, unlike many Triestine intellectuals, the Italian-speaking commercial classes were "cosmopolitan" in outlook and did not favor inclusion in Italy because they believed Trieste's economic prosperity rested on its favored position in the Habsburg Empire. In contrast, many Italian workers in Trieste came to assume their interests would be better served by an internationalist socialist regime than an Italian (or Yugoslav) nationalist one. In Istria the ethnic struggle did coincide roughly with one level of class conflict, as most absentee landowners were Italian while the peasantry were predominantly Croatian. Slavic nationalism was virtually synonymous with social reform there. For further consideration of these cross-currents of class and related aspects of the Italian nationalist movement in the Julian Region in the nineteenth century, see Novak, *Trieste*, pp. 15–16; Rusinow, *Italy's Austrian Heritage*, pp. 20–30; Duroselle, *Conflit de Trieste*, pp. 77–84; de Castro, *La Questione di Trieste*, 1:37–44. Of particular interest is Vivante's now classic study *Irredentismo adriatico*.

9   For the relationship between irredentism and post-1865 Italian diplomacy see Lowe and Marzari, *Italian Foreign Policy*, pp. 15–19, 96–98; Seton-Watson, *From Liberalism to Fascism*, pp. 100–103, 137, 204–5, 242.

10  The implications of intensified Italian irredentism after 1890 are discussed in Tergestinus, "Venezia Giulia," pp. 208–9; Rusinow, *Italy's Austrian Heritage*, pp. 20–30; Lowe and Marzari, *Italian Foreign Policy*, pp. 127–30; Vivante, *Irredentismo adriatico*, pp. 166–220; Sestan, *Venezia Giulia*, pp. 95–103; Seton-Watson, *From Liberalism to Fascism*, pp. 406–7. Personal testimony to the powerful impact of irredentist sentiment on official circles is provided in Salandra, *La neutralità italiana*, pp. 28–37; Giolitti, *Memoirs of My Life*, pp. 205–8.

11  For the rise and impact of a Slavic nationalist movement in the Julian Region see de Castro, *La Questione di Trieste*, 1:33–37; Duroselle, *Conflit de Trieste*, pp. 73–84; Novak, *Trieste*, pp. 17–19; Rusinow, *Italy's Austrian Heritage*, pp. 22–29; Sestan, *Venezia Giulia*, pp. 81–93; Vivante, *Irredentismo adriatico*, pp. 155–220, passim; *La Marche Julienne*, pp. 75–237, passim.

12  For the Julian Region's economic significance before the First World War see Moodie, *Italy's Austrian Heritage*, pp. 105–33; Novak, *Trieste*, pp. 12–13; Vivante,

*Irredentismo adriatico,* pp. 221–62; Mihelić, *The Political Element in the Port Geography of Trieste,* pp. 13–21; Roletto, *Trieste ed i suoi problemi,* pp. 17–34. For the importance of the Suez Canal and favorable Austrian economic policy in the development of the Triestine economy, see Lo Giudice, *Trieste, l'Austria ed il canale de Suez.*

13 Vivante, *Irredentismo adriatico,* p. 221.

14 This chapter departs from the method of handling place names described in the preface. Although now in Yugoslavia and known as Rijeka, the city in question was generally recognized by its Italian name at the time. Moreover, Fiume has been the name used in most English-language studies of the problem.

15 There is no monographic study focused specifically on the diplomacy of the Fiume dispute or on American intervention therein, but there is an extensive literature touching on different aspects of the problem. The most relevant works in English are Albrecht-Carrié, *Italy at the Paris Peace Conference;* Kernek, "Wilson and National Self-Determination"; Lederer, *Yugoslavia at the Paris Peace Conference;* Mayer, *Politics and Diplomacy of Peacemaking;* Mamatey, *The United States and East Central Europe;* Živojinović, *America, Italy, and the Birth of Yugoslavia.* With the exception of Mayer, these works generally fail to set Wilson's Fiume policy in a broader interpretative framework. Two works that do make such an attempt are Floto, "Woodrow Wilson: War Aims and the European Left," and Schmitz, "Woodrow Wilson and the Liberal Peace." Floto stresses the domestic political motivations of Wilson's stand on Fiume, an explanation whose limitations Schmitz correctly criticizes. More justifiably, Schmitz explains Wilson's policy as part of a genuine commitment to oppose militarism and imperialism. But he does not give sufficient attention to the limits of that commitment and, by implying that the complementary antirevolutionary thrust of the New Diplomacy was irrelevant in the Italian context, he fails to provide an adequate explanation for Wilson's unwillingness to use economic pressure against Italy. For a fuller exposition of the interpretation of the Wilson administration's Fiume policy outlined in this chapter, see Rabel, "Between East and West," pp. 34–97.

16 For analyses of the internal and external forces that shaped Italy's war aims and contributed to its disastrous wartime experience, see Bosworth, *Italy, The Least of the Great Powers;* Bosworth, *Italy and the Approach of the First World War;* Gottlieb, *Studies in Secret Diplomacy during the First World War;* Page, *Italy and the World War;* Renzi, "Italy's Neutrality and Entrance into the Great War"; Seton-Watson, *From Liberalism to Fascism,* pp. 413–97, passim; Toscano, *Il Patto di Londra;* Webster, *Industrial Imperialism in Italy.* The phrase *sacro egoismo* was coined by Prime Minister Antonio Salandra during a speech in October 1914 to describe the guiding principles of Italian foreign policy. Though the significance of his comment has been inflated out of proportion, the concept of *sacro egoismo* offers a convenient, shorthand description of the central thrust of liberal Italy's opportunistic diplomacy as the least of Europe's great powers.

17 The evolution of the Wilson administration's policies on self-determination as

they related to Italy were determined by a complex interaction between the liberal ideals of the New Diplomacy and the pressure of military exigencies during World War I. For a more detailed interpretation of that interaction, see Rabel, "Between East and West," pp. 47–68.

18  For evidence of the intimate relationship between Italian diplomacy and the domestic sociopolitical situation in the immediate postwar period, see Speranza, *The Diary of Gino Speranza*, 2:205–34; Page's correspondence from November 1918 to January 1919 in the Thomas Nelson Page Papers; Ray Stannard Baker to Colonel Edward House, 22 November, 6 December, 12 December 1918, box 3, Ray Stannard Baker Papers. For secondary analyses of this relationship, see Maier, *Recasting Bourgeois Europe*, pp. 109–15; Mayer, *Politics and Diplomacy*, pp. 198–226; Seton-Watson, *From Liberalism to Fascism*, pp. 505–27.

19  Wilson's attitude toward the Brenner frontier remains perplexing. He apparently accepted Italian demands in the north as early as December 1918 when he met with Italian leaders in Paris. See Albrecht-Carrié, *Italy at the Paris Peace Conference*, pp. 81, 85. Wilson later attributed this violation of the principle of self-determination to "insufficient study." Seymour, *The Intimate Papers of Colonel House*, 4:435n. For an interesting analysis of Wilson's motives for the Brenner concession, see Kernek, "Wilson and National Self-Determination," pp. 255–64. Almost as if to compensate for this concession to the Italians on the grounds of national security, Wilson thereafter never wavered from the recommendations made by his territorial experts on Italy's eastern claims in a report of January 1919. The report (reprinted in Albrecht-Carrié, *Italy at the Paris Peace Conference*, pp. 367–68) is of particular interest as a classic application of Wilsonian principles of self-determination and economic justice to a specific problem. Its conclusions rested on the mistaken assumption that the Wilsonian program would be implemented in toto, thereby transcending European political realities and balance-of-power considerations. As it happened, the combination of a resurgent Allied Right, a revolutionary threat on the Left and domestic political opposition in the United States thwarted the realization of that program.

20  Wilson's fear of driving the Yugoslavs "into the hands of the Bolshevists" has received little attention in studies of the Fiume dispute. For evidence of this concern, see Rabel, "Between East and West," pp. 85–86.

21  The division of opinion concerning Fiume within the American delegation at Paris is analyzed from differing perspectives in Albrecht-Carrié, *Italy at the Paris Peace Conference*, pp. 119–31; Birdsall, *Versailles, Twenty Years After*, pp. 27–28; Floto, *Colonel House in Paris*, pp. 220–25; Mayer, *Politics and Diplomacy*, pp. 695–97; Rabel, "Between East and West," pp. 78–83. Minutes of the meetings of the Council of Four concerning Italy's claims are printed in *FRUS: The Paris Peace Conference*, 5:80–101, 106–9, 135–37; Mantoux, *Les Délibérations du Conseil des Quatre*, 1:300–315, 328–29, 337–39.

22  Wilson's statement of 23 April 1919 is printed in Baker, *Woodrow Wilson and World Settlement*, 3:287–90. For an interpretation suggesting that Wilson's Ital-

ian manifesto was intended primarily for domestic consumption to rally liberal support in the United States, see Floto, "Wilson: War Aims and the European Left," pp. 142–43.
23 For the complicated efforts to resolve the deadlock on Fiume after the Paris Peace Conference and the reasons for a direct Italo-Yugoslav settlement, see Rabel, "Between East and West," pp. 88–95; Albrecht-Carrié, *Italy at the Paris Peace Conference*, pp. 285–309, 323–26.
24 It is beyond the scope of this study to examine closely these complicated local conflicts, but there is an extensive Italian and Yugoslav literature concerning politiconational developments in the Julian Region during the interwar period. That work has done much to illuminate the sources of the complex national (Italian, Yugoslav, internationalist, autonomist) and ideological (fascist, socialist, communist, liberal) cross-currents which would overlap and clash openly in the area after the outbreak of World War II. Recent scholarship on the interwar period has tended to transcend the narrow polemical tone of earlier studies written against a background of intense national rivalry or Cold War competition. For brief introductions in English to local interwar developments and bibliographical references, see Rusinow, *Italy's Austrian Heritage*, pp. 185–210, 226–38, 266–71; Novak, *Trieste*, pp. 34–45. For local appraisals of Italo-Yugoslav scholarship on the question, see the numerous articles on "Italiani, sloveni e croati ai confini orientali," in *Bollettino dell'Istituto regionale per la storia del movimento di liberazione nel Friuli–Venezia Giulia* 2 (May 1974): 3–41 (hereafter cited as *Bollettino ISML-VG*); the articles on "Fascismo, anti-fascismo e resistenza nella Venezia-Giulia (1914–1945)" in *Bollettino ISML-VG* 4 (August 1976): 6–78.
25 For general accounts of the rise of the Fascist party in the Julian Region and its interwar policies there, see Rusinow, *Italy's Austrian Heritage*, pp. 84–160, 185–210; Apih, *Italia: Fascismo e antifascismo nella Venezia Giulia (1918–43)*, pp. 37–228, passim; Silvestri, *Dalla redenzione al fascismo: Trieste, 1918–1922*. For two contemporary studies of the persecution of Yugoslavs in Italy by a Slovenian expert on the question and by a leading Italian antifascist exile, see Čermelj, *Life-and-Death Struggle of a National Minority*; Salvemini, *Racial Minorities under Fascism in Italy*. See also n. 23.
26 Rusinow, *Italy's Austrian Heritage*, pp. 185–238, 266–80, passim. For further analyses of Italo-Yugoslav relations in the interwar period, see de Castro, *La Questione di Trieste*, 1:125–31; Novak, *Trieste*, pp. 42–45; Hoptner, *Yugoslavia in Crisis*.

### Chapter 2

1 See, for example, Cox, *The Race for Trieste*, pp. 7 and passim; Mastny, *Russia's Road to the Cold War*, p. 282; Smith and Agarossi, *Operation Sunrise*, p. 186.
2 Valdevit, "Gli Alleati e la Venezia Giulia," p. 55, emphasizes the same point. See

also Valdevit, *Questione di Trieste*, pp. 19–89. Valdevit's interpretation of the role of the Julian Region in Allied strategy and diplomacy is similar to that presented in this chapter but focuses more on British policy. Cf. also de' Robertis, *La frontiera orientale italiana;* de' Robertis, *Le grandi Potenze.*

3 FO 371, 30205, R589/73/92, Public Record Office, London (hereafter cited as PRO); FO 371, 30240, R960/960/92, PRO. For secondary analyses of the Anglo-Yugoslav "secret accords" of 1941, see Barker, *British Policy in South-East Europe,* pp. 87–88; Pupo, "Gli 'accordi segreti' anglo-jugoslavi (1941)"; Wheeler, *Britain and the War for Yugoslavia, 1940–1943,* pp. 29–33, 36, 46–47; Woodward, *British Foreign Policy in the Second World War,* 1:532.

4 FO 371, 30240, R1949/960/92, PRO; Cabinet Paper WP(41)45 in CAB 66/15, PRO; cf. FO 371, 29937, R6661/168/22, PRO.

5 Barker, *British Policy in South-East Europe,* p. 5.

6 *FRUS, 1941,* 1:342, 351–52, 367–69. The Foreign Office was aware of possible American objections even when first contemplating the proposal to the Yugoslavs. At the time Cadogan suggested to Churchill that it was unnecessary to inform the Americans as the instructions to Eden did not "commit us to anything definite." FO 371, 30240, R960/960/92, PRO.

It is also important to note that British (and Soviet) approval of the Atlantic Charter was conditional. See Wilson, *The First Summit,* pp. 185, 261–63. Cf. Gaddis, *The United States and the Origins of the Cold War.,* pp. 11–13.

7 See, for example, Dallek, *Franklin D. Roosevelt and American Foreign Policy,* pp. 317–61, passim; Divine, *Roosevelt and World War II,* p. 85; Gaddis, *The United States and the Origins of the Cold War,* pp. 1–31, passim.

8 The "Declaration of the United Nations" stated that all the Allied nations accepted the "common program of purposes and principles embodied in . . . the Atlantic Charter." *FRUS, 1942,* 1:25–26.

9 Rosenman, *The Public Papers and Addresses of Franklin D. Roosevelt,* 12:333, 459.

10 Campbell, "The Italo-Yugoslav Frontier: Alternative Boundaries," 22 December 1942, Report T-198, Territorial Subcommittee Documents, Records of Harley Notter, lot files, Record Group 59, National Archives, Washington D.C. (hereafter cited as NA). For related studies of the Julian problem, see reports T-171, T-182, T-184, T-190, T-217, T-396, and T-471, all in ibid. See also the summary report of 12 May 1943 in *FRUS: The Conferences at Washington and Quebec, 1943,* pp. 791–94.

11 John C. Campbell, letter to the author, 22 December 1986.

12 Minute by Sargent, 31 December 1941, FO 371, 33446, R35/35/92, PRO. For British attempts to avoid encouraging Yugoslav territorial claims and occasional internal disagreements on this policy within the Foreign Office, see FO 371, 30240, R7703/960/92, PRO; FO 371, 33493, R7833/2354/92, PRO; FO 371, 36702, R2608/117/92, PRO; FO 371, 37603, R10530/117/92, PRO; FO 371, 37632, R546/546/92, PRO.

The Royal Yugoslav government-in-exile also pressed its claims in the United States but drew no apparent response. See *FRUS, 1942,* 3:841–44; *FRUS, 1943,* 2:1018–20.

13  Howard, *Mediterranean Strategy,* pp. 40 and passim. Cf. Stoler, *The Politics of the Second Front,* pp. 74–78, 92–102.

14  FO 371, 37276, R8489/362/22, PRO. Roosevelt's suggestion was probably related to discussions between Hull and Eden at Quebec concerning the possible use of Trieste and Rijeka as ports for southern Germany if there was an economic dismemberment of the German Reich after the war. Interestingly, Hull stated in his memoirs that, "I threw this out simply as a thought we had been discussing, not as a decision made or contemplated by our government." Hull, *The Memoirs of Cordell Hull,* 2:1234; *FRUS: The Conferences at Washington and Quebec, 1943,* pp. 927–28. A paper was prepared within the State Department's postwar planning division in October 1943 entitled "The Economy of the Port of Trieste" but there is no evidence that it was explicitly inspired by Roosevelt's comments. See T-396, Territorial Subcommitte Documents, Records of Harley Notter, lot files, RG 59, NA.

For Roosevelt's idiosyncratic personal diplomacy and his bypassing of the State Department see, for example, Gaddis, *The United States and the Origins of the Cold War,* pp. 102 and passim; Kuniholm, *The Origins of the Cold War in the Near East,* pp. 121–25; De Santis, *The Diplomacy of Silence,* pp. 159, 203.

15  FO 371, 37276, R8489/362/22, PRO; FO 371, 37601, R1019/84/92, PRO. A paper from the former file encapsulating the results of the Foreign Office's ongoing study of the Italo-Yugoslav frontier question from late 1943 to mid-1944 has been published (with an analytical introduction) in Valdevit, "Un documento del Foreign Office sul confine orientale."

16  For introductory accounts of the complex local struggles in the Julian Region after 1943, see Novak, *Trieste,* pp. 70–129, passim; Rusinow, *Italy's Austrian Heritage,* pp. 281–309, 323–65. For more detailed Italian studies from diverse ideological perspectives, see Coceani, *Mussolini, Hitler, Tito alle porte orientali d'Italia;* Pacor, *Confine orientale: Questione nazionale e resistenza nel Friuli–Venezia Giulia;* Collotti, *Il littorale adriatico nel Nuovo Ordine Europeo, 1943–1945;* de Castro, *La Questione di Trieste,* pp. 172–96.

17  The phrase is borrowed from Smith and Agarossi, *Operation Sunrise,* p. 5.

18  Roosevelt's comment in *FRUS, 1943,* 2:383. Numerous historians have discussed the important implications of the Anglo-American handling of the Italian armistice. See, for example, Ellwood, *Italy, 1943–1945,* pp. 29–30, 43–47; Kolko, *The Politics of War,* pp. 39, 52, 128, 130–31; McNeill, *America, Britain, and Russia: Their Cooperation and Conflict, 1941–1946,* p. 310; Miller, *The United States and Italy, 1940–1950,* pp. 67–73; Warner, "Italy and the Powers, 1943–49," p. 37; Gaddis, *The United States and the Origins of the Cold War,* pp. 88–91. Cf. Arcidiacono, "The 'Dress Rehearsal'." Mastny, *Russia's Road to the Cold War,* pp. 106–8, suggests that Stalin was not yet thinking in terms of distinct spheres of

influence because he remained uncertain how far his military power would reach in Eastern Europe. If the Allies had agreed to a genuinely representative three-power military commission in Italy, they might have been in a stronger position to claim greater involvement in the administration of Soviet-occupied areas.

19 *FRUS: The Conferences at Cairo and Teheran, 1943*, pp. 480–81, 493, 504–5. Cf. Barker, "L'opzione istriana," pp. 11–12. For Hopkins's comments see Sherwood, *Roosevelt and Hopkins: An Intimate History*, p. 780. For the explanation of Roosevelt's interest in "that Adriatic business," see Stoler, *Politics of the Second Front*, pp. 144–45. Cf. Feis, *Churchill, Roosevelt and Stalin*, pp. 260–64.

20 In his memoirs Churchill noted: "Decisions had now [June 1944] to be taken about our next move in the Mediterranean, and it must be recorded with regret, that these occasioned the first important divergence on high strategy between ourselves and our American friends." *Triumph and Tragedy*, p. 50. Churchill was disregarding similar Anglo-American disagreements at Teheran and a British historian has more appropriately dubbed this post-Normandy debate "the *last* great controversy over 'the Mediterranean Strategy'" [my italics]. Howard, *Mediterranean Strategy*, p. 60.

21 Churchill, *Triumph and Tragedy*, pp. 56–57 [his italics]. Cf. documents C-717, R-573, C-718, R-574, C-721, R-577 in Kimball, *Churchill and Roosevelt*, 3:212–23, 225–30, 232. See also Barker, "L'opzione istriana," pp. 17–23; Howard, *Mediterranean Strategy*, pp. 60–68; Mastny, *Russia's Road to the Cold War*, p. 196.

22 Memorandum by Stone for G-5, AFHQ, 28 July 1944, partially reprinted in Coles and Weinberg, *Civil Affairs*, p. 590.

23 State Department to Murphy, 9 August 1944, 740.00119 Control (Italy)/8-944, RG 59, NA.

24 FO 371, 40845, U6754/6752/70, PRO. This file reveals the Foreign Office's general concern about Washington's reluctance to accept postwar occupational responsibilities in Europe. Eden explicitly stressed the need to keep the Americans informed so as to prevent them refusing to accept an occupation commitment in the Julian Region. See also Valdevit, "Gli Alleati e Venezia Giulia," p. 61.

25 Minutes of the Anglo-Yugoslav meetings of 12 and 13 August 1944 in Murphy to State Department, 28 August 1944, 740.00119 Control (Italy)/8-2844, RG 59, NA. See also Churchill, *Triumph and Tragedy*, pp. 81–82. For secondary interpretations of the significance of these meetings for the Julian issue, see Valdevit, "Gli Alleati e Venezia Giulia," pp. 61–62; Harris, *Allied Military Administration*, pp. 328–29. American officials held similar meetings with Yugoslav representatives in early September, touching on the subject of Yugoslavia's postwar boundaries. One American participant reported after these discussions that Tito "would fight if necessary for Trieste," but the State Department did not budge from its firm policy. *FRUS, 1944*, 4:1401, 1403–5. See also the assurance given to the Italian government in Stone to Visconti Venosta, 11 September 1944, 740.00119 Control (Italy)/10-1144EG, RG 59, NA.

26 Memorandum by Grew to Hopkins, 16 September 1944, and memorandum by

Leahy to Matthews, 19 September 1944, both reprinted in Coles and Weinberg, *Civil Affairs*, pp. 590–91.

27  Documents C-772, R-611, and C-774 in Kimball, *Churchill and Roosevelt*, 3:299–302, 305; Churchill, *Triumph and Tragedy*, pp. 109, 133–34, 137–38; Barker, "L'opzione istriana," pp. 27–37. For American military assessments of the Adriatic proposal, see the planning documents in 384 Mediterranean (26 Oct. 43), sec. 1-A, ABC Files, RG 165, NA.

28  For more detailed accounts of the Churchill-Stalin discussions, see Churchill, *Triumph and Tragedy*, pp. 196–212; Kimball, "Naked Reverse Right," pp. 1–7; Mastny, *Russia's Road to the Cold War*, pp. 207–12; Albert Resis, "The Churchill-Stalin Secret 'Percentages' Agreement on the Balkans, Moscow, October 1944," pp. 368–87; Woodward, *British Foreign Policy*, 3:146–53. According to Mastny, Stalin also suggested to Churchill that the British make a landing in the upper Adriatic and eventually join the Red Army near Vienna—the very proposal Churchill had advocated repeatedly. Mastny argues, moreover, that Stalin's willingness to sanction equal British influence in Yugoslavia was intended to dampen "the zeal the Yugoslav Communists displayed in building a state closely fashioned after the Soviet model. . . . that zeal, which inspired Tito to behave as his partner rather than his underling." For evidence of Moscow's uneasy wartime relations with the Yugoslav Communists, see Djilas, *Conversations with Stalin*.

29  Mastny, *Russia's Road to the Cold War*, p. 45. A similar argument is put forward persuasively in Garson, "The Atlantic Alliance, Eastern Europe, and the Origins of the Cold War," pp. 296–320. Cf. Lundestad, *The American Non-Policy towards Eastern Europe, 1943–1947*, pp. 39–44.

30  Coles and Weinberg, *Civil Affairs*, p. 591. For representative examples of the British field reports, see the report by Captain D. Prescott on operations with the Partisans in Istria, November 1944, in WO 202, 205, PRO; report by Major H. Vincent of 29 November 1944, and Vincent to Commander G. A. Holdsworth, 15 November 1944, in WO 202, 316, PRO; report by Major Tucker of 23 October 1944 in WO 204, 2000, PRO. For similar American field reports, see the reports numbered L45159, L48022, L49479, and L52572, in Office of Strategic Services (OSS) Reports, RG 226, NA.

31  FO 371, 40601, U8634/57/70, PRO; FO 371, 40735, U8838/491/70, PRO.

32  *FRUS: The Conferences at Malta and Yalta, 1945*, pp. 888–89.

33  Djilas, *Conversations with Stalin*, p. 114.

34  *FRUS: The Conferences at Malta and Yalta, 1945*, pp. 963–64; Smyth, "The Treatment of Italy," 31 August 1944, CAC 248, Records of Harley Notter, microfilm T-1221, lot files, RG 59, NA; Problem Sheet on Italy, 22 January 1945, box 3, Records of the Office of Western European Affairs relating to Italy, 1943–51, lot files, RG 59, NA.

For general studies of Anglo-American relations in Italy, see Ellwood, *Italy, 1943–1945*; Kogan, *Italy and the Allies*; Miller, "The Search for Stability," pp. 264–86; Miller, *The United States and Italy*; Warner, "Italy and the Powers."

35  De Santis, "In Search of Yugoslavia." For other studies of British and American policies toward Yugoslavia, see Auty and Clogg, *British Policy towards Wartime Resistance in Yugoslavia and Greece*; Barker, *British Policy in South-East Europe*; Larson, *United States Foreign Policy toward Yugoslavia, 1943–1963*; Modisett, "The Four-Cornered Triangle"; Radovanovic, "American Attitudes toward the Wartime Resistance in Yugoslavia, 1941–1945"; Roberts, *Tito, Mihailović, and the Allies, 1941–1945*.
36  *FRUS, 1945*, 4:1103-4; Macmillan, *War Diaries*, pp. 698–99.
37  Minutes of Tito-Alexander meeting, 21 February 1945, 740.0011EW, microfilm 982, roll 214, RG 59, NA, and in FO 371, 48810, R4632/6/92, PRO; *FRUS, 1945*, 4:1106–7, 1111; FO 371, 48813, R7933/6/92, PRO. Cf. "Background Statement on Alexander-Tito Talks," *New York Times*, 20 May 1945, p. 17. See also Cox, *Race for Trieste*, p. 17; Harris, *Allied Military Administration*, pp. 330–32; Smith and Agarossi, *Operation Sunrise*, pp. 173–74.
38  *FRUS, 1945*, 4:1107–8; Kirk to secretary of state, 26 February 1945, 740.0011EW, microfilm 982, roll 214, RG 59, NA.
39  Velebit, cited in Campbell, *Successful Negotiation*, p. 84. For Anglo-American evaluations of Yugoslav objectives in the Julian Region and attempts to gain total control of the resistance movement there, see the reports by Major H. Vincent of 29 November 1944, and by Major R. Macpherson of 30 December 1944, in WO 202, 316, PRO; report by Captain H. Gibb, 5 January 1945, in WO 202, 317A, PRO; OSS Report GB-4786, 29 April 1945, WO 202, 316, PRO; report by Captain H. Gibb, 26 February 1945, WO 202, 520, PRO; reports by Major Tucker of 23 October 1944 and Major R. Macpherson of 4 December 1944, both in WO 204, 2000, PRO; Major General D. Noce, G-3 Division, AFHQ, to chief of staff, 16 January 1945, in WO 204, 2000, PRO. For a detailed analysis of the significance for Anglo-American policymaking of these developments relating to the resistance movement in the Julian Region, see Valdevit, "Resistenza e Alleati fra Italia e Jugoslavia." For other interpretations of Yugoslav aims in the Julian Region, see Duroselle, *Conflit de Trieste*, pp. 156–57; MacLean, *Disputed Barricade*, p. 302; Wilson, *Tito's Yugoslavia*, p. 34.
40  *FRUS, 1945*, 4:1108–10.
41  Ibid., pp. 1113–15, 1117–19; Offie to Dunn, 4 March 1945, 740.0011EW, microfilm 982, roll 214, RG 59, NA.
42  Foreign Office memorandum, "Arrangements to be made in the Province of Venezia Giulia on the Eviction of the Germans," PHP(45)11(o), 12 March 1945, in CAB 81/46, PRO; APW(45)31 and APW(45) sixth meeting, in CAB 87/69, PRO. British concerns that the United States would not participate in AMG of the Julian Region were reinforced by a War Department statement to the Combined Civil Affairs Committee that "no additional U.S. military personnel is available for the administration of military government or civil affairs" in that area. CCAC 148/2, 14 March 1945, CCS 383.21 Italy (10-18-44), sec. 1, RG 218, NA. For general British efforts to ensure a greater American role in postwar international affairs, see

Anderson, *The United States, Great Britain and the Cold War*; Hathaway, *Ambiguous Partnership*.

43  Churchill to Eden, Prime Minister's Personal Minute, M196/5, 11 March 1945, Eden to Churchill, PM/45/111, 15 March 1945, Churchill to Eden, Prime Minister's Personal Minute, M216/5, Eden to Churchill, PM/45/118, 18 March 1945 all in PREM 3, PRO; Woodward, *British Foreign Policy*, 3:364–65.

44  For a detailed account of the politicomilitary implications of these negotiations, see Smith and Agarossi, *Operation Sunrise*. Cf. Dulles, *The Secret Surrender*.

45  *FRUS, 1945*, 4:1120–21.

46  Truman, *Year of Decisions*, pp. 17, 243.

47  *FRUS, 1945*, 4:1121–23; Sargent to Major General L. C. Hollis, 23 April 1945, and Prime Minister's Personal Minute, D123/5, 25 April 1945, both in FO 371, 48812, R4247/6/92, PRO; Duroselle, *Conflit de Trieste*, p. 160.

48  Kirk to State Department, 27 and 28 April 1945, 740.0011EW/4-2745, 2845, microfilm 982, roll 271, RG 59, NA; *FRUS, 1945*, 4:1123–25; Alexander to Combined Chiefs of Staff (CCS), 26 April 1945, printed in Coles and Weinberg, *Civil Affairs*, p. 594; Macmillan, *War Diaries*, p. 745.

49  *FRUS, 1945*, 4:1123–25.

50  CCS to AFHQ, FAN 536, 28 April 1945, printed in Coles and Weinberg, *Civil Affairs*, pp. 594–95; *FRUS, 1945*, 4:1126.

51  Alexander to Clark, 30 April 1945, reprinted in Coles and Weinberg, *Civil Affairs*, p. 595; Kirk to State Department, 29 April 1945, 740.00119 Control (Italy)/4-2945, RG 59, NA. For evidence of Alexander's determination to seize Trieste itself, see Alexander, *The Alexander Memoirs*, pp. 151–52.

52  *FRUS, 1945*, 4:1130–32; Churchill to Alexander, 1 May 1945, PREM 3, 495/6, PRO; Churchill, *Triumph and Tragedy*, p. 439. Churchill wrote to Truman that same day in similar terms about the liberation of Prague. Churchill, *Triumph and Tragedy*, p. 442. For an analysis of Churchill's general "cable campaign" to win American support for the pursuit of political objectives during the final phases of the European war, see Anderson, *The United States, Great Britain, and the Cold War*, pp. 40–51, 56–58, 61–62.

For the PCI's wartime policies on the Julian Region, see Pallante, *Il Partito Comunista Italiano*, pp. 259 and passim; Pallante, "Concezioni e posizioni del PCI." Cf. Terzuolo, "Relations between the Communist Parties of Italy and Yugoslavia, 1941–1960"; Terzuolo, "Resistance and the National Question in the Venezia Giulia and Friuli, 1943–1945."

53  Tito to Alexander, enclosed in Makins to Matthews, 2 May 1945, 740.00119 Control (Italy)/5-145, RG 59, NA. Also reprinted in Coles and Weinberg, *Civil Affairs*, pp. 595–96.

54  Entry of 30 April 1945, reel 9, Diaries of Henry Lewis Stimson (microfilm), Harry S Truman Library, Independence, Missouri (hereafter cited as Stimson Diaries); *FRUS, 1945*, 4:1127–32; Kirk to State Department, 29 April 1945, RG 59; 740.00119 Control (Italy)/4-2945, RG 59, NA.

55 For a firsthand description of the final military operations of World War II in the Julian Region and of the fall of Trieste, see Cox, *Race for Trieste*, pp. 9–19, 156–205. Cf. Novak, *Trieste*, pp. 133–60.
56 John C. Campbell, letter to author, 22 December 1986.

## Chapter 3

1 For an alternative interpretation, see Valdevit, *Questione di Trieste*, pp. 89–102. In contrast, Cox, *Race for Trieste*, overstates the extent to which the Trieste crisis can be explained in strictly Cold War terms.
2 Cox, *Race for Trieste*, pp. 168–69, 186–217; Kay, *Italy*, pp. 537–55; Kirk to State Department, 2 May 1945, 740.00119 Control (Italy)/5-245, RG 59, NA.
3 Tito to Alexander, 3 May 1945, and Alexander to Tito, 4 May 1945, in Alexander to CCS, 4 May 1945, both reprinted in part in Coles and Weinberg, *Civil Affairs*, p. 596. See also Cox, *Race for Trieste*, pp. 199–200; Harris, *Allied Military Administration*, pp. 335–36.
4 Alexander to Tito, in Alexander to CCS, 4 May 1945, Tito to Alexander, in Alexander to CCS, 5 May 1945, Alexander to CCS, 5 May 1945, all reprinted in Coles and Weinberg, *Civil Affairs*, pp. 596–98; Harris, *Allied Military Administration of Italy*, pp. 335–37; *FRUS, 1945*, 4:1142–44.
5 *FRUS, 1945*, 4:1149, 1151; Alexander to CCS, 10 May 1945, reprinted in Coles and Weinberg, *Civil Affairs*, p. 598.
6 *FRUS, 1945*, 4:1130–33.
7 Ibid., pp. 1133–35; memorandum by Lincoln to General Hull, 3 May 1945, ABC 387.4 Italy (2 Sep 43), sec. 9-A, ABC Decimal File, 1941–1948, Plans and Operations Division (Army Staff), RG 165, NA; Stimson Diaries, 2 May, 7 May 1945.
8 Truman, *Year of Decisions*, p. 245; *FRUS, 1945*, 4:1128.
9 *FRUS, 1945*, 4:1136, 1139–40, 1142–45, 1148, 1150–51. For a contemporary British evaluation of the State Department's "quite unrealistic" policy, see Macmillan, *War Diaries*, p. 751. Macmillan feared that interdepartmental conflict in Washington and the president's caution might lead to "another Greece—with us carrying the baby, as usual."
10 Ibid., pp. 1132–33.
11 Eden to Macmillan, 5 May 1945, Eden to Washington embassy, 4 May 1945, Foreign Office to Washington embassy, 7 May 1945, Washington embassy to Foreign Office, 7 May 1945, all in WO 204, 44, PRO.
12 *FRUS, 1945* 4:1148.
13 Memorandum by Cannon, 6 May 1945, RG 59, 740.00119 Control (Italy)/5-645, NA.
14 *FRUS, 1945*, 4:1151–53.
15 For varying interpretations of how, why, and when a broad anti-Soviet animus emerged among State Department officers, see Davis, *The Cold War Begins*, pp.

255–87, 369–95; De Santis, *Diplomacy of Silence*, pp. 106–54; Yergin, *Shattered Peace*, pp. 83–91; Gaddis, *The United States and the Origins of the Cold War*, pp. 171–73, 188–236.

16  *FRUS, 1945*, 4:1128, 1154–55; Truman, *Year of Decisions*, pp. 246–47; Messer, *End of an Alliance*, p. 76. For further analyses of how Truman's views on foreign policy were influenced by his advisers in this period, see, for example, Gaddis, *The United States and the Origins of the Cold War*, pp. 198–206; Kuniholm, *Origins of the Cold War in the Near East*, pp. 232–33, 235; Yergin, *Shattered Peace*, pp. 79–86.

17  *FRUS, 1945*, 4:1156–57; Truman, *Year of Decisions*, pp. 247–48; press release, 12 May 1945, *Department of State Bulletin*, 15 May 1945, p. 902. The press statement was probably intended mainly to reassure the Italian government, which had been pressing Washington for action. For a discussion of Rome's efforts to influence British and American policymakers, see de Castro, *La Questione di Trieste*, 1:329–41.

18  *FRUS, 1945*, 4:1157–58; Eden to Churchill, 14 May 1945, WO 204, 44, PRO; Churchill to Truman, 12 May 1945, PREM 3, 495/1, T895/5, PRO.

19  *FRUS, 1945*, 4:1160; Eden to Churchill, 14 May 1945, WO 204, 44, PRO; Truman, *Year of Decisions*, p. 248.

20  Truman Diary, 22 May 1945, reprinted in Messer, *End of an Alliance*, p. 82; Gaddis, *Strategies of Containment*, pp. 15–17.

21  *FRUS, 1945*, 4:1161, 1163–64, 1165–67; Truman, *Year of Decisions*, pp. 248–49.

22  *FRUS, 1945*, 4:1167–68.

23  Ibid., pp. 1168–70. Truman, *Year of Decisions*, p. 249. For Washington's attempts to coordinate its political efforts on this issue with military action, see the memoranda from General George Marshall to Truman of 17 May and 18 May 1945, both in folder 125, Chairman's File (Admiral Leahy), 1942–1948, Records of the United States Joint Chiefs of Staff, RG 218, NA.

24  The unusual and potentially volatile relationship between the two occupying forces in Trieste is described at length in Novak, *Trieste*, pp. 161–94, passim; Cox, *Race for Trieste*, pp. 206–57, passim; Kay, *Italy*, pp. 553–66. See also the intelligence reports on events in Trieste during the Yugoslav occupation in the Confidential File, box 1, Post and Counselor Files, Trieste, Federal Records Center, Suitland, Maryland (hereafter cited as FRC); memorandum by Dunlop, RC, Venezie Region for Executive Commissioner, AC, 13 May 1945, in Coles and Weinberg, *Civil Affairs*, p. 599.

25  Report by Harding on "Influence of Yugoslav Mal-Administration on 13 Corps Troops," 15 May 1945, WO 204, 44, PRO; Alexander to CCS, 17 May 1945, reprinted in part in Coles and Weinberg, *Civil Affairs*, p. 600; Truman, *Year of Decisions*, p. 249. For the views of New Zealand soldiers in Trieste, see Rabel, "Between War and Peace."

26  *FRUS, 1945*, 4:1170–71.

27  Stevenson to Foreign Office, 27 May 1945, WO 204, 44, PRO; *FRUS, 1945*, 4:1175.

For evidence of Moscow's relative indifference, see the conciliatory cable from Stalin to Truman of 23 May 1945, in *FRUS, 1945*, 4:1172–73. Although Truman, *Year of Decisions*, p. 251, wrote that "it disappointed me," the cable was moderate in tone and Stalin was almost perfunctory in his support of Tito. Many writers have, in fact, suggested that disagreement over Trieste was one of the first sources of the Soviet-Yugoslav antagonism which would culminate in the complete break of 1948. See, for example, Armstrong, *Tito and Goliath*, pp. 53, 64–65; Campbell, *Tito's Separate Road*, p. 11; Lendvai, *Eagles in Cobwebs*, p. 82; Maclean, *Disputed Barricade*, pp. 304–7; Dennison Rusinow, *The Yugoslav Experiment, 1948–1974*, p. 16.

28  *FRUS, 1945*, 4:1171–74; memorandum by Grew to Truman, 21 May 1945, RG 59, 740.00119 Control (Italy)/5-2145, NA; Alexander to CCS, 23 May 1945, reprinted in Coles and Weinberg, *Civil Affairs*, pp. 600–601.

29  Memorandum by Jones to Cannon, Matthews, and Phillips, 24 May 1945, 740.00119 Control (Italy)/5-2445, RG 59, NA; memorandum by Grew to Truman, 26 May 1945, 740.00119 Control (Italy)/5-2645, RG 59, NA; Kirk to State Department, 27 May 1945, 740.00119 Control (Italy)/5-2745, RG 59, NA; Alexander to CCS, 27 May 1945, file no. 76 Tito (Yugoslavia), White House Records of Fleet Admiral Leahy, RG 218, NA; Stimson and Forrestal to secretary of state, 29 May 1945, 740.00119 Control (Italy)/5-2945, RG 59, NA; memorandum by Grew to Truman, 29 May 1945, 740.00119 Control (Italy)/5-2945, RG 59, NA; Churchill to Alexander, 29 May, 2 June 1945, PREM 3, 495/8, PRO. Churchill's cables illustrated his conviction that Britain would have to rely on the Americans to counter Soviet expansion now that British power was waning.

30  Patterson to State Department, 2 June 1945, 740.00119 Control (Italy)/5-2945, RG 59, NA; *FRUS, 1945*, 4:1179, 1181–82. Text of Belgrade Agreement on Venezia Giulia between the Yugoslav Foreign Minister and the United States and British Ambassadors, 9 June 1945, reprinted in Coles and Weinberg, *Civil Affairs*, p. 601. See also map 1.

31  In this context Yergin, *Shattered Peace*, p. 91, has noted that "Grew was attempting to have the Trieste issue, a limited and local problem, treated as the first stage in what he saw as the major and inevitable conflict of the postwar years."

32  Kuniholm, *Origins of the Cold War in the Near East*, pp. xix–xx. Cox, *Race for Trieste*, p. 264, has speculated that "the lesson of Trieste" influenced the Truman administration's actions in Iran and Greece in 1946–47, thereby suggesting that the "positive" model described by Kuniholm was itself based on an implicit prototype of Cold War policymaking exemplified in Trieste. He offers no documentary evidence for this claim. See, however, Truman's interview with Herbert Feis on 20 November 1950 at the time of the Korean conflict. The president stated that "he had felt the weight and threat of Soviet aggression steadily during his five years of office. Twice before he had stood up to it—come what might—when Communists were about to march into Trieste and when they were about to go after Iran; . . ." Cited in Feis, *From Trust to Terror*, p. 10.

## Chapter 4

1. For a detailed analysis of the character of AMG in Zone A from 1945 to 1946, see Valdevit, "Politici e militari." Cf. Novak, *Trieste*, pp. 202–33.
2. "Proclamation No. 1," printed in Allied Military Government, Thirteenth Corps, Venezia Giulia, *The Allied Military Government Gazette* 1 (15 September 1945): 3–6 (hereafter cited as *AMG Gazette*); Proposed Supplementary Directive, AFHQ to HQ, Thirteenth Corps and HQ, AC, 29 July 1945, partially reprinted in Coles and Weinberg, *Civil Affairs*, p. 606; Harris, *Allied Military Administration*, pp. 345–46.
3. *FRUS, 1945*, 4:1186–87; appendix 1 of Agreement between Chief of Staff, AFHQ, and the Jugoslav Chief of Staff, 20 June 1945, partially reprinted in Coles and Weinberg, *Civil Affairs*, pp. 601–2. See also Novak, *Trieste*, pp. 200–201; Harris, *Allied Military Administration*, pp. 342–43.
4. The text of the Belgrade agreement is reprinted in Coles and Weinberg, *Civil Affairs*, p. 601. Documentation pertaining to the dispute over article 3 may be found in *FRUS: The Conference of Berlin (the Potsdam Conference), 1945*, 1:842–46.
5. This diplomatic correspondence may be followed in *FRUS: The Conference of Berlin (The Potsdam Conference), 1945*, 1:192–93, 846–54. These documents include a cable from Stalin to Truman on 21 June protesting Anglo-American treatment of Yugoslavia with respect to Trieste.
6. Ibid., pp. 854–56.
7. Directive, AFHQ to HQ, Eighth Army, 26 June 1945, reprinted in part in Coles and Weinberg, *Civil Affairs*, pp. 604–5.
8. "General Order No. 6," 12 July 1945, *AMG Gazette* 1 (15 September 1945): 32; "Notice No. 2," 14 June 1945; ibid., 2 (1 October 1945): 12; Alexander to CCS, 18 July 1945, ABC 387.4 Italy (2 Sept 43), sec. 8-B, RG 165, NA (also reprinted in Coles and Weinberg, *Civil Affairs*, pp. 605–6); Thirteenth Corps Administrative Instructions 12, 5 August 1945, reprinted in Coles and Weinberg, *Civil Affairs*, p. 608; Proposed Supplementary Directive, AFHQ to HQ Thirteenth Corps and HQ, AC 29 July 1945, reprinted in Coles and Weinberg, *Civil Affairs*, p. 606; telephone interview with Alfred Connor Bowman (senior civil affairs officer in Trieste from July 1945 to June 1947), 27 March 1982.
9. Harding to AFHQ, 12 August 1945, TI 304/137/47, file 222, box 2, AMG (Italy), Region XIII: Venezia Giulia, RG 331, FRC. For further evidence of AMG–Venezia Giulia's autonomy from AMG structures in Italy, see Valdevit, "Politici e militari," p. 88. Kirk's comments in *FRUS, 1945*, 4:1192–94.
10. Minutes of a meeting at HQ, AMG, Thirteenth Corps, 28 July 1945, reprinted partially in Coles and Weinberg, *Civil Affairs*, p. 607; "General Order No. 11," *AMG Gazette* 1 (15 September 1945): 45–48; Bowman, *Zones of Strain*, pp. 93–94. General Order No. 11 is also partially reproduced in Coles and Weinberg, *Civil Affairs*, pp. 608–10, accompanied by the observation that it was "an inter-

11  AFHQ to CCS, 25 August 1945, partially reprinted in Coles and Weinberg, *Civil Affairs*, pp. 606–7; Bowman, *Zones of Strain*, p. 92; Bowman telephone interview, 27 March 1982; CCS to SACMED, 29 August 1945, reprinted partially in Coles and Weinberg, *Civil Affairs*, p. 607.
12  Minutes of meeting at AFHQ, Thirteenth Corps, 1 September 1945, partially reprinted in Coles and Weinberg, *Civil Affairs*, p. 610; Bowman, "Venezia Giulia and Trieste," p. 13.
13  Valdevit, "Politici e militari," pp. 91–92; Bowman, SCAO Report, Thirteenth Corps, August 1945, reprinted partially in Coles and Weinberg, *Civil Affairs*, pp. 94–96.
14  Minutes of meeting at HQ, AMG, Thirteenth Corps, 8 September 1945, reprinted partially in Coles and Weinberg, *Civil Affairs*, p. 611; Bowman, SCAO, Thirteenth Corps, report for September 1945, reprinted in ibid., p. 611; Bowman, *Zones of Strain*, pp. 95–96.
15  Lieutenant Colonel D. A. M. Street, Allied Information Service, Trieste, to all section heads, 15 October 1945, 11304/137/47, file 222, AMG (Italy), Region XIII, RG 331, FRC.
16  See Sullivan to Foreign Office, 4 January 1946, and the internal Foreign Office debate on the question in FO 371, 59337, R312/3/92, 530/3/92, PRO.
17  Churchill's speech cited in Gaddis, *The United States and the Origins of the Cold War*, p. 308. The phrase "democracy's vital outpost in Venezia Giulia" was used in a State Department memorandum at about the same time as Churchill's speech. Memorandum by Hawkins to Dowling, 19 February 1946, box 1, Records of Office of Western European Affairs Relating to Italy, 1943–51, lot files, RG 59, NA.
18  Patricia Ward, "James F. Byrnes and the Paris Conferences," in Clements, *Byrnes and the Origins of the Cold War*, p. 60. For general discussions of the significance of the CFM meetings in the development of the Cold War, see Messer, *End of an Alliance*, pp. 115–216, passim; Ward, *Threat of Peace*.
19  Acheson, *Present at the Creation*, p. 194; Campbell, Oral History Interview, Harry S Truman Library. Extensive reports of the CFM meetings concerning Trieste may be found in *FRUS, 1945*, 2; *FRUS, 1946*, 2.
20  *FRUS, 1945*, 2:229–36, 240–42, 248–55; Byrnes, *Speaking Frankly*, pp. 97, 124; Bohlen, *Witness to History*, p. 253; Ward, *Threat of Peace*, p. 30.
21  Byrnes, *Speaking Frankly*, pp. 127–28; Bohlen, *Witness to History*, p. 254; Ward, *Threat of Peace*, pp. 92–93, 95–96, 99; *FRUS,1946*, 2:703–53. For American impressions of Soviet obstinacy, see Campbell Oral History, pp. 86–91.
22  Minute by Colville, 8 May 1946, FO 371, 59502, R6875/307/92, PRO. See also Campbell Oral History, pp. 99, 102–5. Though Soviet and Yugoslav sources are not readily accessible, it became evident in the wake of the Soviet-Yugoslav schism that a lack of sufficient support for Yugoslav claims to Trieste had long been a source of Yugoslav grievances.

23 Campbell Oral History, pp. 60–61; memorandum by Stone to Truman, 18 April 1946, subject file (Italy), President's Secretary's File, Truman Papers. Cf. "United States Support of Italy in the Peace Treaty Negotiations, 1945–1946," Research Project no. 59, April 1948, Division of Historical Policy Research, Department of State, subject file (Italy), PSF, Truman Papers; memorandum by Matthews on United States Policy toward Italy, 10 September 1945, 740.00119 Control (Italy)/9-1045, RG 59, NA.

24 For examples of American perspectives on the significance of the Trieste issue in the Italian peace treaty negotiations, see Campbell Oral History, pp. 92, 101, 109; "United States Support of Italy in the Peace Treaty Negotiations," pp. 3–5, PSF, Truman Papers; memorandum by Stone for Truman, 18 April 1946, subject file (Italy), PSF, Truman Papers; memorandum by Hawkins to Dowling, 19 February 1946, box 1, Records of Office of Western European Affairs Relating to Italy, 1943–51, lot files, RG 59, NA; "Politico-Military Implications of the Venezia Giulia Situation," OPD Study, 13 March 1946, ABC 387.4 Italy (2 Sep 43) sec. 8-C, RG 156, NA. Cf. Lord Inverchapel to Foreign Office, Weekly Political Summary, 22–29 June 1946, FO 371, 51608, AN2107/1/45, PRO. For Italian political pressures on the United States on the Trieste issue, see *FRUS, 1946*, 2:728; memorandum by Matthews to Byrnes et al., 25 May 1946, 760H.6515/5-2546, RG 59, NA; Sir Noel Charles to Foreign Office, 16 May 1946, FO 371, 60705, ZM1666/1286/22, PRO. Key's comment is in *FRUS, 1946*, 2:729.

25 *FRUS, 1945*, 5:1229, 1233, 1266, 1277; *FRUS, 1946*, 6:869–70, 887–88; Acheson to Patterson, 17 May 1946, 740.00119 Control (Italy), RG 59, NA. Examples of Patterson's reporting may be found in *FRUS, 1945*, 5:1291–94, but see also his personal correspondence (which includes evidence of remarkable naiveté on his part) in the Papers of Richard C. Patterson Jr., boxes 1 and 2, Harry S Truman Library. See also Campbell Oral History, pp. 103–5; Bohlen, *Witness to History*, p. 253.

26 For a description of local Slavic-Italian competition to influence the peace negotiations during the 1945–47 period, see Novak, *Trieste*, pp. 252–57; Byington to Department of State, 28 March 1946, 740.00119 Control (Italy)/3-2846, RG 59, NA. For the frontier incidents see, for example, State Department to American embassy, Belgrade, 9 March 1946, 740.00119 Control (Italy)/3-846, RG 59, NA; "Protest against Entry of Yugoslav Forces into Zone A," *Department of State Bulletin* 15 (September 1, 1946): 414–15 (hereafter cited as *DSB*). For Harding's concern and his statement, see *FRUS, 1946*, 6:873–78, 882. For evidence of similar concern in Washington, see the record of a meeting between Byrnes, Forrestal, and Patterson, 8 March 1946, Matthews-Hickerson Files, lot files, RG 59, NA.

27 The fears of American CFM delegates are discussed in Ward, *Threat of Peace*, pp. 104–5. The plane incidents and their effects are described in "Protests against Yugoslav Attack on American Planes and Detention of American Personnel," *DSB* 15 (1 September 1946): 415–19; "Facts Relating to Flights of American

Planes over Yugoslav Territory," *DSB* 15 (15 September 1946): 501–5; Acheson, *Present at the Creation*, pp. 195–96; Byrnes, *Speaking Frankly*, pp. 144–46. For local AMG support for the concept of internationalization, see Valdevit, "Politici e militari," pp. 112–19.

28 Byrnes, *Speaking Frankly*, pp. 132–34; *FRUS, 1946*, 2:570–76, 598–601, 614–16, 703–12, 715–25, 731–38, 752–53; Ward, *Threat of Peace*, pp. 108–13. The United States, of course, was counting on a majority influence at the peace conference.

29 *FRUS, 1946*, 3:689–91, 697–99, 700–702, and passim; *FRUS, 1946*, 4:592–653; Byrnes, *Speaking Frankly*, pp. 147–48; John C. Campbell, letter to author, 22 December 1986; Ward, *Threat of Peace*, p. 147. For the text of the Italian peace treaty, see United States Department of State, *Treaties and Other International Agreements of the United States, 1776–1949*, 4:311–402.

30 *FRUS, 1946*, 2:1113–58, 1166–96, 1200–1226, 1234–78, passim; Ward, *Threat of Peace*, pp. 159–63; Byrnes, *Speaking Frankly*, pp. 151–54; Bohlen, *Witness to History*, pp. 255–56; Campbell, letter to author, 22 December 1986.

31 Italian peace treaty as cited in n. 29 above.

32 LaFeber, *America, Russia, and the Cold War, 1945–1975*, pp. 50–74; Gaddis, *The United States and the Origins of the Cold War*, pp. 323, 346–52; President Truman's address in *Public Papers of the Presidents of the United States: Harry S Truman, 1947*, pp. 176–80; [George F. Kennan] "X," "The Sources of Soviet Conduct," pp. 566–82.

33 *FRUS, 1946*, 4:840–44; *FRUS, 1947*, 4:79; memorandum by McClintock to Rusk, 14 April 1947, 860S.00/1447, RG 59, NA; Novak, *Trieste*, pp. 277–78. Although the United States was partly responsible for the failure to select a governor, John Campbell has noted that "American officials did not, to my knowledge, pre-plan or foresee the impasse over the naming of a governor." Campbell, letter to author, 22 December 1986.

34 Novak, *Trieste*, pp. 259–60; *FRUS, 1947*, 4:80.

35 Memorandum for Record, P & O 092 TS (24 Jul 47), 24 July 1947, ABC 093 Trieste (3 July 1946) sec. 1-C, RG 319, NA; CCS to AFHQ, 17 July 1947, in Coles and Weinberg, *Civil Affairs*, p. 613. For the general relationship between the decline of British power and the acceptance by the United States of an increasing range of international commitments, see Anderson, *The United States, Great Britain, and the Cold War, 1944–1947*, especially pp. 144–84; Hathaway, *Ambiguous Partnership*. Cf. Richard A. Best, Jr., *"Cooperation with Like-Minded Peoples:" British Influence on American Security Policy, 1945–1949*.

36 Bowman, *Zones of Strain*, p. 7.

### Chapter 5

1 "Proclamation No. 1 to the People of the Free Territory of Trieste, British–United States Zone," printed in "Report of the Administration of the British–United

States Zone of the Free Territory of Trieste, 15 September to 31 December 1947, by Major General T. S. Airey, C.B., C.B.E., Commander, British–United States Zone, Free Territory of Trieste," United Nations, Security Council, *Official Records, Supplement for August 1948*, document S/679 (18 February 1948), pp. 41–42 (hereafter cited as *AMG Report*, followed by appropriate document number and date). For the Anglo-American interpretation of the relevant provisions of the Italian peace treaty, see Munnecke, "Legal Challenge," pp. 6–10. See also Novak, *Trieste*, pp. 275–76. See map 2 for the new boundaries of Zone A and Zone B of the FTT.

2. Munnecke, "Legal Challenge," p. 6; memorandum by Joyce of "Meeting at Duino Castle between 8:45 P.M., 15 September, and 12:30 A.M., 16 September 1947," 19 September 1947, 860S.00/9-2247, RG 59, NA.
3. Joyce, "Meeting at Duino," 19 September 1947, 860S.00/9-2247, RG 59, NA; *FRUS, 1947*, 4:98–99.
4. Memorandum by R. H. Hillenkoeter, director of Central Intelligence, 17 September 1947, Document CIADCI RHHLTR 470917, Central Intelligence Agency Records, Washington, D.C.; entry of 15 September 1947, Leahy Diary, Papers of William D. Leahy, Library of Congress, Washington, D.C. (hereafter cited as Leahy Diary).
5. *FRUS, 1947*, 4:98; Leahy Diary, 15 September 1947.
6. Joyce to State Department, 20 September 1947, 860S.00/9-2047, RG 59, SD, NA; FO 371, 61035, AN3245/17/45 and AN3448/17/45, PRO. Interestingly, one of these four congressmen was Richard M. Nixon, future vice president and president of the United States.
7. Joyce to State Department, 20 September 1947, 860S.00/9-1947, RG 59, NA; State Department to Trieste, 22 September 1947, 860.99/9-1947, RG 59, NA.
8. "A Study on Morale and Confidence, Free Territory of Trieste, in Connection with the Planning and Advisory Staff's Memorandum No. AMG/FTT/PL/341/1 of 28 October 1947," by Colonel H. P. P. Robertson, 800 Public Opinion File, Records of the USPOLAD to the commander, British–United States Zone, Free Territory of Trieste, RG 84, FRC. For further evidence of the increasingly anticommunist tenor of AMG see, for example, Joyce to State Department, 20 September 1947, 860S.00/9-2047, RG 59, NA; Joyce to State Department, 5 December 1947, 860S.00/12-547, RG 59, NA.
9. Joyce to State Department, 20 September 1947, 860S.00/9-2047, RG 59, NA; Airey to Sullivan, 4 November 1947, enclosed in Joyce to State Department, November 1947, 801.500, Trieste Post, RG 59, FRC. See also *FRUS, 1947*, 4:122.
10. Joyce to Dowling, 5 September 1947, 860S.00/9-547, RG 59, NA; Airey to Sullivan, 4 November 1947, 801.500, Trieste Post, RG 84, FRC.
11. *FRUS, 1947*, 4:97, 102.
12. Ibid., pp. 118–20, 121–22; Joyce to State Department, 15 November 1947, 801.500, Trieste Post, RG 84, FRC. After meeting with Airey Sullivan withdrew his conclusion.

13  *FRUS, 1947*, 4:122–25.
14  Memorandum from director of Office of European Affairs to Marshall, 14 November 1947, 860S.00/10-3147, RG 59, NA.
15  FO 371, 67345, R15601/10/92, R15729/10/92, PRO.
16  Memorandum from director of Office of European Affairs to Marshall, 14 November 1947, 860S.00/10-3147, RG 59, NA; *FRUS, 1947*, 3:502.
17  Miller, "Taking Off the Gloves," p. 36. Cf. Varsori, "La Gran Bretagna e le elezioni politiche italiane del 18 aprile 1948." For a near contemporary study of this question by an occasional State Department employee who frequently dealt with Trieste, see Campbell, *The United States in World Affairs, 1948–49*, pp. 41–49. Other former State Department officials who dealt with the Trieste issue have also stressed the need to understand the crisis mentality prevailing in American policymaking circles at the time of the Italian election. Telephone interview with Joseph N. Greene, 30 November 1986; telephone interview with Leonard Unger, 9 January 1987.
18  Joyce to State Department, 2 March 1948, 860S.00/3-248, RG 59, NA; *FRUS, 1948*, 3:509–10; minute by G. Campbell, 1 March 1948, in FO 371, 72475, R2634/29/70, PRO; minute by G. Wallinger, 1 March 1948, in FO 371, 72486, R3071/44/70, PRO.
19  Aide-mémoire from British embassy in Washington, 12 March 1948, 860S.00/3-1248, RG 59, NA; FO 371, 72486, R3265/44/70, R3282/44/70, PRO; *FRUS, 1948*, 3:512–14. See also the State Department's cables to the ambassadors in Moscow and Belgrade, 13 March 1948, 860S.00/3-1348, RG 59, NA.
20  *FRUS, 1948*, 3:775–79. Two paragraphs concerning covert actions are omitted in this published version of NSC 1/3. For an original copy, consult box 2, National Security Council Documents, NA. Miller, "Taking Off the Gloves," p. 47, is not necessarily correct in claiming that NSC 1/3 recommended that "the United States support the return to Italy of the Free Territory of Trieste." The document only refers to "Trieste" and does not stipulate whether the United States should favor partition or the return of the *whole* FTT to Italy.
21  Developments during the period from 12 March to 20 March 1948 may be traced in detail in the files numbered 860S.00/3-1248 to 860S.00/3-2048, RG 59, NA. See also *FRUS, 1948*, 3:512–17; FO 371, 72487, PRO.
22  "Statement by the Governments of the U.S., U.K., and France," *DSB* 18 (28 March 1948): 425; *FRUS, 1948*, 3:517–18. The transparency of the Tripartite Proposal's purpose and its possible negative impact were underlined in a Foreign Office minute of 30 April 1948: "In the Cold War, the rallying of Western public opinion is a major consideration; and most people in the West regard our Trieste proposals not as a constructive and justified solution but as a rather shady electoral maneuvre." FO 371, 72491, R5275/44/70, PRO.
23  *FRUS, 1948*, 3:519–20; Novak, *Trieste*, p. 282; *DSB* 18 (25 April 1948): 549. James Miller has noted aptly that "the three-power declaration was a masterstroke of propaganda and diplomacy in that the Soviet Union was forced to side

with its increasingly restive communist ally, Yugoslavia, which claimed the entire area, or support a Western initiative to aid the PCI's chances." This dilemma may explain why the Soviet Union delayed replying to the Tripartite Proposal and based its rejection of the Western move on a procedural question. Miller, "Taking off the Gloves," p. 50, overstates his case when he concludes that "Stalin chose to denounce the Western move and let the PCI suffer the consequences." At the time the Foreign Office cabled Washington that the "Soviet reply avoids acceptance or refusal of our proposal (either of which would be embarrassing to them) by starting a dispute about procedure. Our main objective must be to get the Soviet Government to reveal their opinion on our substantive proposals as soon as possible." FO 371, 72489, R4707/44/70, PRO.

24  Dunn to State Department, 4 April 1948, 860S.00/4-48, RG 59, NA; Caffery to State Department, 18 April 1948, 865.014/4-748, RG 59, NA; *FRUS, 1948*, 1:186; Eden, *Full Circle*, pp. 198–99.

25  Telephone interview with Greene, 30 November 1986; telephone interview with Unger, 9 January 1987; Campbell, letter to author, 22 December 1986. Eden, *Full Circle*, p. 199; *DSB* 18 (18 April 1948): 522; *FRUS, 1948*, 3:522–23; *DSB* 18 (25 April 1948): 549.

26  State Department to Trieste, 7 May 1948, 860S.00/5-748, RG 59, NA; minute by G. T. C. Campbell, 19 May 1948, in FO 371, 72492, R6270/44/70, PRO. Cf. also Joyce to State Department, 7 May 1948, 860S.00/5-748, RG 59, NA.

27  *FRUS, 1948*, 3:559, 563, 568–69, 575. For a more detailed analysis of increased Italian economic influence over Zone A, see Novak, *Trieste*, pp. 283–90.

The Yugoslavs protested that these economic agreements violated the Italian peace treaty. See, for example, "Note to the President of the Security Council," from the government of Yugoslavia, 28 July 1948, Security Council, *Official Records, Supplement for August 1948*, document S/927.

28  *FRUS, 1948*, 3:560–61, 568–69; Joyce to State Department, 5 May 1948, 850 ECA Trieste/850 FTT, Mission to Trieste, Office of the Director, File Programs, Trieste 1948–1949, RG 286, FRC; Airey to Chiefs of Staff, 13 May 1948, P&O 091 Trieste, sec. 1, RG 319, NA.

29  The pro-Italian implications of the changes in AMG structure are set out, for instance, in Joyce to State Department, 16 July 1948, 860S.00/7-1648, RG 59, NA. For Airey's recommendations that the FTT be returned to Italy, see *AMG Report*, S/781 (24 May 1948), p. 64; *AMG Report*, S/953 (6 August 1948), p. 132. More detailed discussion of increased Italian influence on the administration of Zone A may be found in Novak, *Trieste*, pp. 291–98.

30  For general analyses of the Tito-Stalin schism, see Armstrong, *Tito and Goliath*; Dedijer, *The Battle Stalin Lost*. For a documentary record of the immediate origins of the Tito-Stalin break, see Bass and Marbury, *The Soviet-Yugoslav Controversy*, pp. 1–46. See also Halperin, *Triumphant Heretic*, pp. 62–68; Campbell, *Tito's Separate Road*, pp. 10–29.

31  Campbell Oral History, pp. 104–05, 130–31; Charles G. Stefan, "The Emergence

of the Soviet-Yugoslav Break: A Personal View from the Belgrade Embassy;" NSC 18, box 2, National Security Council Documents, NA. The secretary of state approved NSC 18 on 11 July 1948 and the National Security Council concurred in its conclusions on 2 September. This document was the basis for United States policy toward Yugoslavia until mid-1949. For an analysis of the cautious American response, see Lees, "The American Decision to Assist Tito," pp. 409–14.

32  Joyce to State Department, 3 July 1948, 860S.00/7-348, RG 59, NA; Joyce to State Department, 21 July 1948, 860S.00/7-2148, RG 59, NA; State Department to Joyce, 23 July 1948, 860S.00/7-2148, RG 59, NA. Cf. Airey to CCS, 1 December 1948, 860S.00/12-148, RG 59, NA; State Department to Joyce, 2 December 1948, 860S.00/12-148, RG 59, NA; FO 371, 72496, R9565/44/70, PRO.
33  FO 371, 72495, R8311/44/70, PRO.
34  State Department to American embassy, Paris, 21 July 1948, 860S.00/7-1948, RG 59, NA.
35  Baldwin to State Department, 30 December 1948, 860S.00/12-3048, RG 59, NA; memorandum by E. P. Stein, 2 March 1949, 860S.00/3-2949, RG 59, NA; Baldwin to State Department, 860S.00/3-2949, RG 59, NA; *FRUS, 1949*, 4:504–7; State Department to London, 30 July 1948, 860S.00/7-3048, RG 59, NA; *FRUS, 1948*, 3:546–48; *FRUS, 1949*, 4:497–99.
36  Baldwin to State Department, 29 March 1949, 860S.00/3-2949, RG 59, NA. See also the relevant dispatches in the files numbered 860S.00/9-1448 to 860S.00/6-2249, RG 59, NA.
37  Armstrong, *Tito and Goliath*, pp. 88–110; Dedijer, *The Battle Stalin Lost*, pp. 133–216, passim.
38  Campbell Oral History, pp. 131–38; Paterson, *Soviet-American Confrontation*, pp. 140–42; Armstrong, *Tito and Goliath*, pp. 125–26; Halperin, *Triumphant Heretic*, pp. 140–44; Lees, "The American Decision to Assist Tito," pp. 414–22.
39  *FRUS, 1949*, 4:507–11; *FRUS, 1949*, 5:905.
40  *FRUS, 1949*, 4:507–11; *FRUS, 1949*, 5:905; Kirk to State Department, 14 July 1949, 760S.61/7-1449, RG 59, NA; memorandum by Unger of conversation with Lord Jellicoe, 18 July 1949, 860S.00/7-1849, RG 59, NA; memorandum by Greene of conversation with Boyd, 19 October 1949, 860S.00/10-1949, RG 59, NA.
41  *FRUS, 1949*, 4:522–25.
42  Reams to State Department, 2 December 1949, 860S.00/12-149, RG 59, NA; Baldwin to State Department, 11 November 1949, 860S.00/11-1349, RG 59, NA; Major General L. C. Allen to State Department, 8 December 1949, 860S.00/12-849, RG 59, NA.
43  Baldwin to State Department, 11 November 1949, 860S.00/11-1349, RG 59, NA.

### Chapter 6

1  *FRUS, 1950*, 3:1302–3. For the internal Foreign Office discussions leading to the presentation of this aide-mémoire, see FO 371, 88153, RT 1015/1, PRO.

2. Memorandum of conversation by Llewellyn Thompson, 18 January 1950, 750G.00/1-1850, RG 59, NA; *FRUS, 1950,* 3:1305–10. For evidence of some support for the British position within the State Department, see F. Williamson to T. Achilles, 24 January 1950, 750G.00/1-2450, RG 59, NA.
3. *FRUS, 1950,* 3:1310–11.
4. *FRUS, 1950,* 4:1386; *FRUS, 1950,* 3:1311–14. On 9 March an American official in the Rome embassy informed a British colleague that the possibilities of Italo-Yugoslav agreement on a Trieste settlement at the time were as "dead as a doornail." The British appeared to take a similar view even before receiving the American reply to their note of 18 January. FO 371, 88154, RT 1015/46, PRO.
5. Holmes to State Department, 2 February 1950, 750G.00/2-250, RG 59, NA; State Department to London, 20 February 1950, RG 59, NA; *FRUS, 1950,* 3:1303, 1319–22.
6. Unger to State Department, 22 April 1950, 750G.00/4-2250, RG 59, NA. See also Unger to State Department, 3 June 1950, 750G.00/6-250, RG 59, NA. For similar analyses of Soviet motives, see Judd to State Department, 17 March 1950, 750G.00/3-1750; Douglas to State Department, 21 April 1950, 750G.00/4-2150; Kirk to State Department, 22 April 1950, 750G.00/4-2250, all in RG 59, NA.
7. *FRUS, 1950,* 3:1324–25; *FRUS, 1950,* 4:460–65; FO 371, 88161, RT 1015/207; State Department to London, 12 May 1950, 750G.00/5-950, RG 59, NA. The Anglo-American reply to the Soviet note is printed in *DSB* (26 June 1950): 1054–58.
8. Memorandum of conversation by Greene, 24 October 1950, 750G.00/10-2450, RG 59, NA; *FRUS, 1950,* 3:1329–34, 1337–44; FO 371, 88162, RT 1015/236, 244, and 88163, RT 1015/251, PRO.
9. De Castro, *La Questione di Trieste,* 2:3–7; Novak, *Trieste,* pp. 353–55; Campbell Oral History, pp. 140–53. Campbell stresses (p. 51) that Washington was especially concerned in 1950 and 1951 that "the Korean pattern" might be repeated in Yugoslavia. For the evolution of American aid policy toward Yugoslavia, see Brands, "Redefining the Cold War," pp. 41–47.
10. Dunn to State Department, 21 December 1950, 750G.00/12-2150, RG 59, NA; *FRUS, 1951,* 4:218, 221–22; de Castro, *La Questione di Trieste,* 2:7–22.
11. Novak, *Trieste,* p. 358; *FRUS, 1951,* 4:227–28; State Department to Dunn, 10 July 1951, 750G.00/7-1051, RG 59, NA.
12. *FRUS, 1951,* 4:228–36, 238–39, 243; memoranda by Byington of conversations with Porter (British embassy), 24 August 1951, 750G.00/8-2051, and 25 August 1951, 750G.00/8-2551, RG 59, NA; Dunn to State Department, 26 August 1951, 750G.00/8-2651, RG 59, NA; memorandum by Byington of conversation with Luciolli (Italian embassy), 30 August 1951, 750G.00/8-3051, RG 59, NA; memorandum by Byington of conversation with Porter, 30 August 1951, 750G.00/8-3051, RG 59, NA.
13. Dunn to State Department, 4 September 1951, 750G.00/9-451, RG 59, NA; minutes of meetings with De Gasperi, 24–26 September 1951, box 66, Dean Acheson

Papers, Harry S Truman Library, Independence, Missouri (published in *FRUS, 1951*, 4:675–80, 699–703, 713–16); Acheson, *Present at the Creation*, pp. 572–73; de Castro, *La Questione di Trieste*, 2:33–36.

14 *FRUS, 1951*, 4:258, 265–67; memorandum by Perkins to Acheson, 17 January 1952, 750G.00/1-1752, RG 59, NA; State Department to Allen, and enclosures, 24 January 1952, 750G.00/1-2452, RG 59, NA; memorandum by Barbour of conversation with Allen, W. Knight, Byington, and Marcy, 6 March 1952, 750G.00/3-652, RG 59, NA; summary of the secretary's daily meetings, 11 January and 26 March 1952, Records of the Office of the Executive Secretariat, lot files, RG 59, NA. See also Novak, *Trieste*, pp. 361–63; de Castro, *La Questione di Trieste*, 2:114–31.

15 FO 371, 88161, RT 1015/221, and 88166, RT 10110/8, 9, PRO. Cf. Novak, *Trieste*, pp. 350–52.

16 Unger to State Department, 8 June 1950, 750G.00/6-850, RG 59, NA; Dunn to State Department, 21 December 1950, 750G.00/3-951, RG 59, NA; *FRUS, 1950*, 3:1339–42; telephone interview with Greene, 30 November 1986. See also Valdevit, *Questione di Trieste*, pp. 237–41.

17 *FRUS, 1950*, 3:1341. For the AMG's "new" approach, see Novak, *Trieste*, pp. 363–71, passim. Cf. Valdevit, *Questione di Trieste*, pp. 241–42.

18 Higgs to State Department, 23 March 1952, 750G.00/3-2352, RG 59, NA; memorandum by Perkins to Williamson, 25 March 1952, 750G.00/3-2552, RG 59, NA; memorandum by Perkins to Acheson, 25 March 1952, 750G.00/3-2552, RG 59, NA; Higgs to State Department, 28 March 1952, 750G.00/3-2852, RG 59, NA.

19 Gifford to State Department, 2 April 1952, 750G.00/4-252, RG 59, NA; Greene, "Negotiating Paper for London Talks on Zone A Administration of the FTT," 2 April 1952, 750G.00/4-252, RG 59, NA; State Department to Trieste, 28 April 1952, 750G.00/4-2852, RG 59, NA; Holmes to State Department, 7 May 1952, 750G.00/5-752, RG 59, NA. See also Valdevit, *Questione di Trieste*, pp. 247–49; Novak, *Trieste*, pp. 384–404; de Castro, *La Questione di Trieste*, 2:163–246, passim.

20 Higgs to State Department, 27 March 1952, 750G.00/3-2752, RG 59, NA. See also memorandum from Perkins to Acheson, 28 March 1952, 750G.00/3-2852, RG 59, NA, outlining a proposal for the transfer to Italian authority of administration of Zone A. Cf. Valdevit, *Questione di Trieste*, pp. 248–50.

21 Gifford to State Department, 24 and 25 June 1952, 750G.00/6-2452, RG 59, NA; Allen to State Department, 1 July 1952, 750G.00/6-3052, RG 59, NA; State Department to London, 1 August 1952, 750G.00/8-152, RG 59, NA; memorandum by Perkins for acting secretary of state, 20 August 1952, 750G.00/8-2052, RG 59, NA; Allen to State Department, 16 September 1952, 750G.00/9-1652, RG 59, NA. Interestingly, Acheson appeared to feel that Yugoslav obstinacy on Trieste should not be ignored in other areas of Washington's relations with Belgrade. When discussing aid to Yugoslavia with his officials in mid-1952, he observed that "with Trieste as it is . . . we should not rush out to give a great deal to the

194 | Notes

Yugoslavs." Summary of the secretary's daily meeting, 14 July 1952, Records of the Office of the Executive Secretariat, lot files, RG 59, NA.

22  Eden, *Full Circle*, pp. 200–203. Ironically, the Trieste dispute would be resolved two years later in a manner corresponding almost exactly to this British proposal of late 1952. State Department to London, 30 September 1952, 750G.00/9-3052, RG 59, NA; State Department to London, 8 October 1952, 750G.00/10-852, RG 59, NA.

23  Memorandum by Perkins for acting secretary of state, 16 October 1952, 750G.00/10-1652, RG 59, NA; memorandum by Matthews of conversation with R. B. Knight and Ambassador Tarchiani, 12 November 1952, 750G.00/11-1252, RG 59, NA. Eden, *Full Circle*, p. 203, suggests that the Italian government was quite aware of its bargaining strength with the Americans and he notes that "he was not surprised" when the American approach to Rome in December failed.

24  State Department to London, 3 December 1952, 750G.00/12-252, RG 59, NA; State Department to Rome, 6 December 1952, 750G.00/12-652, RG 59, NA; Dunn to State Department, 17 December 1952, 750G.00/12-1752, RG 59, NA; State Department to London, 23 December 1952, 750G.00/12-1752, RG 59, NA; de Castro, *La Questione di Trieste*, 2:346–57, passim.

25  Bunker to State Department, 23 January 1953, 750G.00/1-2353, RG 59, NA; memorandum by Bonbright for Matthews, 23 January 1953, 750G.00/1-2353, RG 59, NA; State Department to Bunker, 26 January 1953, 750G.00/1-2653, RG 59, NA.

26  For Tarchiani's original suggestion, see the memorandum by Byington of conversation with Matthews and Tarchiani, 28 January 1953, RG 59, NA; State Department to Rome, 27 February 1953, 750G.00/2-453, RG 59, NA; Bunker to State Department, 26 March 1953, 750G.00/3-653, RG 59, NA; memorandum by Bonbright for Dulles, 20 April 1953, 750G.00/4-2053, RG 59, NA; Dillon to State Department, 24 April 1953, 750G.00/4-2453, RG 59, NA; State Department to Rome, 14 May 1953, 750G.00/5-1453, RG 59, NA; memorandum by Byington of conversation with Beeley (British embassy), 19 May 1953, 750G.00/5-1953, RG 59, NA. See also Novak, *Trieste*, pp. 416–17; de Castro, *Questione di Trieste*, 2:461–85, passim.

27  Memorandum by Byington for Wainhouse, 3 July 1953, 750G.00/7-253, RG 59, NA; Dwight D. Eisenhower, *Mandate for Change*, p. 413; telephone conversation, 5 September 1953, box 5, Dwight D. Eisenhower Diary Series, Ann Whitman File, Dwight D. Eisenhower Papers, Dwight D. Eisenhower Library, Abilene, Kansas (hereafter cited as DDE Diary); Novak, *Trieste*, pp. 418–35; memorandum by W. Knight of conversation with Sensi (Italian embassy), 2 September 1953, 750G.00/9-253, RG 59, NA.

28  State Department to Rome, 30 August 1953, 750G.00/8-2953, RG 59, NA; memorandum by W. Knight of conversation with Merchant and Luciolli, 1 September 1953, 750G.00/9-153, RG 59, NA; State Department to Rome, 2 September 1953, 750G.00/9-253, RG 59, NA.

29  For general accounts of Luce's career (including references to her role in the final stages of the Trieste dispute), see Hatch, *Ambassador Extraordinary*; Shadegg, *Clare Boothe Luce*. Both biographies were written with her assistance and are highly favorable portraits of her public career. Although Luce was arguably the leading female Cold Warrior of her time, a critical, scholarly biography of this significant figure remains to be written.

C. D. Jackson was also a relatively influential Cold Warrior whose career has, until recently, not attracted scholarly attention. See Cook, *Declassified Eisenhower*, pp. 122–31, 178–81, 193–95, and passim. Cook bases her brief analysis of Jackson's activities on his personal papers, now housed in the Eisenhower Library.

30  Luce, cited in Hatch, *Ambassador Extraordinary*, p. 226. See also ibid., pp. 205, 215–19; Cook, *Declassified Eisenhower*, pp. 192–94; Shadegg, *Clare Boothe Luce*, p. 243. For an Italian view that the major factor in the 1953 election outcome was the desire for "a patriotic satisfaction on the vital question of Trieste," see Tarchiani to Matthews, 16 June 1953, 750G.00/6-1653, RG 59, NA.

31  Luce to State Department, nos. 765 and 782, 4 September 1953, 750G.00/9-453, RG 59, NA.

32  Telephone conversation, Eisenhower and Dulles, 5 September 1953, box 5, DDE Diary; Luce to Jackson, and enclosure, 7 September 1953, box 57, C. D. Jackson Papers, Dwight D. Eisenhower Library, Abilene, Kansas. Luce's "poem" has been published in Cook, *Declassified Eisenhower*, p. 193; and Shadegg, *Clare Boothe Luce*, p. 247 (with variations). Eisenhower, *Mandate for Change*, p. 409, even cites it in his memoirs.

33  Memorandum by Jackson for Eisenhower, 29 September 1953; memorandum by Eisenhower for Dulles, 30 September 1953, all in box 1, Dulles-Herter Series, Whitman File, Dwight D. Eisenhower Papers (hereafter cited as DDE Papers).

34  State Department to London, 11 September 1953, 750G.00/9-1153, RG 59, NA; Aldrich to State Department, 16 September 1953, 750G.00/9-1653, RG 59, NA; State Department to London, 24 September 1953, 750G.00/9-2453, RG 59, NA; memorandum by Scott to Dulles, 25 September 1953, 750G.00/9-2553, RG 59, NA; memorandum by Scott to Dulles, 28 September 1953, 750G.00/9-2853, RG 59, NA; memorandum by Nes of conversation with Byington, Barbour, Freund, W. Knight, Cheetham (Foreign Office), and Salt (British embassy), 1 October 1953, 750G.00/10-153, RG 59, NA; memorandum by Nes of conversation with Byington, Freund, Knight, Cheetham, and Salt, 2 October 1953, 750G.00/10-253, RG 59, NA; State Department to Rome, 6 October 1953, 750G.00/10-653, RG 59, NA; State Department to Belgrade, 6 October 1953, 750G.00/10-653, RG 59, NA; Wallner to State Department, 8 October 1953, 750G.00/10-853, RG 59, NA. Eden, *Full Circle*, pp. 204–5; Novak, *Trieste*, pp. 427–28. The text of the announcement of 8 October 1953 is reprinted in *DSB* 19 (19 October 1953): 529.

35  Eisenhower Diary Notes, 8 October 1953, box 4, DDE Diary. Also reprinted in Eisenhower, *Mandate for Change*, p. 414.

36  Luce to State Department, 10 October 1953, 750G.00/10-1053, RG 59, NA; Wallner

to State Department, 13 October 1953, 750G.00/10-1353, RG 59, NA; Wallner to State Department, 9 October 1953, 750G.00/10-953, RG 59, NA; Wallner to State Department, 10 October 1953, 750G.00/10-1053, RG 59, NA; memorandum by Barbour of conversation with Dulles, Merchant, K. Popović (Yugoslav foreign minister), V. Popović (Yugoslav ambassador), and M. Bruner (Yugoslav embassy).

37  Halperin, *Triumphant Heretic*, pp. 160–61; Eisenhower, *Mandate for Change*, p. 414.

38  Memorandum by Barbour of conversation with Dulles, Merchant, K. Popović, V. Popović, and Bruner, 12 October 1953, 750G.00/10-1253, RG 59, NA; memorandum by Barbour of conversation with Dulles, Merchant, K. Popović, and V. Popović, 13 October 1953, 750G.00/10-1353, RG 59, NA; Eden, *Full Circle*, p. 205.

39  Luce to State Department, 18 October 1953, 750G.00/10-1853, RG 59, NA; memorandum by Barbour of conversation with Dulles, Merchant, V. Popović, and Bruner, 20 October 1953, 750G.00/10-2053, RG 59, NA; memorandum by Byington of conversation with Eisenhower, Dulles, Secretary of Defense Wilson, Admiral Radford, Cutler, and Merchant, 22 October 1953, with attached memorandum for Eisenhower from Dulles, 750G.00/10-2253, RG 59, NA; Bohlen to State Department, 13 October 1953, 750G.00/10-1353, RG 59, NA; Bohlen to State Department, 18 October 1953, 750G.00/10-1853, RG 59, NA. See also Novak, *Trieste*, pp. 433–35, 448–49; de Castro, *La Questione di Trieste*, 2:585–650, passim.

40  State Department to Rome, 26 October 1953, 750G.00/10-2653, RG 59, NA; memorandum by Merchant to Dulles, 26 October 1953, 750G.00/10-2653, RG 59, NA; memorandum by Merchant of conversation with Dulles and Makins (British ambassador), 26 October 1953, 750G.00/10-2653, RG 59, NA; State Department to Belgrade, 30 October 1953, 750G.00/10-3053, RG 59, NA. The painstaking process by which the State Department tried to lay down the groundwork for a five-power conference may be traced in detail in the files for November and December 1953 in 750G.00, RG 59, NA. For a detailed report on the Trieste riots, see Unger to State Department, 18 November 1953, 750G.00/11-1853, RG 59, NA.

41  For the original suggestion and its evolution see State Department to Rome and Belgrade, 2 November 1953, 750G.00/11-253, RG 59, NA; State Department to Belgrade, 24 November 1953, 750G.00/11-2453, RG 59, NA; memorandum by Nes of conversation with Barbour, Byington, Holmes, Salt, and Ruffin (French embassy), 26 November 1953, 750G.00/11-2653, RG 59, NA; State Department to Belgrade, 5 December 1953, 750G.00/12-553, RG 59, NA; State Department to Rome, 28 December 1953, 750G.00/12-2253, RG 59, NA; memorandum by Merchant to Dulles, 31 December 1953, 750G.00/12-3153, RG 59, NA; Durbrow to State Department, 7 January 1953, 750G.00/1-754, RG 59, NA; Riddleberger to State Department, 15 January 1953, 750G.00/1-1554, RG 59, NA.

The background and course of the negotiations are described by firsthand participants in Eden, *Full Circle*, pp. 205-9; Campbell, *Successful Negotiation*, pp. 23-144, passim. Eden, *Full Circle*, p. 209, described the outcome of this negotiating process as "a classic example of the true function of diplomacy, an open agreement secretly arrived at."

42  Letter of instructions from Acting Secretary of State W. B. Smith to Thompson, 28 January 1954, 750G.00/1-2854, RG 59, NA (published in Campbell, *Successful Negotiation*, pp. 170–74).

43  Campbell, *Successful Negotiation*, pp. 170–74.

44  Campbell, *Successful Negotiation*, pp. 26–28 and passim; Eden, *Full Circle*, p. 207. Thompson described the State Department's initial instructions as "hopeless." He believed that "basically they were favorable to Italy and did not give us room to negotiate with the Yugoslavs." Campbell, *Successful Negotiation*, p. 26. Leonard Unger, Thompson's "expert" adviser during the talks, has also expressed the same view (telephone interview with Unger, 9 January 1987). See also State Department to London, 25 February 1954, 750G.00/2-1354, RG 59, NA.

45  Campbell, *Successful Negotiation*, passim; Eden, *Full Circle*, p. 207; copy of Agreed Record of Positions Reached at Discussions between the U.S., U.K., and Yugoslavia in London, 2 February–31 May 1954, in Butterworth to State Department, 2 June 1954, 750G.00/6-254, RG 59, NA. One of the American negotiators in London has recently confirmed that the offer of economic assistance was indeed a key factor in securing Yugoslav agreement to the compromise on Trieste — not only because of the actual money involved but also because of its symbolic importance as an indication that the United States was willing to be friendly toward Yugoslavia and assist it with its economic problems. Telephone interview with Unger, 9 January 1987.

46  State Department to Rome, 4 June 1954, 750G.00/6-454, RG 59, NA; memorandum by Merchant to Dulles, 1 July 1954, 750G.00/7-154, RG 59, NA; memorandum by Elbrick to Dulles, 19 July 1954, 750G.00/7-1954, RG 59, NA; Campbell, *Successful Negotiation*, pp. 18, 62–63, 99, 116–17; Novak, *Trieste*, pp. 453–54.

47  Velebit and Brosio, cited in Campbell, *Successful Negotiation*, pp. 99, 102, 103, 116; Eisenhower, *Mandate for Change*, p. 417; telephone interview with Unger, 9 January 1987. Ironically, *sottile* means "subtle" in Italian. Memorandum by Elbrick to Dulles, 3 August 1954, 750G.00/8-354, RG 59, NA.

48  Memorandum by Collins to Tyler, 10 August 1954, 750G.00/8-1054, RG 59, NA; Luce to Eisenhower, 31 August 1954, published partially in Eisenhower, *Mandate for Change*, pp. 417–18; Eisenhower to Smith, 3 September 1954, Dulles-Herter Series, Whitman File, DDE Papers (also published partially in Eisenhower, *Mandate for Change*, p. 419).

49  Shadegg, *Clare Boothe Luce*, pp. 250–52; Campbell, *Successful Negotiation*, pp. 128–29, 131–32; Robert Murphy, *Diplomat among Warriors*, p. 422. As Luce's personal papers remain closed to most scholars, Shadegg's improbable but intriguing account of the anonymous informant who called on Luce in Rome cannot be corroborated from other sources. See also memorandum by Merchant to Smith, 2 September 1954, 750G.00/9-254, RG 59, NA.

50  Smith to Eisenhower, 3 September 1954; Eisenhower to Smith, 6 September

1954; Smith to Eisenhower, 10 September 1954, all in box 3, Dulles-Herter Series, Whitman File, DDE Papers.

51 Murphy, *Diplomat among Warriors*, pp. 423–24; Eisenhower's letter is reprinted in Campbell, *Successful Negotiation*, pp. 422–25; Murphy to State Department, 20 September 1954, 750G.00/9-2054, RG 59, NA; memorandum by Scott to Dulles, 25 September 1954, 750G.00/9-2554, RG 59, NA.

52 Thompson's diplomatic skills were also recently stressed by Leonard Unger, as was the fact that Luce and the pro-Italian lobby within American policymaking circles placed considerable pressure on the negotiators in London to obtain concessions for Italy (telephone interview with Unger, 9 January 1987). Eisenhower to Thompson, 7 October 1954, 750G.00/10-954, RG 59, NA; Luce to State Department for Thompson, 5 October 1954, 750G.00/10-554, RG 59, NA. For studies of the Trieste talks, see Campbell, *Successful Negotiation*; Duroselle, *Conflit de Trieste*. Leonard Unger is also completing a brief study of those talks to be published by the Johns Hopkins University Press.

53 For the detailed terms of the settlement, see "Memorandum of Understanding between the Governments of Italy, the United Kingdom of Great Britain and Northern Ireland, the United States of America, and Yugoslavia Regarding the Free Territory of Trieste," United Nations, Treaty Series, vol. 235 (1956), no. 3297. Also printed in Campbell, *Successful Negotiation*, pp. 154–67. For the new Italo-Yugoslav frontier of 1954, see map 2.

54 For the Soviet reaction, see Bohlen to State Department, 14 October 1954, 750G.00/10-1454, RG 59, NA; Luce to State Department, 20 October 1954, 750G.00/10-2054, RG 59, NA.

55 Novak, *Trieste*, pp. 466–68.

56 Campbell, *Successful Negotiation*, pp. 20–21; *Keesings Contemporary Archives* 21 (17–23 November 1975): 27452.

57 Remarks by the Honorable John Foster Dulles at a pre-Columbus Day celebration in New York, 11 October 1954, box 88, Selected Correspondence and Related Materials, John Foster Dulles Papers, Princeton University, Princeton, N.J. (hereafter cited as Dulles Papers).

58 Eisenhower, *Mandate for Change*, p. 419; remarks by Dulles in New York, 11 October 1954, box 88, Selected Correspondence and Related Materials, Dulles Papers. See also press statement on Trieste agreement, 5 October 1954, and press release of message to Italian Foreign Ministers, 6 October 1954, in box 88, Selected Correspondence and Related Materials, Dulles Papers.

# Bibliography

**Archives and Manuscript Collections**

Duke University, Durham, North Carolina

George Allen Papers. Thomas Nelson Page Papers.

Library of Congress, Washington, D.C.

Ray Stannard Baker Papers. Robert Lansing Papers. William Leahy Papers.

National Archives, Diplomatic Branch, Washington, D.C.

*Record Group 59.* Central Decimal File. Matthews-Hickerson Files. Harley Notter Papers. Office of Strategic Services, Reports. Office of the Executive Secretariat, Records. Office of Western European Affairs, Records Relating to Italy, 1943–1952. Myron Taylor Papers.

*Record Group 353.* Secretary of State's Committee, Records, 1944–1947 (Microfilm: M-1054).

National Archives, Dwight D. Eisenhower Library, Abilene, Kansas

John Foster Dulles Papers. Dwight D. Eisenhower Papers. C. D. Jackson Papers. White House Office: Office of the Special Assistant for National Security Affairs, Records, 1952–1961.

## National Archives, Federal Records Center, Suitland, Maryland

*Record Group 84.* United States Political Adviser to the Commander, British/United States Zone, Free Territory of Trieste, Records.
*Record Group 331.* Allied Military Government (Italy): Region XIII (Venezia Giulia), Files.

## National Archives, Modern Military Branch, Washington, D.C.

*National Security Council, Records.*
*Record Group 165.* Operations Division Files.
*Record Group 218.* United States Joint Chiefs of Staff, Records. White House Records of Fleet Admiral William D. Leahy (Leahy Papers).
*Record Group 226.* Office of Strategic Services, Reports, 1941–1946.
*Record Group 319.* ABC Files, 1942–1948. Plans and Operations Files, 1946–1950.

## National Archives, Harry S Truman Library, Independence, Missouri

Dean Acheson Papers. Richard C. Patterson, Jr., Papers. Henry L. Stimson Papers (microfilm). Myron C. Taylor Papers. Harry S Truman Papers.

## New Zealand National Archives, Wellington, New Zealand

External Affairs Files. World War II Archives.

## Public Record Office, London, England

*Cabinet Office Records.* CAB 65: War Cabinet Minutes. CAB 66: War Cabinet Memoranda. CAB 80: Chiefs of Staff Committee. CAB 81: Post-hostilities Planning Subcommittee. CAB 87: Armistice and Post-war Committee.
*Foreign Office Records.* FO 371: General Correspondence. FO 842: Consular Files, Trieste.
*Prime Minister's Office Records.* PREM 3: Prime Minister.
*War Office Records.* WO 106: Directorate of Military Operations and Intelligence. WO 202: Military Headquarters Papers: Military Missions. WO 204: Military Headquarters Papers: Allied Force Headquarters.

## Princeton University, Princeton, N.J.

Allen W. Dulles Papers. John Foster Dulles Papers. Robert Lansing Selected Papers.

### Interviews and Letters

Alfred Connor Bowman, telephone interview, 27 March 1982. John C. Campbell, letter to the author, 22 December 1986. Joseph N. Greene, telephone interview, 30 November 1986. Leonard Unger, telephone interview, 9 January 1987.

### Oral Histories

National Archives, Harry S Truman Library, Independence, Missouri

John C. Campbell. John Wesley Jones. James W. Riddleberger.

Princeton University, Princeton, N.J.

Julius C. Holmes. Livingston T. Merchant. James W. Riddleberger. Llewellyn Thompson.

United States Army Military History Institute, Carlisle, Pennsylvania

Charles Bolte. Paul W. Caraway. Mark W. Clark. Clyde D. Eddleman. William M. Hoge.

### Other Unpublished Materials

Black, Gregory Dale. "The United States and Italy, 1943–1946: The Drift towards Containment." Ph.D. dissertation, University of Kansas, 1973.

Conrad, Allison Alan. "Allied Military Government of Venezia Giulia and Trieste —Its History and Organization." M.A. thesis, University of Maryland, 1956.

Heim, Keith Merle. "Hope without Power: Truman and the Russians, 1945." Ph.D. dissertation, University of North Carolina at Chapel Hill, 1973.

Lees, Lorraine Mary. "American Foreign Policy towards Yugoslavia, 1941–1949." Ph.D. dissertation, The Pennsylvania State University, 1976.

Modisett, Lawrence E. "The Four-Cornered Triangle: British and American Policy towards Yugoslavia, 1939–1945." 2 vols. Ph.D. dissertation, Georgetown University, 1981.

Pallante, Pierluigi. "Concezioni e posizioni del PCI sulla questione nazionale durante la guerra di liberazione." Paper presented to the Convegno di Studi Storici Italo-jugoslavi, Trieste, Italy, November 1986.

Rabel, Roberto. "Between East and West: Trieste, the United States and the Cold War, 1943–1954." Ph.D. dissertation, Duke University, 1984.

———. "American Liberal Internationalism and European Frontiermaking: A Comparative Study of United States Responses to the Fiume Problem of 1918–19 and the Trieste Crisis of Mid-1945." Paper presented to the Australian and New Zealand American Studies Association Conference, Auckland, New Zealand, May 1986.

———. "Between War and Peace: The New Zealand Experience in Trieste, May–June 1945." Paper presented to the New Zealand Historical Association Conference, Palmerston North, New Zealand, February 1987.

Radovanovic, Connie Kovac. "American Attitudes toward the Wartime Resistance in Yugoslavia, 1941–1945." Ph.D. dissertation, University of Alabama, 1982.

Terzuolo, Eric Robert. "Relations between the Communist Parties of Italy and Yugoslavia, 1941–1960." Ph.D. dissertation, Stanford University, 1980.

**Public Documents and Papers, Documentary Collections, Official Publications, and Pamphlets**

Allied Military Government, British/United States Zone, Free Territory of Trieste (Public Information Division). *Trieste Handbook*. Trieste: Allied Military Government, British/United States Zone, Free Territory of Trieste, 1949.

Allied Military Government, British/United States Zone, Free Territory of Trieste (Information and Public Relations Division). *Trieste Handbook*. Rev. ed. Trieste: Allied Military Government, British/United States Zone, Free Territory of Trieste, 1950.

Allied Military Government, Thirteenth Corps, Venezia Giulia. *The Allied Military Government Gazette*. 2 vols. Trieste: Allied Military Government, Thirteenth Corps, Venezia Giulia, September 1945–September 1947.

Bass, Robert, and Elizabeth Marbury, eds. *The Soviet-Yugoslav Controversy, 1948–58: A Documentary Record*. New York: Prospect Books, 1959.

Clissold, Stephen, ed. *Yugoslavia and the Soviet Union, 1939–1973: A Documentary Survey*. London: Oxford University Press for the Royal Institute of International Affairs, 1975.

Coles, Harry L., and Albert K. Weinberg. *Civil Affairs: Soldiers Become Governors*. Washington, D.C.: Office of the Chief of Military History, Department of the Army, 1964.

*Documents Relating to New Zealand's Participation in the Second World War, 1939–1945*. Vol. 2. Wellington: War History Branch, Department of Internal Affairs, 1951.

Economic Cooperation Administration, European Recovery Program. *Trieste—Country Study*. Washington, D.C.: Government Printing Office, 1949.

Harris, C. R. S. *Allied Military Administration of Italy, 1943–1945*. London: Her Majesty's Stationery Office, 1957.

Kardelj, Edvard. *Trieste and Yugoslav-Italian Relations*. New York: Yugoslav Information Center, 1953.

Kay, Robin. *Official History of New Zealand in the Second World War, 1939–1945: Italy*. Vol. 2, *From Cassino to Trieste*. Wellington: Historical Publications Branch, Department of Internal Affairs, 1967.

Komer, Robert W. *Civil Affairs and Military Government in the Mediterranean Theater*. Washington, D.C.: Office of the Chief of Military History, Department of the Army, 1948.

Mantoux, Paul. *Les Délibérations du Conseil des Quatre (24 mars–28 juin 1919)*. 2 vols. Paris: Editions du Centre National de la Recherche Scientifique, 1955.

Michel, Paul Henri. *La Question de l'Adriatique (1914–1918): Recueil de Documents*. Paris: Alfred Costes, 1938.

*Public Papers of the Presidents of the United States. Harry S Truman*. 6 vols. Washington, D.C.: Government Printing Office, 1961–65.

Rosenman, Samuel I., ed. *The Public Papers and Addresses of Franklin D. Roosevelt, 1928–1945*. 13 vols. New York: Harper, 1938–1950.

United Nations, Security Council. Quarterly Reports on "... the Administration of the British–United States Zone of the Free Territory of Trieste ... by Major General T. S. Airey ..." *United Nations Security Council Official Records*, 1948–1951. Documents S/679 (February 18, 1948), S/781 (May 25, 1948), S/953 (August 6, 1948), S/1174 (January 5, 1949), S/1242 (February 3, 1949), S/1318 (May 6, 1949), S/1374 (August 11, 1949), S/1473 (March 9, 1950), S/2062 (March 29, 1951).

United States, Department of State. *The Department of State Bulletin*, 1945–1954.

―――. *Foreign Relations of the United States*. Annual vols., 1914–1919, 1941–1951. Washington, D.C.: Government Printing Office, 1928–1933, 1958–1977.

―――. *Foreign Relations of the United States: The Conference of Berlin (The Potsdam Conference), 1945*. 2 vols. Washington, D.C.: Government Printing Office, 1960.

―――. *Foreign Relations of the United States: The Conferences at Cairo and Teheran, 1943*. Washington, D.C.: Government Printing Office, 1961.

―――. *Foreign Relations of the United States: The Conferences at Malta and Yalta, 1945*. Washington, D.C.: Government Printing Office, 1955.

―――. *Foreign Relations of the United States: The Conferences at Washington and Quebec, 1943*. Washington, D.C.: Government Printing Office, 1970.

―――. *Foreign Relations of the United States: The Paris Peace Conference*. Vols. 1–9, 11–12. Washington, D.C.: Government Printing Office, 1942–1947.

―――. *Treaties and Other International Agreements of the United States, 1776–1949*. Vol. 4. Compiled by Charles I. Bevans. Department of State Publication No. 8512. Washington: Government Printing Office, 1970.

Woodward, Llewellyn. *British Foreign Policy in the Second World War*. 5 vols. London: Her Majesty's Stationery Office, 1970–1976.

**Memoirs, Autobiographies, Diaries, and Correspondence**

Acheson, Dean. *Present at the Creation: My Years in the State Department*. New York: Norton, 1969.

Alexander, Field Marshal Sir Harold, Earl of Tunis. *The Alexander Memoirs, 1940–1945*. Edited by John North. New York: McGraw-Hill, 1962.
Baker, Ray Stannard. *Woodrow Wilson and World Settlement*. 3 vols. Garden City, N.Y.: Doubleday, Page, 1922–1923.
———. *Woodrow Wilson, Life and Letters*. 8 vols. New York: Doubleday, Doran, 1927–1939.
Bohlen, Charles E. *Witness to History, 1929–1969*. New York: Norton, 1973.
Bowman, Alfred Connor. *Zones of Strain: A Memoir of the Early Cold War*. Stanford, Calif.: Hoover Institution Press, 1982.
Byrnes, James F. *Speaking Frankly*. New York: Harper, 1947.
Churchill, Winston. *Triumph and Tragedy*. London: Cassell, 1954.
Cox, Geoffrey. *The Road to Trieste*. London: William Heinemann, 1947.
Dedijer, Vladimir. *The Battle Stalin Lost: Memoirs of Yugoslavia, 1948–1953*. New York: Viking, 1971.
De Simone, Pasquale. *Memorie sull'Istria della Resistenza e dell'Esodo*. Gorizia: Budin, 1971.
Djilas, Milovan. *Conversations with Stalin*. New York: Harcourt, Brace and World, 1962.
Eden, Anthony. *Full Circle: The Memoirs of Anthony Eden*. Boston: Houghton Mifflin, 1960.
Eisenhower, Dwight D. *Mandate for Change, 1953–1956: The White House Years*. Garden City, N.Y.: Doubleday, 1963.
Giolitti, Giovanni. *Memoirs of My Life*. Translated by Edward Storer. London: Chapman and Dodd, 1923.
Grew, Joseph G. *Turbulent Era: A Diplomatic Record of Forty Years, 1904–1945*. 2 vols. Boston: Houghton Mifflin, 1952.
House, Edward Mandell, and Charles Seymour, eds. *What Really Happened at Paris: The Story of the Paris Peace Conference, 1918–1919, by American Delegates*. New York: Scribners, 1921.
Hull, Cordell. *The Memoirs of Cordell Hull*. 2 vols. New York: Macmillan, 1948.
Kimball, Warren, ed. *Churchill and Roosevelt: The Complete Correspondence*. 3 vols. Princeton, N.J.: Princeton University Press, 1984.
Leahy, William. *I Was There*. New York: McGraw-Hill, 1950.
Macmillan, Harold. *War Diaries: Politics and War in the Mediterranean, January 1943–May 1945*. London: Macmillan, 1984.
Murphy, Robert. *Diplomat Among Warriors*. New York: Doubleday, 1964.
Salandra, Antonio. *L'intervento [1915]: Ricordi e pensieri*. Verona: Mondadori, 1930.
———. *La neutralità italiana [1914]: Ricordi e pensieri*. Milan: Mondadori, 1928.
Seymour, Charles, ed. *The Intimate Papers of Colonel House*. 4 vols. Boston: Houghton Mifflin, 1926–1928.
Speranza, Gino. *The Diary of Gino Speranza: Italy, 1915–1919*. Edited by Florence Colgate Speranza. 2 vols. New York: Columbia University Press, 1941.
Tarchiani, Alberto. *Dieci anni tra Roma e Washington*. Verona: Mondadori, 1955.

Truman, Harry S. *Memoirs*. Vol. 1: *Year of Decisions*. New York: Doubleday, 1955.
Wilson, Woodrow. *The Papers of Woodrow Wilson*. Edited by Arthur S. Link. Princeton, N.J.: Princeton University Press, 1966–.

### Secondary Works

Books

Albrecht-Carrié, René. *Italy at the Paris Peace Conference*. New York: Columbia University Press, 1938.
Anderson, Terry H. *The United States, Great Britain, and the Cold War, 1944–1947*. Columbia and London: University of Missouri Press, 1981.
Apih, Elio. *Italia: Fascismo e antifascismo nella Venezia Giulia (1918–1943)*. Bari: Laterza, 1966.
Armstrong, Hamilton Fish. *Tito and Goliath*. New York: Macmillan, 1951.
Auty, Phyllis and Richard Clogg, eds. *British Policy towards Wartime Resistance in Yugoslavia and Greece*. New York: Harper and Row, 1975.
Barker, Elisabeth. *British Policy in South-East Europe in the Second World War*. New York: Harper and Row, 1976.
Best, Richard A., Jr. *"Cooperation with Like-Minded Peoples:" British Influences on American Security Policy, 1945–1949*. Westport, Conn.: Greenwood Press, 1986.
Birdsall, Paul. *Versailles Twenty Years After*. New York: Reynal, 1941.
Bosworth, R. J. B. *Italy, the Least of the Great Powers: Italian Foreign Policy before the First World War*. London: Cambridge University Press, 1979.
———. *Italy and the Approach of the First World War*. London: Macmillan, 1983.
Braudel, Fernand. *The Mediterranean and the Mediterranean World in the Age of Philip II*. 2 vols. New York: Harper and Row, 1973.
Campbell, John C. *Tito's Separate Road: America and Yugoslavia in World Politics*. New York: Harper and Row, 1967.
———. *The United States in World Affairs, 1948–1949*. New York: Harper, 1949.
———, ed. *Successful Negotiation: Trieste 1954*. Princeton, N.J.: Princeton University Press, 1976.
Čermelj, Lavo. *Life-and-Death Struggle of a National Minority: The Yugoslavs in Italy*. Translated by F. C. Copeland. 2d ed. Ljubljana: Tiskarna Ljudske Pravise, 1945.
Clements, Kendrick A., ed. *James F. Byrnes and the Origins of the Cold War*. Durham, N.C.: Carolina Academic Press, 1982.
Coceani, Bruno. *Mussolini, Hitler, Tito alle porte orientali d'Italia*. Bologna: Cappelli, 1948.
Collotti, Enzo. *Il littorale adriatico nel Nuovo Ordine Europeo, 1943–1945*. Milan: Vangelista, 1974.
Colummi, Christiana; Lilliana Ferrari; Gianna Nassisi; and Germano Trani. *Storia di un esodo: Istria, 1945–1956*. Trieste: Istituto Regionale per la Storia del

Movimento di Liberazione nel Friuli–Venezia Giulia, 1980.
Cook, Blanche Wiesen. *The Declassified Eisenhower: A Divided Legacy.* New York: Doubleday, 1981.
Cox, Geoffrey. *The Race for Trieste.* London: William Kimber, 1977.
Croce, Benedetto. *Storia d'Italia dal 1871 al 1915.* 8th ed. Bari: Laterza, 1943.
Dallek, Robert. *Franklin D. Roosevelt and American Foreign Policy, 1932–1945.* New York: Oxford University Press, 1979.
Davis, Lynn Etheridge. *The Cold War Begins: Soviet-American Confrontation over Eastern Europe.* Princeton, N.J.: Princeton University Press, 1974.
De Castro, Diego. *La questione di Trieste: L'azione politica e diplomatica italiana dal 1943 al 1954.* 2 vols. Trieste: LINT, 1981.
Dedijer, Vladimir. *The Battle Stalin Lost: Memoirs of Yugoslavia, 1948–1953.* New York: Viking, 1971.
De' Robertis, Antonio Giulio M. *La frontiera orientale italiana nella diplomazia della seconda guerra mondiale.* Naples: Edizioni Scientifiche Italiane, 1981.
——. *Le grandi Potenze e il confine giuliano, 1941–1949.* Bari: Edizioni Fratelli Laterza, 1983.
De Santis, Hugh. *The Diplomacy of Silence: The American Foreign Service, the Soviet Union, and the Cold War, 1933–1947.* Chicago: University of Chicago Press, 1980.
Divine, Robert A. *Roosevelt and World War II.* Baltimore: Johns Hopkins University Press, 1969.
Dulles, Allen. *The Secret Surrender.* New York: Harper and Row, 1966.
Duroselle, Jean-Baptiste. *Le Conflit de Trieste, 1943–1954.* Brussels: Institut de Sociologie de l'Université Libre de Bruxelles, 1966.
Ellwood, David W. *L'alleato nemico: La politica dell'occupazione anglo-americana in Italia 1943/1946.* Milan: Feltrinelli, 1977.
——. *Italy, 1943–1945.* Leicester: Leicester University Press, 1985.
Feis, Herbert. *Churchill, Roosevelt, Stalin: The War they Waged and the Peace they Sought.* Princeton, N.J.: Princeton University Press, 1969.
——. *From Trust to Terror: The Onset of the Cold War, 1945–1950.* New York: Norton, 1970.
Floto, Inga. *Colonel House in Paris: A Study of American Policy at the Paris Peace Conference, 1919.* Aarhus, Denmark: Universitetsfurlaget i Aarhus, 1973.
Gaddis, John Lewis. *The United States and the Origins of the Cold War, 1941–1947.* New York: Columbia University Press, 1972.
——. *Strategies of Containment: A Critical Appraisal of Postwar American National Security Policy.* New York: Oxford University Press, 1982.
Gottlieb, W. W. *Studies in Secret Diplomacy during the First World War.* London: George Allen and Unwin, 1957.
Halperin, Ernst. *Triumphant Heretic: Tito's Struggle against Stalin.* London: Heinemann, 1958.
Hatch, Alden. *Ambassador Extraordinary: Clare Boothe Luce.* New York: Henry

Holt, 1955, 1956.
Hathaway, Robert M. *Ambiguous Partnership: Britain and America, 1944–1947.* New York: Columbia University Press, 1981.
Hoptner, Jacob B. *Yugoslavia in Crisis, 1934–1941.* New York: Columbia University Press, 1962.
Howard, Michael. *The Mediterranean Strategy in the Second World War.* London: Wiedenfeld and Nicolson, 1968.
Kardelj, Edvard. *Trieste and Yugoslav-Italian Relations.* New York: Yugoslav Information Center, 1953.
Kogan, Norman. *Italy and the Allies.* Cambridge: Cambridge University Press, 1956.
Kohn, Hans. *The Idea of Nationalism: A Study in Its Origins and Background.* New York: Macmillan, 1944.
Kolko, Gabriel. *The Politics of War: The World and United States Foreign Policy, 1943–1945.* New York: Random House, 1968.
Kuniholm, Bruce Robellet. *The Origins of the Cold War in the Near East: Great Power Conflict and Diplomacy in Iran, Turkey, and Greece.* Princeton, N.J.: Princeton University Press, 1980.
La Feber, Walter. *America, Russia, and the Cold War, 1945–1975.* 3d ed. New York: John Wiley and Sons, 1976.
Larson, David L. *United States Foreign Policy toward Yugoslavia, 1943–1963.* Washington, D.C.: University Press of America, 1979.
Lederer, Ivo. *Yugoslavia at the Paris Peace Conference: A Study in Frontiermaking.* New Haven: Yale University Press, 1963.
Lendvai, Paul. *Eagles in Cobwebs: Nationalism and Communism in the Balkans.* Garden City, N.Y.: Doubleday, 1969.
Levin, N. Gordon, Jr. *Woodrow Wilson and World Politics: America's Response to War and Revolution.* New York: Oxford University Press, 1968.
Link, Arthur S., ed. *Woodrow Wilson and a Revolutionary World, 1913–1921.* Chapel Hill, N.C.: University of North Carolina Press, 1982.
Lo Giudice, Giuseppe. *Trieste, l'Austria ed il canale di Suez.* Catania: Università degli Studi, 1979.
Lowe, C.J., and F. Marzari, *Italian Foreign Policy, 1870–1940.* London and Boston: Routledge and Kegan Paul, 1975.
Lundestad, Geir. *The American Non-policy towards Eastern Europe, 1943–1947: Universalism in an Area Not of Essential Interest to the United States.* Tromsö, Oslo, Bergen (Norway): Universitetsforlaget, 1978.
MacLean, Fitzroy. *Disputed Barricade: The Life and Times of Josip Broz Tito, Marshal of Jugoslavia.* London: Harper, 1957.
McNeill, William Hardy. *America, Britain, and Russia: Their Cooperation and Conflict, 1941–1946.* London: Oxford University Press, 1953.
Maier, Charles S. *Recasting Bourgeois Europe: Stabilization in France, Germany, and Italy in the Decade after World War I.* Princeton, N.J.: Princeton University Press, 1975.

Mamatey, Victor S. *The United States and East Central Europe, 1914–1918: A Study in Wilsonian Diplomacy and Propaganda.* Princeton, N.J.: Princeton University Press, 1957.
*La Marche Julienne: Etude de Géographie Politique.* Sušak: L'Institut Adriatique, 1945.
Maserati, Ennio. *L'occupazione jugoslava di Trieste (maggio–giugno 1945).* Udine: Del Bianco, 1963.
Mastny, Vojtech. *Russia's Road to the Cold War: Diplomacy, Warfare, and the Politics of Communism, 1941–1945.* New York: Columbia University Press, 1979.
Mayer, Arno J. *Politics and Diplomacy of Peacemaking: Containment and Counterrevolution at Versailles, 1918–1919.* New York: Alfred A. Knopf, 1967.
Messer, Robert L. *The End of an Alliance: James F. Byrnes, Roosevelt, Truman, and the Origins of the Cold War.* Chapel Hill: University of North Carolina Press, 1982.
Mihelić, Dušan. *The Political Element in the Port Geography of Trieste.* Chicago: Department of Geography, University of Chicago, 1969.
Miller, James Edward. *The United States and Italy, 1940–1950: The Politics and Diplomacy of Stabilization.* Chapel Hill: University of North Carolina Press, 1986.
Moodie, A. E. *The Italo-Yugoslav Boundary: A Study in Political Geography.* London: George Philip and Son, 1945.
Nicolson, Nigel. *Alex: The Life of Field Marshal Earl Alexander of Tunis.* New York: Atheneum, 1973.
Novak, Bogdan C. *Trieste, 1941–1954: The Ethnic, Political, and Ideological Struggle.* Chicago: University of Chicago Press, 1970.
Pacor, Mario. *Confine orientale. Questione nazionale a resistenza nel Friuli–Venezia Giulia.* Milan: Feltrinelli, 1964.
Page, Thomas Nelson. *Italy and the World War.* New York: Charles Scribner's Sons, 1920.
Pallante, Pierluigi. *Il Partito Comunista e la questione nazionale: Friuli–Venezia Giulia, 1941–1945.* Udine: Del Bianco, 1980.
Paterson, Thomas G. *Soviet-American Confrontation: Postwar Reconstruction and the Origins of the Cold War.* Baltimore: Johns Hopkins University Press, 1973.
Reitzel, William. *The Mediterranean: Its Role in America's Foreign Policy.* Port Washington, N.Y.: Kennikat Press, [1948], reprint 1969.
Roberts, Walter R. *Tito, Mihailović, and the Allies, 1941–1945.* New Brunswick, N.J.: Rutgers University Press, 1973.
Roletto, Giorgio. *Trieste ed i suoi problemi: Situazione, tendenze, prospettive.* Trieste: Borsatti, 1952.
Rusinow, Dennison I. *Italy's Austrian Heritage, 1919–1946.* Oxford: Oxford University Press, 1969.
———. *The Yugoslav Experiment, 1948–1974.* London: C. Hurst, for the Royal Institute of International Affairs, 1977.

Salvemini, Gaetano. *Racial Minorities under Fascism in Italy*. Chicago: The Women's International League for Peace and Freedom, Conference on Minorities, 1934.
Schiffrer, Carlo. *Le origini dell'irredentismo triestino (1813–1860)*. Udine: Istituto delle Edizioni Accademiche, 1937.
———. *Venezia Giulia: Study of a Map of the Italo-Yugoslav National Borders*. Rome: Carlo Colombo, 1946.
Sestan, Ernesto. *Venezia Giulia: Lineamenti di una storia etnica e culturale*. 2d ed. Bari: Centro Librario, 1965.
Seton-Watson, Christopher. *Italy from Liberalism to Fascism, 1870–1925*. London: Methuen, 1967.
Shadegg, Stephen. *Clare Boothe Luce: A Biography*. New York: Simon and Schuster, 1970.
Sheppard, G. A. *The Italian Campaign, 1943–1945: A Political and Military Reassessment*. New York: Praeger, 1968.
Sherwood, Robert. *Roosevelt and Hopkins, An Intimate History*. New York: Harper, 1948.
Silvestri, Claudio. *Dalla redenzione al fascismo: Trieste, 1918–1922*. 2d ed. Udine: Del Bianco, 1966.
Smith, Bradley F., and Elena Agarossi. *Operation Sunrise: The Secret Surrender*. New York: Basic Books, 1979.
Stoler, Mark. *The Politics of the Second Front: American Military Planning and Diplomacy in Coalition Warfare, 1941–1943*. Westport, Conn.: Greenwood, 1977.
Toscano, Mario. *Il Patto di Londra: Storia diplomatica dell'intervento italiano*. 2d rev. ed. Bologna: Zanichelli, 1934.
Ulam, Adam B. *Expansion and Coexistence: Soviet Foreign Policy 1917–73*. 2d ed. New York: Praeger, 1974.
Valdevit, Giampaolo. *La questione di Trieste 1941–1954: Politica internazionale e contesto locale*. Milan: Franco Angeli, 1986.
Vivante, Angelo. *Irredentismo adriatico*. Florence: Parenti, [1912] 1954.
Ward, Patricia Dawson. *The Threat of Peace: James F. Byrnes and the Council of Foreign Ministers, 1945–1946*. Kent: Ohio State University Press, 1979.
Webster, Richard A. *Industrial Imperialism in Italy, 1908–1915*. Berkeley: University of California Press, 1975.
Wheeler, Mark C. *Britain and the War for Yugoslavia, 1940–1943*. Boulder, Colo.: East European Monographs, 1980.
Wilson, Duncan. *Tito's Yugoslavia*. Cambridge: Cambridge University Press, 1979.
Wilson, Theodore. *The First Summit: Roosevelt and Churchill at Placentia Bay, 1941*. Boston: Houghton Mifflin, 1969.
Wittner, Lawrence. *American Intervention in Greece, 1943–1949*. New York: Columbia University Press, 1982.
Woolf, S. J., ed. *The Rebirth of Italy, 1943–1950*. New York: Humanities Press, 1972.
Yergin, Daniel. *Shattered Peace: The Origins of the Cold War and the National Security State*. Boston: Houghton Mifflin, 1977.

Živojinović, Dragan R. *America, Italy, and the Birth of Yugoslavia (1917–1919)*. Boulder, Colo.: East European Monographs, 1972.

Articles

Arcidiacono, Bruno. "The 'Dress Rehearsal': The Foreign Office and the Control of Italy, 1943–1944." *Historical Journal* 28 (1985): 417–27.
Barker, Elisabeth. "L'opzione istriana: obiettivi politici e militari della Gran Bretagna in Adriatico (1943–1944)." *Qualestoria* 10 (February 1982): 3–44.
Brands, Henry W., Jr. "Redefining the Cold War: American Policy toward Yugoslavia, 1948–60." *Diplomatic History* 11 (Winter 1987): 41–53.
Bowman, Alfred C. "Venezia Giulia and Trieste." *Military Government Journal* 1 (June 1948): 9–15.
De Santis, Hugh. "In Search of Yugoslavia: Anglo-American Policy and Policy-making 1943–45." In *The Second World War: Essays In Military and Political History*. Edited by Walter Laqueur, pp. 320–42. London: Sage, 1982.
"Fascismo, antifascismo e resistenza nella Venezia Giulia (1914–1945)." *Bollettino dell'Istituto regionale per la storia del movimento di resistenza nel Friuli–Venezia Giulia* 4 (August 1976) 6–78.
Floto, Inga. "Woodrow Wilson: War Aims, Peace Strategy, and the European Left." In *Woodrow Wilson and a Revolutionary World, 1919–1921*. Edited by Arthur S. Link. Chapel Hill: University of North Carolina Press, 1982.
Gaddis, John Lewis. "The Emerging Post-revisionist Synthesis on the Origins of the Cold War." *Diplomatic History* 7 (Summer 1983): 171–90.
Garson, Robert. "The Atlantic Alliance, Eastern Europe, and the Origins of the Cold War: From Pearl Harbour to Yalta." In *Contrast and Connection: Bicentennial Essays in Anglo-American History*. Edited by H. C. Allen and Roger Thompson, pp. 296–320. Athens, Ohio: Ohio University Press, 1976.
Haines, C. Grove. "Trieste—A Storm Center of Europe." *Foreign Policy Reports* 22 (April 1, 1946): 14–24.
Hammett, Hugh B. "America's Non-policy in Eastern Europe and the Origins of the Cold War." *Survey* 19 (Autumn 1973): 144–62.
"Italiani, sloveni e croati ai confini orientali." *Bollettino dell'Istituto regionale per la storia del movimento di liberazione nel Friuli–Venezia Giulia* 2 (May 1974): 3–41.
[Kennan, George F.] "X." "The Sources of Soviet Conduct." *Foreign Affairs* 25 (July 1947): 566–82.
Kernek, Sterling J. "Woodrow Wilson and National Self-Determination Along Italy's Frontier: A Study in the Manipulation of Principles in the Pursuit of Political Interests." *Proceedings of the American Philosophical Society* 126 (August 1982): 243–300.
Kimball, Warren F. "Naked Reverse Right: Roosevelt, Churchill, and Eastern Europe from TOLSTOY to Yalta—and a Little Beyond." *Diplomatic History* 9 (Winter

1985): 1–24.
Lees, Lorraine M. "The American Decision to Assist Tito, 1948–1949." *Diplomatic History* 2 (Fall 1978): 407–22.
Mark, Edward. "Charles E. Bohlen and the Acceptable Limits of Soviet Hegemony in Eastern Europe: A Memorandum of 18 October 1945." *Diplomatic History* 3 (Spring 1979): 201–13.
Miller, James Edward. "The Search for Stability: An Interpretation of American Policy in Italy, 1943–1946." *Journal of Italian History* 1 (Autumn 1978): 264–86.
———. "Taking Off The Gloves: The United States and the Italian Elections of 1948." *Diplomatic History* 7 (Winter 1983): 35–55.
Munnecke, Charles M. "Legal Challenge in Trieste: Military Government Establishes a New Concept of International Law in Occupied Areas." *Military Government Journal* 2 (Summer 1949): 6–10.
Pupo, Raoul. "Gli 'accordi segreti' anglo-jugoslavi (1941)." *Qualestoria* 7 (March 1979): 18–20.
Rabel, Roberto. "Prologue to Containment: The Truman Administration's Response to the Trieste Crisis of May 1945." *Diplomatic History* 10 (Spring 1986): 141–60.
Renzi, William A. "Italy's Neutrality and Entrance into the Great War: A Re-examination." *American Historical Review* 73 (June 1968): 1414–32.
Resis, Albert. "The Churchill-Stalin Secret 'Percentages' Agreement on the Balkans, Moscow, October, 1944." *American Historical Review* 83 (April 1978): 368–87.
Schmitz, David F. "Woodrow Wilson and the Liberal Peace: The Problem of Italy and Imperialism." *Peace and Change* 12 (forthcoming, 1987).
Semple, Ellen Churchill. "The Barrier Boundary of the Mediterranean Basin and its Northern Breaches as Factors in History." *Annals of the Association of American Geographers* 5 (1915): 27–59.
Siracusa, Joseph M. "The Meaning of TOLSTOY: Churchill, Stalin, & the Balkans, Moscow, October 1944." *Diplomatic History* 3 (Fall 1979): 443–63.
Stefan, Charles G. "The Emergence of the Soviet-Yugoslav Break: A Personal View from the Belgrade Embassy." *Diplomatic History* 6 (Fall 1982): 387–404.
Tergestinus [pseud.]. "La Venezia Giulia nella tradizione italiana (1815–1915)." *Nuova Antologia* 80 (March 1945): 197–209.
Terzuolo, Eric R. "Resistance and the National Question in the Venezia Giulia and Friuli, 1943–1945." In *Nation and Ideology: Essays in Honor of Wayne S. Vucinich*. Edited by Ivo Banac, John G. Ackerman, and Roman Szponluk, pp. 411–34. Boulder, Colo.: East European Monographs, 1981.
Valdevit, Giampaolo. "Gli Alleati e la Venezia Giulia, 1941–1945." *Italia Contemporanea* 142 (March 1981): 55–88.
———. "Un documento del Foreign Office sul confine orientale." *Qualestoria* 7 (July 1979): 11–23.
———. "Politici e militari Alleati di fronte alla questione della Venezia Giulia (giugno 1945–luglio 1946)." *Qualestoria* 9 (October 1981): 83–119.
———. "Resistenza e Alleati fra Italia e Jugoslavia." *Qualestoria* 8 (March 1980):

3–12.
Varsori, Antonio. "La Gran Bretagna e le elezioni politiche italiane del 18 aprile 1948." *Storia Contemporanea* 13 (February 1982): 5–70.
Warner, Geoffrey. "Italy and the Powers, 1943–49." In *The Rebirth of Italy 1943–50.* Edited by S. J. Woolf, pp. 30–56. New York: Humanities Press, 1972.
Zeeman, Bert. "Britain and the Cold War: An Alternative Approach—The Treaty of Dunkirk Example." *European History Quarterly* 16 (1986): 343–67.
Zeno, Livio. "La Questione di Trieste e l'azione di Carlo Sforza." *L'Osservatore Politico Letterario* 24 (April 1978): 15–30.

# Index

Acheson, Dean, 87, 137–38, 193 n.21
Adriatic region: Italian claims in, 9; Julian Region as outlet to, 2, 7–8, 25, 44; Northern, vii, 40, 45–46; proposed operations in, 27–28, 31–32, 178 n.28; and United States, 151–52; Yugoslav claims in, 87
AFHQ. *See* Allied Force Headquarters
Airey, Terence S., 98, 103–5, 107, 115, 121, 123, 125, 139–41
Alexander, Harold: and AMG in Julian Region, 36–47 passim, 54, 68, 76–81; negotiations with Tito, 37, 54–57, 60, 66; and Trieste crisis of May 1945, 55–58, 60, 64–71
Allen, George, 133, 140, 143
Allied Commission, 36, 76, 80, 89
Allied Control Commission, 29
Allied Force Headquarters (AFHQ), 33, 54, 78, 80–81, 98
Allied Military Government (AMG): in Italy, 29–31, 39, 75–76, 79–80; planning for in Julian Region, 29–31, 33–34, 37, 43–45, 47–48, 50, 54, 56–58, 60, 66, 70, 165; possible Yugoslav role in, 39–40, 68; Pula's inclusion in, 68–71; Yugoslav opposition to in Julian Region, 29–30, 33, 36–37, 42–43, 46–47, 54–55, 67, 165. *See also* Allied Military Government, Free Territory of Trieste; Allied Military Government, Zone A, Julian Region
Allied Military Government, Free Territory of Trieste (AMG-FTT): agreements with Italian government, 119–20, 142; costs of, 143–44, 163; Italian influence on, 119–21, 123, 139–43; planned elections of 1951, 136–37; policy of, 103–8, 118–21, 125, 139–43; termination of, 160, 163. *See also* Free Territory of Trieste
Allied Military Government, Thirteenth Corps. *See* Allied Military Government, Zone A, Julian Region
Allied Military Government–Venezia Giulia (AMG–VG). *See* Allied Military Government, Zone A, Julian Region
Allied Military Government, Zone A, Julian Region, 69, 74–85, 91, 96–100, 103. *See also* Allied Military Government
Allies: inter-Allied relations in World War II, 18, 21, 25–28, 33, 35–37, 48, 52–53, 75; and Italian campaign, 23, 26–28, 31–32, 36, 38–39, 41–43, 49–50; and occupation of Julian Region, vii, 29–30, 32, 36, 65–67, 71, 83; and occupation policy in Italy, 25–26; in World War I, 11–12. *See also* Great Britain; Soviet Union; United States

Alto Adige (South Tyrol), 9
AMG. *See* Allied Military Government
Anglo-American policy. *See* Allies; Foreign Office; Great Britain; State Department; United States
Anticommunism, anticommunists: and AMG, 81, 84, 106, 129, 139; in Julian Region, 25, 66; and United States, 70, 74, 77, 129, 165
Armistice and Post-War Committee of the British cabinet, 40–41
Atlantic Charter, x, 20–22, 24, 29, 34, 38, 47, 50, 58, 60, 70–71, 164, 175 n.8
Attlee, Clement, 86
Austria, 34, 37–39, 44–46, 59, 66, 70, 135
Austro-Hungarian Empire, 3, 5–7, 9, 25, 170 n.1, 171 n.8
Austro-Italian frontier, 2, 10
Axis powers, 21. *See also* Germany; Italy; Japan

Badoglio, Pietro, 23
Baldwin, Charles F., 125, 128–29
Balkans, 2, 92; and Great Britain, 18, 28, 32; and Italy, 9, 15; and Soviet Union, 32, 86; and United States, 28, 31, 47, 49, 56, 59, 62
Barker, Elisabeth, 19
Bebler, Aleš, 128
Belgrade agreement, 75–78, 82, 84
Berlin, 112, 161
Bevin, Ernest, 109–11, 133
Bidault, Georges, 91, 115
Bohlen, Charles, 90, 94
Bologna, 41
Bolshevism, Bolsheviks, 11, 40
Bowman, Alfred Connor, 80–83, 100
Brenner Pass, 9–10, 173 n.19
Brosio, Manlio, 156–57
Byrnes, James F., 86–87, 90, 92–94

Cadogan, Alexander, 20, 175 n.6
Caffery, Jefferson, 117
Cammarata thesis, 141
Campbell, G. T. C., 123
Campbell, John C., 22, 87, 89–90, 93–94, 117

Cannon, Cavendish, 59–61, 109
Capodistria. *See* Koper
Casablanca Conference, 23
CCS. *See* Combined Chiefs of Staff
Central Europe, 2, 7, 30, 95
Central Intelligence Agency (United States), 115, 158
Central powers, 9–10
CFM. *See* Council of Foreign Ministers
Chetniks, 25
Chiefs of Staff (Great Britain), 27
China, 86
Christian Democratic party. *See* Italian Christian Democratic party
Churchill, Winston S.: and Italy, 35, 40, 45–46; and Julian Region in World War II, 30–31, 40–46; and Mediterranean strategy, 27, 34, 49, 57, 177 n.20; and proposed dash for Trieste, 44–46; and proposed Istrian landing, 26–28, 32, 178 n.28; and Roosevelt, 20, 24, 26–27, 31–32; and Soviet Union, 32, 45–46, 178 n.28; and spheres of influence, 32, 35, 45, 85; and Tito, 29–30, 32, 37, 40, 42; and Trieste crisis of May 1945, 61–65, 68–69, 165; war aims of, 18, 27, 31–35, 45–46, 49–50, 180 n.52; and Yugoslav border claims, 20; and Yugoslavia, 32, 40, 45–46
Cittanova d'Istria. *See* Novigrad
Clemenceau, Georges, 11
Combined Chiefs of Staff (CCS), 33, 39, 42–44, 55, 58, 65, 67–68, 78–79, 81–82, 98
Combined Civil Affairs Committee (CCAC), 41, 179 n.42
Cominform. *See* Communist Information Bureau
Commerce Department (United States), 126
Communism: American opposition to, 50, 72, 84, 105, 121, 124–25; clash with liberalism, x, 73, 100, 105, 113; containment of, 73, 106, 108, 163, 166–67, 183 n.32; and Eastern Europe, 60, 90, 114; and Free Territory of Trieste, 105–8, 121, 124–25; and Italy, 113–14, 117, 136, 147, 162; in Julian

Region, 25, 75, 79–85, 100; threat to West of, 9, 50, 61–62, 72–73, 165, 183 n.32; and Yugoslavia, 29, 99, 122–23. *See also* Anticommunism; Communist Information Bureau; Eastern bloc; Italian Communist party; Soviet Communist party; Yugoslav Communist party
Containment policy, x, 53, 73, 96, 106–7, 110, 129, 162–63, 166–67
Council of Foreign Ministers (CFM), 86–87, 89–94, 97
Court of Cassation (Italian), 141
Cox, Geoffrey, 54, 183 n.32
Croatia, Croats, xiii, 2, 4, 6, 14–15, 25. *See also* Yugoslavia
Czechoslovakia, 112

Dalmatia, 5, 9, 11, 18, 39
Danubian region, 2, 7–8, 22, 44
Danzig, 93
D'Annunzio, Gabriele, 13
Declaration of the United Nations, 21, 175 n.8
De Gasperi, Alcide, 89, 114–15, 137–38, 143–44, 146, 149
Democratic party (United States), 12
Devin. *See* Duino
Dowling, Walter C., 110–11
Duino (Devin), 76–77, 92
Dulles, John Foster, 148–50, 153, 158, 161–62
Dunn, James, 104, 110, 113, 115–16, 132, 140–41
Duroselle, Jean-Baptiste, viii

Eastern (Soviet) bloc, vii, 89, 97, 99, 116, 131, 162
Eastern Europe: communism in, 60, 90, 114; and Soviet Union, 26, 28, 33–34, 60, 64, 68, 90, 96, 177 n.18; and United States, 24, 26, 64, 72, 110
East-West relations: general tensions in, 49, 53, 74, 86, 96, 126; and Trieste problem, vii–viii, 61, 72–74, 83, 85, 87, 93–94, 99–101, 164–66
EDC. *See* European Defense Community
Eden, Anthony, 29, 34, 39–41, 62–63, 117, 143–44, 156, 170 n.5, 175 n.6, 176 n.14, 177 n.24, 196 n.41
Eisenhower, Dwight D., 27, 65, 147, 149–53, 157–59, 162. *See also* Eisenhower administration
Eisenhower administration, 147–48, 155, 161, 167. *See also* Eisenhower, Dwight D.
Ethnic principle, 22, 138, 143–44, 155, 170 n.5
European Defense Community (EDC), 144, 147, 157, 161
European Recovery Program. *See* Marshall Plan
Export-Import Bank (United States), 126

Fascism, Fascist party, 13–15, 25, 66, 77, 79, 83
Finland, 86
Fiume. *See* Rijeka
Foreign Office (Great Britain): Foreign Press and Research Service of, 18; and Free Territory of Trieste, 106, 109–15, 119, 123–24, 132–33, 137, 140, 143–44, 155–57, 189 n.22; and Italy, 113, 189 n.22; and Julian Region in World War II, 18–19, 23–24, 29, 33–34, 40–43, 55, 175 n.6, 177 n.24; Southern Department of, 111; and Trieste crisis of May 1945, 58, 60, 64, 67, 71; and Yugoslavia, 18–19, 23, 29, 40–42
France, 3, 9, 11, 86, 143, 154; and Italian peace treaty, 88–89, 91–94, 134; and Tripartite Proposal, 114–15, 117, 123; in World War II, 26–28
Free Territory of Trieste (FTT), xiii; crisis of late 1953 concerning, 150–53; failure to come into being, viii, 99, 102–3, 108, 121, 166; governorship of, 93–98, 101, 103, 108–9, 111-12, 116, 124–25, 134, 153, 187 n.33; and Italian elections of 1948, 113–18, 129–30; Italian peace treaty negotiations concerning, viii, 91–95, 101; negotiations of 1954 concerning, 153–62; permanent statute of, 95, 134; preparations for, 95–98; provisional statute of, 96, 103.

*See also* Allied Military Government, Free Territory of Trieste; Free Territory of Trieste, Zone A; Free Territory of Trieste, Zone B; Yugoslav Military Government, Free Territory of Trieste

Free Territory of Trieste, Zone A, 102, 129; communism in, 105–8, 111, 124–25, 134, 139; economy of, 119–20; elections of 1949 in, 125; Italians in, 105–7, 121, 125, 139–43; proposed Allied withdrawal from, 150–52; proposed annexation by Italy of, 129, 136, 139, 144–45, 150–52, 156–57; riots in, 142, 153; Slovenes in, 106–7, 145; Yugoslav claims in, 133, 161. *See also* Allied Military Government, Free Territory of Trieste; Free Territory of Trieste

Free Territory of Trieste, Zone B, 108, 117, 133, 152; Italian claims in, 136–37, 145–46, 151, 161; proposed annexation by Yugoslavia of, 144–47, 150, 156–57. *See also* Free Territory of Trieste; Yugoslav Military Government, Free Territory of Trieste

Freyberg, Bernard C., 54

Friuli, 38

Fulton, Missouri, 85

Gaddis, John Lewis, 64

Garibaldi-Natisone division, 38

Gavrilović, Milan, 18

Germany, 5, 86, 176 n.14; and Cold War, 154, 161; ethnic presence in Julian Region, xiii, 3; expansion in 1930s, 15, 93; and Julian Region in World War II, 25, 30, 33, 43, 47–48; surrender in Italy of, 41, 43; surrender in Trieste of, 48, 50; in World War II, 18–19, 27–28, 32, 36, 38, 42, 46, 49–50

Gorica. *See* Gorizia

Gorizia (Gorica), 18, 20, 54, 62

Great Britain, xii, 9, 11: and Anglo-Yugoslav "secret agreements," 18–20; and Cold War, xi, 112; and Free Territory of Trieste, 106, 108–15, 118–19, 123–24, 126, 132–61 passim, 189 n.22; and Italian peace treaty, 88–89, 91, 111; and Italy, 35, 113–18, 144, 189 n.22; and Julian Region during World War II, 17–20, 23–24, 29–34, 37, 40, 165, 179 n.42; and Julian Region from 1945 to 1947, 84–85, 91, 101; and Mediterranean region, 23, 28, 35, 49, 57, 98, 109, 177 n.20; and Soviet Union, 17–18, 33–34; and Trieste crisis of May 1945, vii, 58, 60, 64, 67, 71, 165; World War II aims of, 18–19, 28, 40, 49, 57; and Yugoslavia, 18–19, 29, 34–36, 40–42. *See also* Foreign Office; War Office

Greece, 16, 19, 34, 57, 59, 72, 96, 98, 107, 181 n.19, 183 n.32

Grew, Joseph, 47, 56–57, 61–62, 72, 165, 183 n.31

Habsburg Empire. *See* Austro-Hungarian Empire

Halifax, Lord, 58

Harding, John, 66, 76, 91

Harding, Warren, 12

Harrison, Geoffrey W., 155–57

Herter Committee, 104

Hitler, Adolf, 16, 18, 35, 59, 61

Hoge, William, 140

Hopkins, Harry, 27, 63

Hull, Cordell, 24, 176 n.14

Hungary, 7, 59

Inverchapel, Lord, 111

Iran, 72–73, 183 n.32

Irredentism. *See* Nationalism: Italian; Nationalism: Yugoslav

Isola. *See* Izola

Isonzo (Soča) River, 46–48, 54

Istria (Istra), 2, 4–5, 18–20, 25–27, 31–33, 37, 171 n.8

Istra. *See* Istria

Italian Christian Democratic party (DC), 38, 117, 129, 144–46, 148, 156, 165–66

Italian Communist party (PCI), 25, 35, 38, 46, 88, 113–14, 116, 190 n.23

Italian Liberal party (PLI), 146

Italian peace treaty, xiii, 101–2, 129; and Julian Region, vii–viii, 74–75, 85–98,

103–4, 108, 121, 125, 127, 141, 165; proposed revision of, 110, 116–18, 135, 137, 141, 160; ratification of, 75, 83, 95; West accused of violating, 116, 134, 190 n.27
Italian Republican party (PRI), 146
Italian Socialist party (PSI) 113, 146
Italy, xiii; and armistice of 1943, 23, 25–26, 36; association with Western powers, 26, 68, 99, 107, 120, 131, 136–37, 166; in civil administration of Trieste, 77–80, 82–83; claims to Julian Region, vii, 10–13, 28, 87, 89, 93, 99, 128, 136–37, 145–46, 151, 161, 170 n.5; elections of 1948 in, 113–18, 124, 129, 165, 189 n.22, 190 n.23; elections of 1953 in, 144–48; ethnic presence in Julian Region, xiii, 4–5, 9–10, 14–15, 80, 82–83, 98, 105–6; and Free Territory of Trieste, 119–20, 133, 136–48, 150–53, 156–57, 158–61; and Italian peace treaty, 87–89, 93–95, 97, 99, 135; and Julian Region between the wars, 14–15; negotiations with Yugoslavia concerning Free Territory of Trieste, 109, 126–27, 131, 136–38, 143–44, 150, 153; political stability of, xii, 13, 57–58, 60, 70, 88–89, 112, 166; and Trieste crisis of May 1945, 57–60, 70–71, 182 n.17; and Tripartite Proposal, 113, 115–17, 126, 128–29, 133, 136–37, 148, 151; and World War I, 9–10, 172 n.16; and World War II, 16, 23, 25–28, 32, 35, 54; and Yugoslavia, 12–13, 15–16, 54, 91, 128, 134, 145–46, 149, 151, 153–55, 161–62, 167. *See also* Italian peace treaty; Nationalism: Italian; Partisans: Italian
Izola (Isola), 155

Jackson, C. D., 147–49, 195 n.29
Jakšić, Pavle, 54
Japan, 57, 59, 63, 86
Joint Chiefs of Staff (United States), 27, 68, 128
Jovanović, Arso, 76
Joyce, Robert P., 103–5, 107, 109–10, 113, 123–24
Jugoslav Committee for National Liberation (JCNL), 38
Julian Region: civil administration of, 75–77; definition of, 2, 169 n.1; economy of, 3, 7–8; ethnic composition of, 3–4, 14, 89, 170 n.5, 171 n.8; geography of, xii–xiii, 2; history to 1940 of, 2–16 passim, 171 n.8, 174 n.24; strategic importance of, 3, 28, 31, 164, 166; in World War II, 25, 28, 31, 36–38, 42–43, 47–48. *See also* Allied Military Government, Zone A, Julian Region; Istria; Trieste; Yugoslav Military Government, Zone B, Julian Region
Julijska Krajina (Julian March). *See* Julian Region

Kennan, George, 96
Key, David, 89
Kingdom of the Serbs, Croats, and Slovenes. *See* Yugoslavia
Kirk, Alexander, 36–50 passim, 56–57, 59–61, 77, 80, 165
Koper (Capodistria), 145, 155
Korea, 148, 161, 183 n.32
Kuniholm, Bruce, 72, 183 n.32

League of Nations, 11–12
Leahy, William, 104
Lee, John H., 103
Liberal democracy, ix–x, 11, 14, 25, 84, 99–100, 105, 113, 165–66
Liberal internationalism, x, 11–12, 14, 164, 173 n.17
Liberalism. *See* Liberal democracy; Liberal internationalism
Ljubljana Gap, 27–28
Lloyd George, David, 11
London memorandum of understanding. *See* Memorandum of understanding
Luce, Clare Booth, 147–49, 152, 157–59, 161, 167, 195 n.29, 197 n.49, 198 n.52
Luce, Henry, 147
Luciolli, Mario, 147

Macmillan, Harold, 36, 181 n.9
Marshall, George C., 47, 96
Marshall Plan, 96, 107, 112, 119–20
Mastny, Vojtech, 33, 176 n.17, 178 n.28
Matthews, H. Freeman, 57–58
Mayer, Arnold, 10
Mazzini, Giuseppe, 5
Mediterranean region: and Great Britain, 23, 27–28, 35, 49, 57, 98, 109, 177 n.20; and Soviet Union, 86; and United States, 84, 89, 98, 114–15
Mediterranean theater, 23, 26–28, 49
Memorandum of understanding: of 1952, 142–43; of October 1954 (London agreement), 160–61
Merchant, Livingston, 147
Messer, Robert, 62
Middle East, 57, 115
Mihailović, Draža, 25
Miller, James, 113, 189 n.20, 189 n.23
Monfalcone, (Tržič), 48, 54, 62
Morgan, William D., 55, 58, 76–77, 80
Morgan line, 69, 91
Molotov, Vyacheslav, 92, 94
Molotov Plan, 97
Mosely, Philip, 138
Munich analogy, 61, 72
Murphy, Robert, 158–59
Mussolini, Benito, 13–16, 23, 25

Naples, 30
National Security Council (United States), 114–15, 122, 191 n.31
Nationalism, ix, 3–4, 14, 170 n.5; Italian, 4–7, 10, 13, 25, 89–90, 101, 130, 139–42, 171 n.8; Yugoslav, 4–7, 14, 15, 90, 101, 130, 171 n.8
NATO. *See* North Atlantic Treaty Organization
Nazism, Nazis, 50, 70
Near East, 72
New Diplomacy, 9–12, 172 n.15, 173 n.17. *See also* Liberal internationalism; Wilson, Woodrow
New Zealand Division, British Eighth Army, 48, 50, 52–54
Normandy landings. *See* Operation Overlord

North Atlantic Treaty Organization (NATO), 131, 137, 142, 144, 147–49, 151, 157
Northern Tier, 72
Notter, Harley, 21
Novak, Bogdan, viii
Novigrad (Cittanova d'Istria), 92

Operation Anvil, 27
Operation Husky, 23
Operation Overlord, 26–28
Operation Sunrise, 41, 43
Organization for European Economic Cooperation (OEEC), 119–20
Orlando, Vittorio, 10–11
Osimo accords of 1975, 161
Osoppo division, 38

Pacific theater, 63
Pact of London of 1915, 9, 18
Paris peace conferences: of 1919, x, 8, 10–11; of 1946, 93–94
Partisans: Italian, 38, 48, 66; Yugoslav, 25–26, 29, 31, 33, 35–36, 38, 48, 50, 67. *See also* Yugoslav Fourth Army
Patterson, Richard C., 58, 67, 90
Patterson, Robert, 90
Pella, Giuseppe, 146–50
Piazza Unità, 160
Piran (Pirano), 146, 155
Pirano. *See* Piran
Pola. *See* Pula
Poland, 59, 64, 72
Potsdam Conference, 86
Pula (Pola), 24, 44–47, 49, 61–62, 65, 68–71, 98, 171 n.7
Punta Sottile (Tenki Rtič), 156–57, 159

Quebec conferences, 24, 30, 32, 49, 176 n.14

Rapallo, Treaty of, 13
Reams, Robert Borden, 126, 128, 132
Republican Fascist party, 25
Republican party (United States), 145, 147
Rijeka, (Fiume), x, 7–8, 10–14, 18, 24, 49, 170 n.1, 172 n.14, 172 n.15

*Risorgimento*, 4–5
Robertson, H. P. P., 106–7
Roman Empire, 3–4
Romania, 26
Rome, Treaty of, 13
Roosevelt, Franklin D.: death of, 42; and Italy, 26, 35; and Julian Region, 23–24, 31, 49, 165, 176 n.14; and proposed Istrian landing, 26–28, 31–32; war aims of, 20, 21, 24, 26–28, 32
Russia, 9

SACMED. *See* Supreme Allied Military Command in the Mediterranean
*Sacro egoismo*, 8–10, 13, 172 n.16
Salandra, Antonio, 172 n.16
Sargent, Orme, 42
Scelba, Mario, 156–58
Security Council. *See* United Nations Security Council
Self-determination, xii, 9–10, 22, 49, 60, 88, 99, 164, 172 n.17, 173 n.19
Serbia, 25. *See also* Yugoslavia
Sforza, Carlo, 15, 113, 117, 133
Shadegg, Stephen, 157, 197 n.49
Sicily, 23
Slovene Ninth Corps, 38
Slovenia: anticommunism of, 25, 66; and civil administration of Trieste area, 80, 82; in FTT, 106–7, 145, 157; in Julian Region, xii, 2, 4, 6, 14–15, 70–80, 82–83; in World War II, 33. *See also* Yugoslavia
Smith, Walter Bedell, 157–58
Socialism, 14, 82
Southeastern Europe, ix, 7, 15, 19–20, 25, 31–33, 35, 47, 49, 159, 162
South Europe, 162
South Slavs, 4, 6. *See also* Yugoslavia
South Tyrol. *See* Alto Adige
Soviet bloc. *See* Eastern bloc
Soviet Communist party, 122–23
Soviet Union: and AMG in Julian Region, 44–45, 84; and Cold War, xi, 86, 88, 97, 99, 112, 163; expansionist policies of, 59–61, 68, 70, 90, 104, 124, 154, 183 n.32; and Free Territory of Trieste, 97, 101, 108–11, 124–25, 127, 134–35, 152–53, 160, 162; and Italian peace treaty, 86–89, 91–95, 97, 99, 116–17; and Italy, 26, 41, 60, 68, 88–89, 115; and Julian Region during World War II, 44–45, 48; and Julian Region from 1945 to 1947, 77; and spheres of influence, 32, 34, 59; and Trieste crisis of May 1945, 48, 57–58, 61, 64–65, 67–69, 73, 183 n.27; and Tripartite Proposal, 114–19, 121, 123–24, 128, 134, 189 n.23; wartime advances of, 28, 32, 34, 45–46; and Western powers, xi, 34, 41, 45–46, 60, 87–88, 93, 97, 99, 151, 162, 166, 168; and Yugoslavia before the split in June 1948, 36, 41, 45–46, 48, 59–61, 68, 88–90, 92, 99, 108, 178 n.28, 183 n.27, 185 n.22; and Yugoslavia after mid-1948, 122–28, 130–31, 133, 160, 166. *See also* Communism; Eastern bloc; Soviet Communist party
Spheres of influence: Churchill and, 32, 35, 45, 85; Eastern (Soviet), 34, 59, 64, 87; Stalin and, 32, 34, 68, 176 n.18; Truman administration and, 53, 60, 64, 71, 165; Western, 60, 64, 72–73, 84, 87, 99, 102. *See also* Eastern bloc; Western bloc
Stalin, Joseph: and proposed Istrian landing, 26–27; and spheres of influence, 32, 34, 68, 176 n.18; and Tito, 58, 122, 138, 178 n.28, 183 n.27; and Tripartite Proposal, 190 n.23; and Western powers, 34, 63, 68, 86
State Department (United States): Advisory Committee on Postwar Foreign Policy, 21; and AMG policy, 30–31, 42, 45, 48, 56–57, 70, 77, 165, 177 n.25; European divisions of, 57, 59, 110, 127; and Free Territory of Trieste, 104–5, 108–29 passim, 132–62 passim; and Italy, 42, 50, 57, 114–15, 136–38, 147–48, 197 n.44; and Julian Region in World War II, 21–24, 29–31, 37, 39, 41–44, 47, 49, 70, 165; Policy Planning Staff of, 122; and Trieste crisis of May 1945, 56–63, 68–69, 71–73; and Yugoslavia, 42, 90, 122–23

Stettin, 85
Stimson, Henry, 47, 50, 56–57, 61
Stoler, Mark, 27
Stone, Ellery W., 29, 36, 80, 89
Sullivan, William, 103–5, 109–10, 140
Supreme Allied Command in the Mediterranean (SACMED), 36, 39, 76–77, 82, 103

Tarchiani, Alberto, 146
Teheran Conference 1943, 26–27, 32, 177 n.20
Thirteenth Corps, British Eighth Army, 66, 76, 78, 80
Thompson, Llewellyn E., 155–57, 159, 197 n.44, 198 n.52
Tito, Josip Broz: and Free Territory of Trieste, 124, 144–47, 150–51, 158–59; and Julian Region in World War II, 36–47 passim; negotiations with Alexander, 37, 54–57, 60, 66; position after break with Stalin, 135, 138, 140; and Soviet Union, 36, 41, 57–59, 88, 122, 124, 126, 134, 138, 149, 166, 178 n.28; talks with Churchill, 29–30, 37; and Trieste crisis of May 1945, x, 50, 52, 54–55, 59–61, 64–65, 67–71; and Western powers, 29, 36, 40–42, 90, 126, 133, 135–37, 140, 148–50, 152, 159, 166
Titoists, 125
Toynbee, Arnold, 18, 24
Treaty of Rapallo, 13
Treaty of Rome, 13
Trentino, 5, 9
Trident Conference, 23
Trieste (Trst): as Cold War problem, vii–xii, 17, 50, 53, 74–75, 83–102 passim, 105, 107–8, 110, 130–32, 135, 151, 154, 162, 163–68, 183 n.31, 183 n.32, crisis of May 1945, vii, 48, 53–73; economy of, 7–8, 22, 95, 119–20, 171 n.8, 176 n.14; final negotiations of 1954 concerning, 131, 153–62 passim, 197 n.41, 198 n.52; historiography of dispute over, vii–ix, 174 n.24; Italian civil administration in, 77–80, 82–83, 121; liberation of, 48, 50, 52, 54, 56; local situation during May 1945 crisis, 65–67; and "race" for, 43–48, 56; Yugoslav civil administration in, 75–84; Yugoslav occupation of, vii, 48, 52–55, 58–62, 65–67, 75, 80, 165. *See also* Free Territory of Trieste, Zone A; Julian Region
Tripartite Proposal, 114–30, 133–34, 136–38, 143, 148, 151, 189 n.22. *See also* Italy: elections of 1948
Triple Alliance, 5
Trst. *See* Trieste
Truman, Harry S: and Free Territory of Trieste, 104, 138, 145; and Julian Region in World War II, 42, 44–45, 47; at Potsdam, 86; and Soviet Union, 57, 62–63, 73, 183 n.32; talks with De Gasperi, 137–38; and Trieste crisis of May 1945, 56–57, 61–65, 68, 72–73, 145, 165, 183 n.32; and Truman Doctrine, 96, 98. *See also* Truman administration
Truman administration, 63, 73, 126, 145–46, 165, 183 n.32. *See also* Spheres of influence; State Department; Truman, Harry S
Tržić. *See* Monfalcone
Turkey, 18, 72, 96

Umag (Umago), 146
Umago. *See* Umag
Unger, Leonard, 127, 134, 197 n.44, 197 n.45, 198 n.52
United Nations Relief and Rehabilitation Administration (UNRRA), 90
United Nations Security Council: and administration of Free Territory of Trieste, 92, 95, 98, 101, 125; Airey's reports to, 121; and governorship of Free Territory of Trieste, 93, 97–98, 108, 111–12, 116, 153; and 1954 settlement, 161
United States: and Cold War, viii–xii, 49–50, 53, 60–61, 69–70, 72–76, 85–90, 96, 98–102, 110, 112–13, 118, 123, 129–32, 150–51, 154, 162–63, 165–68, 183 n.32; and Free Territory of Trieste, xi, 97–98, 102–30 passim,

131–62 passim, 166, 187 n.33, 189 n.20; and general policy toward Julian Region, x, 1, 163–64, 166–68; and Italian peace treaty, 74, 85–94, 99–101, 111; and Italy during World War II, 22, 35, 42, 50, 59; and Italy after World War II, 70, 88–89, 99, 101–2, 107, 110, 112–18, 129, 131, 134–38, 142–43, 145, 147–52, 157, 162–63, 166–67; and Julian Region during and after World War I, 9–12, 14, 16; and Julian Region during World War II, x, 17–18, 22, 29–34, 39, 46–51, 70, 164–65, 179 n.42; and Julian Region from 1945 to 1947, 84–85, 91, 101, 165–66; and Soviet Union, 1, 17–18, 33–34, 48, 58–61, 63–65, 72–73, 87, 93, 99, 151, 162, 166, 168; territorial policy of in World War II, 21, 24, 29, 34, 48, 59–60, 68, 70; and Trieste crisis of May 1945, vii, 53, 55–65, 68–73, 164–65; World War I aims of, 8–9, 164; World War II aims of, 20, 49, 164, 177 n.24; and Yugoslavia during World War II, 22, 29, 35–36, 48; and Yugoslavia after World War II, xii, 59, 89–91, 99, 101–2, 104, 110, 122–28, 130–31, 134–35, 140, 143, 145, 148, 151–52, 157–59, 162–63, 166–67, 191 n.31, 193 n.21, 197 n.45. *See also* State Department; War Department
Ustashi, 25

Valdevit, Giampaolo, ix
Velebit, Vladimir, 38, 155, 157
Venetian Slovenia, 170 n.1
Venezia Giulia (Julian Venetia). *See* Julian Region
Venice, 3, 5, 70
Vidali, Vittorio, 134
Vienna, 7, 28, 45, 178 n.28

Wallinger, Geoffrey, 111, 113
Ward, Patricia, 86
War Department (United States), x, 47, 56, 59, 179 n.42
War Office (Great Britain), 33
Welles, Sumner, 20

Western bloc, vii, 26, 88–89, 94, 99, 111, 113, 122, 124, 131, 135–36, 167. *See also* North Atlantic Treaty Organization; Spheres of influence; Western powers
Western Europe, 54, 61, 96, 113, 115, 120, 144, 150–51, 163, 167
Western powers: and Italian peace treaty, 88, 95, 134; and Italy, 107, 131, 136–37, 166 and Trieste problem, 69, 91, 93, 101, 106, 108–9, 111, 124, 135–36, 138, 143–44, 154, 162; and Tripartite Proposal, 116, 121, 128, 136, 138, 160, 190 n.33. *See also* France; Great Britain; United States; Western bloc
Wilson, Woodrow, x, 8–11, 31, 47, 164, 172 n.15, 172 n.17, 173 n.19
Winterton, John, 141–42, 161

Yalta Conference, 34–37
Yugoslav Communist party, 25, 46, 90, 122–23, 178 n.28
Yugoslavia: attempted occupation of Free Territory of Trieste, 103–5; break with Soviet Union, 122–28, 130–31, 133, 167, 185 n.22; claims to Julian Region, vii, 10, 13–14, 18–19, 23, 28, 40, 65, 87, 93, 99, 161, 170 n.5, 176 n.12; and Free Territory of Trieste, 97, 103–6, 108, 127–28, 132–36, 138, 142–44, 146, 150–53, 156–61, 190 n.27; and Italian peace treaty, 86–88, 90–95, 97–99; and Italy, 12–13, 15–16, 91, 112, 128, 134, 145, 149, 151, 153–55, 161–62, 167; and Julian Region during World War II, 29–30, 33, 36, 38, 41–50, 54–55; and Julian Region from 1945 to 1947, 77, 84; occupation of Julian Region by, 38–39, 42–48, 57; occupation of Trieste by, vii, 48, 50, 52–55, 58–62, 65–67, 75, 80, 165; and Soviet Union, 41, 68, 90, 122–28, 130–31, 133, 167, 183 n.27, 185 n.22; and Trieste crisis of May 1945, 48, 54–55, 65–67; and Tripartite Proposal, 114, 116, 118–19, 121, 128, 138, 143; and Western powers, xii, 33, 42, 91, 99, 112,

122, 126, 150–51, 159, 167. *See also* Eastern bloc; Yugoslav Communist party; Yugoslav Fourth Army; Yugoslav Military Government, Trieste; Yugoslav Military Government, Zone B, Free Territory of Trieste; Yugoslav Military Government, Zone B, Julian Region

Yugoslav Fourth Army, 38–39, 43, 52, 54. *See also* Partisans: Yugoslav

Yugoslav Military Government, Trieste, 66–67. *See also* Yugoslavia: occupation of Trieste by

Yugoslav Military Government, Zone B, Free Territory of Trieste, 116, 121, 123–24, 132, 141–42, 150, 152. *See also* Free Territory of Trieste, Zone B; Yugoslavia: and Free Territory of Trieste

Yugoslav Military Government, Zone B, Julian Region, 69, 90–91, 99. *See also* Yugoslavia: and Julian Region from 1945 to 1947

Zadar (Zara), 18

Zara. *See* Zadar

Zone A, Free Territory of Trieste. *See* Free Territory of Trieste, Zone A

Zone A, Julian Region. *See* Allied Military Government, Zone A, Julian Region

Zone B, Free Territory of Trieste. *See* Free Territory of Trieste, Zone B

Zone B, Julian Region. *See* Yugoslav Military Government, Zone B, Julian Region

---

About the Author
Roberto G. Rabel is Lecturer in American History, University of Otago, New Zealand.

---

Library of Congress Cataloging-in-Publication Data
Rabel, Roberto Giorgio, 1955–
Between East and West : Trieste, the United States, and the Cold War, 1943–1954 / Roberto G. Rabel.
p.    cm.
Bibliography: p.
Includes index.
ISBN 0-8223-0831-2
1. World War, 1939–1945—Territorial questions—Italy—Trieste.
2. World War, 1939–1945—Territorial questions—Yugoslavia.
3. United States—Foreign relations—1945–1953.  4. World politics—1945–   5. Trieste (Italy)—History—1918–   I. Title.
D821.Y8R33   1988
940.53'45—dc19         87-31775  CIP

DATE DUE

| OCT 0 2 1992 | MAR 2 7 2001 |
| APR 2 1 1999 | NOV 0 2 2002 |
| MAY 0 3 2000 | OCT 1 4 2001 |